Ian Lowe

The Etchings of Wilfred Fairclough

Ashgate Editions

First published in 1990 by
Ashgate Editions
Gower House, Croft Road, Aldershot, Hants GU11 3HR

Text copyright © 1990 Ian Lowe
Plates copyright © 1990 Wilfred Fairclough

British Library Cataloguing in Publication Data

Lowe, Ian

The Etchings of Wilfred Fairclough
1. English etchings. Fairclough, Wilfred. Catalogues,
indexes
1. Title
796.924

ISBN 0 85967 846 6
ISBN 0 85967 849 0 (limited edition)

Produced for the publishers by
John Taylor Book Ventures, Hatfield, Herts
Designed by Alan Bartram
Made and printed in Great Britain by
BAS Printers Ltd, Over Wallop, Stockbridge, Hants

Contents

Foreword   7

Introduction   9
Beginnings: Blackburn   9
The Royal College of Art: London 1931-34   10
Rome Scholar: Italy 1934-35   13
Rome Scholar: Spain 1935-36   14
Rome Scholar: Italy 1936-37   15
Draughtsman, Etcher and Teacher: 1938-72   18
A Second Career   20

Acknowledgements   25

Notes   26

The plates   29

Catalogue of published plates   79

List of unpublished plates   112

Foreword

When Wilfred Fairclough gave a talk about his own work
at the Royal Society of Painter-Etchers and Engravers on
1 March 1983 he said that 'the world is a pretty marvellous
place if you go about with your eyes open and you can see
the things that are in front of you. There are two sorts of
seeing in my experience: there is the optical seeing, and
there is the seeing of the mind, what might be called the seeing eye. One is absolutely interdependent on the other. With
the inner eye you can see the possibilities of what you are
looking at, and all my life I have gone around looking at the
raw material, spinning it round in my mind, tossing it in the
air, and hopefully it comes back with a little gilding of magic
which will make the ordinary into something just a little bit
extraordinary and maybe make somebody say 'Well, I never
thought of that'.[1] This provides the text for the essay which
follows, because it is the quality of 'magic', united with the
personality of the artist, that I would like to try to describe.
In doing so, I will make frequent use of the artist's own
words, believing that what an articulate and reflective creator
can tell you is an invaluable insight into his way of approach-
ing as well as rendering a subject. As E S Lumsden put it,
'a definitive assertion by the etcher himself must necessarily
be of far more value than suppositions by anyone else'.[2] I
have therefore drawn upon Wilfred Fairclough's lecture and
letters in presenting what is both an appreciation and a portrait. For his generous support and welcome invitation to
contribute to this record of his work as a printmaker I am
deeply grateful.

IAN LOWE
1 March 1990

Beginnings: Blackburn

The 'ordinary' on which Wilfred Fairclough's eyes first looked was his native city of Blackburn in Lancashire, where he was born on 13 June 1907. The only son of Herbert Fairclough and Edith Amy Milton, he had two elder sisters, Ethel and Clara, and two who were younger than himself, Lilian and Gertrude.[3] In 1912, at the age of five, he went to All Saints School in Blackburn. There, when he reached the senior school in 1918, he was fortunate in being taught by Edward Biggs, who recognised his early talent in drawing, from which the path was to lead on to the Blackburn School of Art and Crafts.[4] Biggs, a communist and an atheist, did not force his views on his pupils but encouraged Fairclough to read G B Shaw, H G Wells, Thomas Hardy and W H Hudson.

When Fairclough left school at the age of fourteen he had been a 'half-timer', working alternately during his last year, at school and in a cotton mill. When the mill failed, Biggs suggested to his father that Fairclough should return to school until he was fifteen. He then started work with a local firm of accountants, Nathaniel Duxbury Son and Finch. He arrived at the office at 8.30, lit the senior partner's fire and filled the inkwells, doing the job so well that he did three years as office boy rather than eighteen months. On five nights a week he attended evening classes in book-keeping, commerce and English to assist his training as an audit clerk. What appears to be an unpromising start to a creative life already demonstrates a number of qualities which were later to distinguish the etcher – efficiency, and a business-like approach both to creative work and to presenting the results; even the responsibility for ink looks forward to Fairclough's later activities.

In the autumn of 1925, at the age of eighteen, he engaged in a new series of evening classes, at the Blackburn School of Art and Crafts under Arthur Jackson, 'a dear headmaster' but 'the training was absolutely abysmal':

There was a complete five-year course of nothing else except what in those days was called 'Light and Shade'. I put up with it for a while and then rebelled because I realised that it was a complete waste of time … 'Light and Shade' was done from plaster casts. There was an apple with leaves, there was a lemon, there were a couple of plums. The casts were hung on a post at eye level. The light came over your left shoulder through a piece of tracing paper, and the exercise was to copy that piece of plaster. You copied what you could see, so that, if it was a good copy, you could hang it at ten feet alongside the original plaster cast, and it would be difficult to tell one from t'other. It had nothing whatsoever to do with drawing, nothing at all. And that went on for five years, before you were even allowed to see a model, that was, a live model'.[5]

In July 1928, Fairclough's mother died of cancer, and his father died in the following May. His sister Clara, 'an angel', two years his senior, had followed in her father's footsteps and qualified as a hairdresser. She continued the business, took on the mortgage of the modest house at 165 Bolton Road, and provided a home for her brother. The demanding life of being an audit clerk from 9 till 6, and then attending evening classes from 6.30 until 9.15 pm, after which he returned home to supper, was relieved at the weekends by walking and sketching. A friend, Jenny Fryers, who had been engaged to Edgar Ainsworth who had gone from Blackburn to the Royal College of Art, mentioned that Ainsworth had no School Certificate which Fairclough had been told was a necessary qualification for admission to the college. He resolved to follow the same route and decided to take the Board of Education's drawing examination in May of 1930. There were six papers. For drawing from the antique and life drawing he used the school, but the remaining four subjects he studied at home, working for hours in his bedroom on human anatomy (bones and muscles), architecture, perspective and drawing from memory in preparation for the four-hour long examinations. This was the practical form that his rebellion against the teaching of 'Light and Shade' took, following the retirement of Arthur Jackson at the end of the summer term, and his succession as headmaster by George Reed.

In the Autumn of 1929 he met Joan Cryer, a student teacher attending the School of Art, whom he was later to marry. After he had successfully passed the six parts of the drawing examination in July 1930, he was offered a post as a part-time teacher at the school in which he had been studying for five years. During his year as a part time teacher he was stimulated by E S Lumsden's *The Art of Etching*.[6] With 'the finest, most comprehensive book on etching ever written' in hand, he refaced two old copper plates and made his first experiments in the medium.

He resolved to follow up his success in the drawing examination by taking the Board of Education's pictorial design course, a two-year programme which he crammed into one. He was the only student in Blackburn working for it, and received little instruction. In 1930 during the Christmas holidays he went to London for the first time and combed the museums, buying postcards to aid his course of study. Although only twenty-five per cent of those who sat the examination passed, he was again successful in the examinations in July 1931. As a result he decided to leave Blackburn, and to study at the Royal College of Art in London. He was convinced that the engraving school there was 'the best in the world'. He was determined to get there, and it had never occurred to him to do anything else. 1931 was 'make or break year'.

There were still two hurdles to be overcome by the twenty-four year old Fairclough, with two Board of Education examinations to his credit, as well as five years' work at the Blackburn School of Art and Crafts. The first of these was financial. The Blackburn Town Council Education Committee usually made a grant of £50 to those who succeeded in getting a place at the Royal College of Art, together with a further loan of £30. The family's solicitor, Mr Roger Oddie, agreed to guarantee the loan but the committee refused to make a grant. Joan Cryer's mother stepped into the breach and offered a loan of £60 so that the way was cleared. When Mr Oddie learnt that his offer had been rejected by the Education Committee, he complained, with the result that, from January 1932, Fairclough received an annual grant of £50. As the fees at the Royal College of Art amounted to thirty guineas a year (£31.50), that left £18 10s (£18.50) to provide for board and lodging, hence the need for the loan. In the second year, free admission was granted to certain students, of whom Fairclough was to be one, but he had yet to get a place. Applications for these had had to be made by June, so that in his reply to Fairclough's letter of application, the Registrar of the Royal College of Art, Hubert Wellington,[7] wrote that he was too late for that year. Fairclough's 'hackles went up'. He decided to go to London to try to persuade Mr Wellington at a meeting in mid-October. Wellington explained that the college was full, that term had started, and that it was too late for him to join for that academic year. Fairclough replied that he had 'burnt his boats' in Blackburn, having resigned his part-time teachership, and that he 'could not go back'. In the face of such firmness of purpose, Wellington ended the interview by saying that he would see the Principal, Sir William Rothenstein,[8] the next morning, and told him to return at 11. At that point Fairclough felt that he was in. He duly returned next day at that time and was working in the engraving school a quarter of an hour later, with his jacket off, 'getting down to it', with guidance from one of his fellow students, Esmé Sandercock. It is not surprising that over fifty years later Fairclough remembered Wellington as 'a gem of a man'.[9]

The Royal College of Art: London 1931-34
Work at the college was no easier for Fairclough initially than it had been at Blackburn:

When the students saw my life drawings they were highly critical. I said 'What should I be doing?' They said 'Form, Form!' So I said 'What's Form?' 'Well, you see, Form's *Form*. If you don't know what Form is, you should go back home.'

I made other enquiries and I more or less got the same answer. I was a very worried student, and suddenly light dawned on me like a shaft of sunlight. What was meant was *Shape* – whatever you were doing, whether it were an object or a figure in life drawing. You analysed Shape, and then you put down that analysis of that shape on paper. Now the difference may not be immediately apparent but it was absolutely a fundamental difference of approach. One was what I call blind copying; the other was a creative process, where you were doing and creating something new. It was a very hard life, much harder than Blackburn … From that time on, things began to get a bit better. Now in this battle-cry 'Form', you were not allowed to incorporate any sort of 'colour'. You were permitted to use a certain amount of texture, but 'colour' was out. As far as drawing and getting studies this was fine, but once you wanted to carry the design forward – I was an engraver, so you had to carry this drawing forward in the making of prints – this Form idea had very severe limitations.[10]

The routine at the college in the early 1930s has been described by Fairclough: 'From Monday to Thursday there was no instruction in the engraving school: "you were on your own". The professors visited on Fridays and Saturdays until 3.30 in the afternoon.' His first etching at the college was a *Van Dyck Head*.[11] 'A copy was the first task all new students in the Engraving School (RCA) were given – "to let them find out how the school worked, and where the tools were". Why that could not have been done with an original plate I never puzzled out.' There were also life-drawing classes in the college which the engravers attended. Among the teaching staff was Alan Sorrell, who had won the Rome Scholarship for Painting in 1928.[12] 'In ten minutes he taught me a great deal about drawing'. In his stuttering voice Sorrell told him that it was 'the directions that you look for, not the bits'.[13] In addition the engravers had a life class of their own but without any instruction. A technician was present throughout the week to provide etching materials.

In 1931 the School of Engraving consisted of the Professor, Malcolm Osborne; his assistant, Robert Austin; the teacher of lithography, F H Spear; and the Visitor, Francis Dodd, who was followed in 1932 by Henry Rushbury.[14] It was 'the most influential London art school of the period for printmaking'.[15] It was dedicated to high, traditional standards which had been set by Sir Frank Short.[16] Short had 'directed the etching class until 1926 when he was succeeded by Malcolm Osborne'.[17] Osborne had been trained by Short from 1901 to 1906 and had been followed in his classes by Austin from 1913 to 1915.[18] When Osborne retired in 1948, he was succeeded by Austin as Professor, until his retirement in 1955, so that there was a remarkable degree of continuity.[19] When Fairclough entered the engraving school

Short was President of the Royal Society of Painter-Etchers and Engravers. In addition, Austin had won the Rome Scholarship for Engraving in 1922, its third holder.[20] By the time Fairclough reached the college, Austin was at the height of his career, having produced eighty-nine plates, an achievement which had been crowned by the catalogue of his prints by Campbell Dodgson.[21]

The training he received was that which had been provided at South Kensington for over forty years. Apart from the fact that Osborne and Austin 'were monopolised by the part-time female students', Fairclough has made no criticism of the instruction which he received aside from the difficulty that he experienced over printing, which was only permitted when the professors were in attendance.

At the end of the summer term 1932, Fairclough left the digs which he had rented in Oakley Street, Chelsea for fifteen shillings (75 pence) a week, and returned home to Blackburn. There he made the studies that he was to use during the following year for his etchings of *Shetley Brook No. 1* (5) and for *Scotshaw Brook* (6), a view of the paper mill at Lower Darwen where he also drew the 'smiling pigs' which were to be 'put to good account' six years later in *The Large Cart, Rothenburg* (28).

On his return for the autumn term he lodged at 1 Hollywood Road, opposite St Stephen's Hospital, again for fifteen shillings a week. The house was kept by two elderly seamstresses, the Misses Caley, and it was their front door which provided the setting for *The Doorway (The Arrival)* (4). This was the set subject for the College Diploma Examination in June 1933. It was *The Doorway (The Arrival)* which was to prompt Fairclough's recollection of the etchings of G L Brockhurst:[22]

In the printing room were two prints of Brockhurst's, a portrait and standing female figure. I am not sure but I think that they belonged to Malcolm Osborne. They were very much admired; the technical finesse is quite remarkable. In those days students were not allowed to print except on Fridays and Saturdays when the Prof. was in attendance. Very frustrating! One worked on a plate, printed it on Friday morning, worked like beaver to be able to print again on Saturday morning. After that, a long wait until Friday came round again. Time was too short to wait so long. The Welches had a copper-plate printing workshop at Hammersmith. Father did the general administration, one son looked after all the paper, and the other three brothers each had a room, complete with presses. Frank Welch charged a shilling (five pence) a print on handmade Whatman (paper). I went for a print one Monday morning to find Frank printing Brockhurst's *Adolescence*[23] (a very beautiful fifteen-year old girl sitting nude in front of a mirror). He told me that Brockhurst had been in with the model for the plate. She looked at Frank and asked 'Do you think it is like me?' to which Frank replied 'Very like you – so far as I can see'.[24]

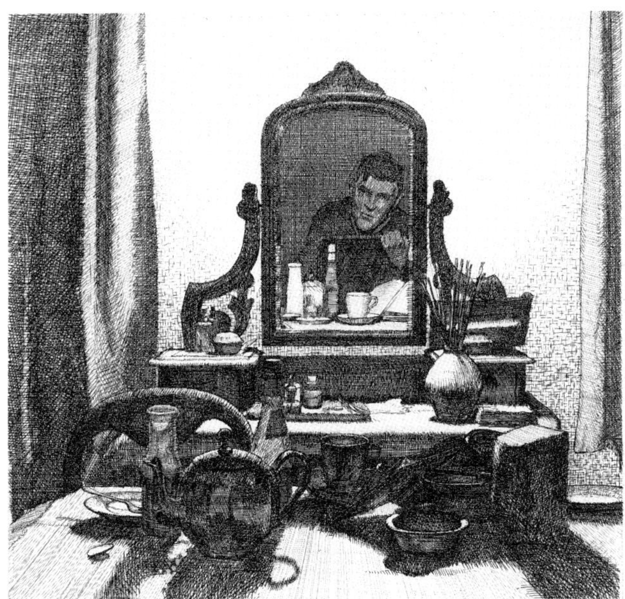

Crockery on Table, Hollywood Road. 1934.
E. $5\frac{1}{4} \times 5\frac{1}{4}$ (L20)

That demonstrates Fairclough's ability to tell a good story, coupled with his sense of humour. 'With no sales for prints, there was no call for printers'.[25] The Welches' workshop closed. 'Frank went to live outside St Albans, Harry moved to a shop in Brook Green Road and I don't know what became of the father and the other two.'[26]

Adolescence was certainly 'a tour de force' in which Brockhurst had 'probably never used his needle with more subtle richness'.[27] Fairclough was to write:

I had the privilege of seeing the actual plate at close quarters and for a short while the technical methods influenced my work (*Joan Dressing her Hair* (2), *The Doorway (The Arrival)* (4) and *Morning* (7)). I would learn from anyone and of course coarsened the method of drawing. The influence was very short-lived. I found the methods Brockhurst used too mechanical and at that time had no knowledge of the acid he used. Working so finely as he did, one look in the nitric bath and the plate would have blown up and disintegrated. It was only very much later that I learned that he used a very weak Dutch bath and bit the plate for a very long time, more or less put the plate in the bath, went to bed, and picked out the plate the following morning. The plate would be pretty black and he then went to work with a burnisher, much in the same way that a mezzotint is worked with scrapers and burnishing.[28]

The influence of Brockhurst can be seen in the composition of the self-portrait, which Fairclough etched, reflected in the mirror (as was *Adolescence*), the table in the foreground covered with the remains of breakfast, *Crockery on Table, Hollywood Road* (*List* 20).

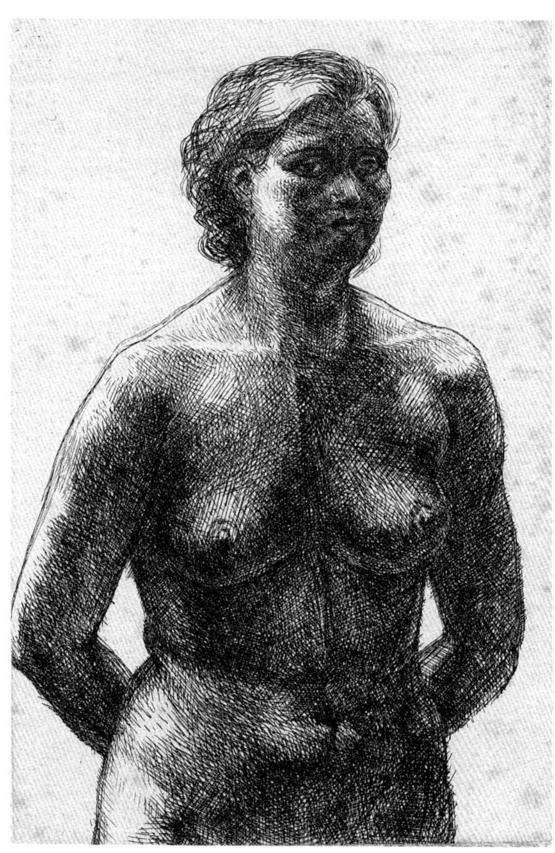

Half-length of Female Lit from rear. 1935.
E. $4\frac{1}{2} \times 3$ (L27)

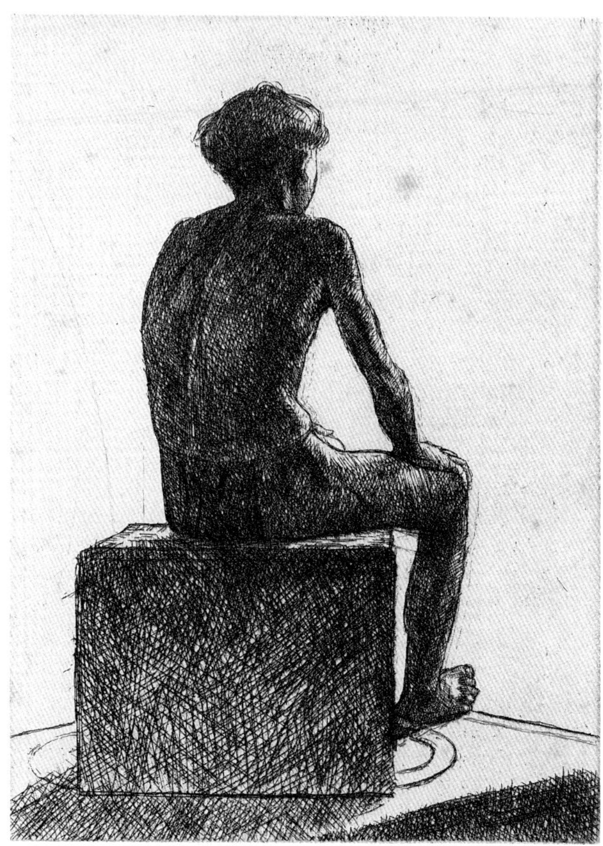

Young Boy. 1933.
E. $4\frac{1}{2} \times 3\frac{1}{4}$ (L9)

It was through the unpublished plates that Fairclough acquired his technical skill, often drawing from the life direct on to the copper plate, as in the studies from the female nude models, and that of a seated *Young Boy* (*List* 9) which was praised by Robert Austin.[29] It was during his second year at the RCA that Fairclough recalled:

I was getting a bit bold. I got a little scrap of copper – about $2 \times 2\frac{1}{2}$ inches – and I laid a ground on it, and did a head and shoulders of a man. I used no contour lines whatever, and I built up an image using tone from black, through grey to white. Robert Austin, who was a very good friend of mine, was also the most serious and vitriolic critic one could wish for, really went to town on me: 'Never do that again. Never do a thing like that again. And if you ever do, don't let me see it'.[30]

Austin could, however, relax and on Saturday afternoons would say 'Pack it up. Let's go and watch Fulham' (football club), while on another occasion he took Fairclough to a boxing night at the Albert Hall to watch the fight between Len Harvey and Jack Peterson.

On the award of his Diploma,[31] Fairclough went to thank Professor Osborne for all his help before leaving the RCA.

Since he had passed the two Board of Education examinations, his course had only taken two, rather than the usual three, years. Osborne said 'But you are coming back, aren't you? You must come back', to which Fairclough replied that he was not able to because he had no money. The situation was that of 1931 in reverse. Further encouraged by Osborne, he was awarded another grant from the Education Committee in Blackburn, and with free admission to the RCA, Fairclough began his postgraduate year in the Autumn of 1933.[32] On Osborne's recommendation he then applied for the Rome Scholarship in Engraving, submitting his application on 30 October:[33] 'Candidates were required to submit: Six prints in any approved medium, three figure compositions, three figure drawings, one drawing of a head, drawings of animals, landscape and architecture. Also one print of a composition, the subject of which was "Morning".'[34] *Morning* (7) shows Joan Cryer doing up her shoe. Osborne and Austin provided references. Both were agreed that Fairclough was 'a very serious student'. Osborne found him 'most industrious', 'enterprising and intelligent and keenly interested in life'. Austin observed that 'He certainly has the

qualities necessary. I feel that he will reach a very high level
(but without the spark of genius which, after all, is most
rare). He is a solid and very responsible person, without frills
and not at all "art studenty" (I don't know if that is a draw-
back). He hasn't parents and how he manages to carry on
his art training with no or little money, I don't know, but it
shows that he is keen and has guts. I like this man a lot...'.[35]

On 5 January 1934 Fairclough was elected an Associate
of the Royal Society of Painter-Etchers and Engravers at the
relatively early age of twenty-six.[36] On 12 January he was
working in the studio at the college when Osborne returned
from the meeting at which the Rome Scholarships had been
awarded.[37] 'Come and talk to me, Fairclough', Osborne said.
When they were in his room, Osborne told him 'You've got
it', and Fairclough burst into tears.[38] Osborne also succeeded
in getting him a grant from the Bird Fund at the Royal
Academy.

Where 1931 had been 'make-or-break year', the first days
of 1934 were a triumphant vindication of the trust which had
been placed in him, and the reward for his hard work and
tenacity. As Austin exclaimed, 'What a week!'.[39] It was in
1934 that Fairclough's work first appeared in *Fine Prints of
the Year*. Noting that etching was 'temporarily out of favour
with the picture-buying public', Malcolm Salaman added
that 'there is a new generation of copper-plate artists ... Let
these be encouraged'.[40] *Winona* (10) was reproduced.[41] The
model for both figures was Joan Cryer. Her dress, which was
borrowed from a fellow student, was of a rich red wool, in
the style of those worn by Dorelia, Augustus John's model.
The studies of drapery in *Winona* (10), *Ruth* (11) and *The
Letter* (12) show the influence of Austin's line engravings as
in *Woman milking a Goat* (1925), *Before Mass* (1926) and
Woman Praying (1927).[42] Also listed as being sent in from
165 Bolton Road, Blackburn were *Shetley Brook No. 1* (5),
Morning (7), *The Letter* (12) and *Plants* (8). 'Mr Fairclough
is a young artist who should make good', concluded
Salaman.[43]

Rome Scholar: Italy 1934-35

The Rome Scholarship in Engraving which Fairclough had
been awarded on 5 January 1934 had been instituted in
1920.[44] Its first holder had been Job Nixon and other holders
who had proved successful printmakers had been Robert
Austin (1922), W E C Morgan (1924), Geoffrey Wedgwood
(1925) and Bouverie Hoyton (1926).[45] The Chairman of the
Faculty was Campbell Dodgson[46] and its members were
established etchers and engravers: Stanley Anderson,
Stephen Gooden, F Ernest Jackson, Harry Morley, Malcolm
Osborne (Fairclough's Professor at the RCA), Henry Rush-

bury (who was later to become Chairman of the Faculty, and
was to propose Fairclough as his successor in 1965), and Ian
Strang.[47] To satisfy such a professional Faculty was no mean
task at the best of times. In the minutes of the Faculty held
on 15 June 1934 it was reported that the age limit had been
raised from twenty-six to twenty-eight (which fortunately,
had admitted Fairclough, who was twenty-six and half when
it was awarded to him), 'in order to admit students whose
comparative maturity would not, in their opinion, prevent
them from successfully fulfilling the purpose of the scholarship'. The wording of the general regulations had been
altered to make it clear that a second year 'must depend upon
satisfactory evidence of progress during the first year'.[48] In
1933 it had been 'evident that the Scholarship was still
attracting the best talent from the Schools of Engraving
throughout the country'. Competition in 1934 had been
'close' and the Faculty were aware of the failure of the holder
of the Scholarship in Engraving in 1931 in whose work they
had been 'gravely disappointed'.[49] It was no sinecure and it
was against this background that Fairclough travelled out to
Rome by rail and boat with the Rome Scholar in Sculpture,
Douglas Bisset, for his first term in October 1934.[50]

While no instruction was given at the School, and scholars
had to work on their own, the facilities were excellent. Fairclough set to work on the view of *Rome from the Pincio* (13)
looking across the Babuino to St Peter's. The Director of the
British School, Colin Hardie, who had been appointed in
February 1933,[51] found that Fairclough, 'being rather older'
had 'a clearer idea of what he wants to do'. 'He feels that
he can work well in Rome and likes the School.'[52] Fairclough
was then twenty-seven, Hardie a year older, and the
Librarian, E K Waterhouse,[53] also appointed in 1933, was
only twenty-nine. After a fortnight's journey to Florence
with Dick Thomas, 1934 Rome Scholar in Painting,[54] Fairclough 'had formed some idea of Italy and what he may
choose in Spring to study e.g. at Assisi and Perugia. I like
both the work and the man and think he will do well'.[55]
When travelling in Italy, Fairclough budgeted for fifteen
shillings (seventy-five pence) a day, the cost of a week's lodging in London, to include rail travel, bed and food. In Perugia, for instance, the cost was four shillings and sixpence
(twenty-two and a half pence) a night, and bed and breakfast
could then be had for the same price in England.[56]

In addition to the winter *Landscape, Acqua Acetosa* (14)
on the Tiber, Fairclough produced three etchings in which
the influence of Austin can be detected, *Praying Peasant*
(15), *Peasant Women* (16) and *Garden Tools* (17). The latter,
although begun in Hyde Park in London, has been metamor-
phosed into a truly Italian subject: the spade leaning against

the tree trunk has no cross bar. The vertical accent and central composition recall Austin's *Scythes* of 1928,[57] which had also been engraved in Rome.

Colin Hardie wrote in 1973: 'Fairclough has remained a friend from those now distant Roman days. Ellis Waterhouse and I had a wonderful time, Arcadian almost'.[58] Of Waterhouse, Fairclough was to recall:

In my first year in Rome I got to know him very well. He was working on his book on Roman Baroque and he took me along with him to see the pictures he was writing about, quite an education! With Colin Hardie and Brian Thomas we did the Villa at Caprarola and visited the famous shrine at Calcati from … which the most holy relic was recently stolen. It was a most hilarious and irreverent pilgrimage.

He had a most wicked and sometimes devastating wit which many people found too much. Xmas Eve 1934 we spent in the Common Room of the British School at Rome drinking cheap Italian wine and eating green figs. A deadly combination. The following day someone suggested a walk before Xmas lunch. A constitutional. E W 'Constitutional? Constipational you mean!'.[59]

In June 1935, while he was travelling back from Italy, Fairclough's application for the renewal of his scholarship for 1935-6 was considered by the Faculty. He submitted:

ETCHINGS
1. *Rome from the Pincio* (13)
2. *Landscape, Acqua Acetosa* (14)
3. *Peasant Women* (16)
4. *Garden Tools* (17)
5. *Praying Peasant* (15)
6. *Valley of the Tescio, Assisi* (18)
7. *Olives at Assisi* (19)
8. *Life Drawing* (two, *List* 26 and 27)

DRAWINGS
Landscape and architecture	18
Figure composition and studies	32
Life drawings	30
Drawings, studies, sketchbook leaves	14 sheets[60]

Both the life drawings were drawn directly on to the plate, the strong female nude with her hands behind her back lit from behind (*List* 27), and the sheet of studies of female nudes, Michelangelesque in feeling. They make a total of nine etchings to show for the first year.[61] The two landscapes at Assisi were also done on to the plate, recalling Muirhead Bone's observation 'One certainly gets a freshness and vivacity in plates done direct, but it precludes the possibility of a carefully digested composition'.[62]

Fairclough reported that he had visited Orvieto, Siena, Florence, Arezzo, Perugia, Assisi, Naples, Pompeii, Paestum, and, from Rome, had been out to Viterbo, Tivoli (a view of which appears in the background of *Praying Peasant* (15)), Frascati, Albano and Tarquinia. His travel for that summer included Venice (to see the exhibition of paintings by Titian), Vienna (to study prints and drawings in the Albertina), Dresden, Berlin, Brussels, and Paris.

In recommending the renewal, Colin Hardie wrote: 'Mr Fairclough has had a good year' and was 'very keen to come back'. 'He has an unobtrusive but shrewdly and humourously observant character.'[63] Campbell Dodgson acknowledged Hardie's 'personal care of the students and for his useful reports on their work' and recorded the presentation of 'some excellent work' by Fairclough. 'The Faculty readily approved the renewal of his Scholarship for a second year, which he had chosen to spend in Spain.'[64]

Rome Scholar: Spain 1935-36
The invasion of Abyssinia by Italy in October 1935 was the reason for Fairclough's 'choice' of Spain. The Directorate of the British School returned to Rome, but the scholars were offered the alternatives of Spain or Greece.[65] Dick Thomas and G W Hooper (Rome Scholar in Painting, 1935) chose Spain, as did Fairclough and Murray Tod (Rome Scholar in Engraving, 1935):[66] 'We were part of the Government's sanctions against Italy'.[67] Fairclough and Tod were in Paris in November when the Honorary General Secretary of the British School, Evelyn Shaw, wrote to say that they were to be housed 'in the most modern and comfortable residence at the University City' and provided with an introduction to the National Academy of Engraving in Madrid.[68] Fairclough wrote from Burgos, which he and Tod found 'very congenial', and a reminder of that visit is to be found in *Bullock Team, Burgos* (55) which has BURGOS/1935 inscribed on the side of the cart.[69]

Madrid, however, was not congenial either in regard to the accommodation or the city itself. The domestic arrangements were more expensive than in Rome and not as satisfactory. The facilities for printmaking were such that they only used them once. By now it was too cold to go out and sketch at Avila and Segovia although they did get to Toledo, a visit which was to bear fruit in 1937 (*El Kantara, Toledo*, 23). 'Apart from the Prado Museum there is no incentive whatsoever for us to stay in Madrid.'[70]

They set off south, to Cordoba and Seville, leaving Madrid on 20 December. It 'rained and rained and rained'.[71] From Ronda, Fairclough wrote in February that there had 'only been ten fine days in the last month'.[72] He warned Shaw that it was difficult for them to advance their plates and that could only be done when they returned to England. Shaw replied that there was no need for them to send their work in until June, noting that they were '"doing" Spain with a vengeance' and that it was 'very good of you to keep me posted', which it was, and sensible too.[73] It also reveals the helpful and friendly side of Shaw.[74] In March 1936, Fairclough sent him a postcard of the cathedral at Palma in Majorca: 'After almost three weeks in Ibiza and Palma we are leaving here today'.[75] They returned to Madrid. Indications of the impending Civil War, which was to break out on 18 July, were evident in 'a church in Alicante which had been wrecked and also the church in Madrid which has been burnt to the ground'.[76] He wrote to Shaw on 19 April that he and Tod were leaving the following day, Tod returning direct to Britain (they had 'travelled together all the time without a cross word'),[77] while he proposed going 'in easy stages', visiting Saragossa, Barcelona and Gerona en route.[78]

After such a difficult, unsettled period he submitted on 17 June: 2 line engravings; 3 etchings, 20 mounted drawings; 21 loose drawings; and 9 sheets of sketchbook notes.[79] The line engravings were *Spanish Mule* (20), the first state of which had been pulled in Madrid, and *Peasant Conversation* (21), both plates as large as those he had done the previous year in Rome, to which he was also to add, from the months in Spain, *El Potro, Cordoba, MCMXXXVI* (22). The etchings were two landscapes at Ronda (*List* 32 and 34) and *Seville: Women Ironing* (*List* 33). In turning to line engraving, a technique in which Austin was acknowledged to be the outstanding practitioner of the period,[80] it is not surprising that compositionally, as well as technically, his influence can be discerned. In *Spanish Mule* (20), it is the way in which the material used has been simplified that recalls the engravings of Austin, an idiosyncratic and individual way of putting the subject on to the plate, shorn of background, with no distracting or extraneous elements, although Fairclough has pointed out that no self-respecting mule would have left the dandelions by its right foot. 'Sunk in their servility', David Jones's description of mules,[81] prompted Fairclough's recollection of those in Stanley Spencer's painting, *Travoys arriving with wounded at a Dressing Station at Smol, Macedonia, September 1916*:[82] 'observe the position of their ears'.[83] In *Peasant Conversation* (21), it is the lines of the drapery, the flecks which shade it, and the placing of the donkey, which recall Austin.

'The Faculty were highly pleased with the skill and promise displayed by Mr Fairclough's work, in view of which, and in order to give him the benefit of travel and study in Italy, they obtained for him a special extension of this award for nine months'; nor had the Faculty 'any hesitation' in renewing Tod's scholarship for a second year.[84] As Shaw wrote to Fairclough, 'no previous Engraver has had his Rome Scholarship exceptionally renewed'.[85]

On 12 July 1936, Wilfred Fairclough and Joan Cryer were married. In 1932 she had followed him to the Royal College of Art, and was now teaching in London and living at 32 Cathcart Road, London SW10 from whence her husband was to send in his exhibits.

Rome Scholar: Italy 1936-37

When Fairclough returned to the British School at Rome in October there were three Rome Scholars, he and Tod being joined by H Andrew Freeth, who had won the scholarship from 'a provincial school of art':[86]

Fifty-five years ago myself, Murray Tod and Cowern met as freshers at the RCA in the Engraving School. Freeth never went to the College but was a very close friend of Cowern from Birmingham. The four of us were very close. In 1934 I went off to Rome, in 1935 Murray Tod followed, and Freeth in 1936, and Cowern in 1937 completed the quartet. One of those times when the light seemed to shine on a small group of friends – and now I am the sole survivor.[87]

They belonged to a group which, against the failed market for etchings, has been called 'the elect': 'Those young etchers whose work was good enough to be exhibited in England and America, to appear in *Fine Prints of the Year*, to be chosen as presentation plates for the Print Collectors' Club (as was *The Spanish Beggar* (24) in 1938), to be appreciated by the scholar-collectors, Malcolm Salaman or Campbell Dodgson, or especially to win the Rome Scholarship ...'.[88] On his way back to Rome, Fairclough visited Paris, Lucerne, whence he was to return in the 1980s,[89] and Lugano, Milan, Florence and Viterbo. He took with him the studies which he had made in Spain, and started work on what was to be his largest plate so far, *El Kantara, Toledo* (23). Colin Hardie, who had returned to Oxford on being elected a fellow of Magdalen College,[90] had been succeeded as Director by C A Ralegh Radford, who recorded that Fairclough was at work on two Spanish subjects, a line engraving (*The Spanish Beggar* (24)) and an etching (*El Kantara, Toledo* (23)).[91] In *Fine Prints of the Year*, Campbell Dodgson wrote of the latter '... Wilfred Fairclough ... has just completed his tenure of a scholarship at the British School at Rome. The study for his excellent *El Kantara Bridge, Toledo* (Pl.17)[92] was made at a period when, as I mentioned last year, the School was temporarily closed and the Rome Scholars enjoyed the hospitality of Spain, just before the Civil War. Toledo is out of reach of etchers at present: it has done good service to many of them in the last half century.'[93]

In March 1937, Fairclough went to Sicily, visiting Palermo, Cefalù, Segesta, Selinunte, Agrigento and Monreale, while his return journey to England in June took him to Rimini, Ravenna, Ferrara, Padua, Verona, Venice, Bolzano, Munich, Nürnberg and the Rhine Valley. On his way along the Romantische Strasse two subjects were to result from the journey, *Farriers* (27) and *The Large Cart, Rothenburg* (28), which, together with those already mentioned, and with *Palma Cathedral* (26), were to provide the climax to Fairclough's achievements between 1934 and 1938.

In his final report Campbell Dodgson recorded: 'At the expiration of his award the Faculty, who were much impressed by the quantity and quality of his work, expressed their warm appreciation of the use which Mr Fairclough had made of his opportunities throughout the period of his Scholarship'.[94] He had fully justified their confidence and trust and brought further lustre to the Rome Scholarship in Engraving.

Fairclough was now unemployed. He turned down the offer of a job at Sheffield because the pay would have been insufficient to help him repay his loans from Blackburn Corporation. The headmaster to whom he had been sent at Raynes Park County Grammar School in London told him that the job he had to fill was not for him, that he wouldn't stay, and that he would then have to find someone else.

Fairclough had plates to work on, and, just as Edward Biggs had befriended him when he was eleven, and Malcolm Osborne, when he was twenty-four, so now he was to be helped by Reginald Brill, Rome Scholar in Painting (1927), who had been appointed Principal at the Kingston-upon-Thames School of Art in 1935.[95] Past Rome scholars used to throw parties and at one given by Edward Armstrong RIBA (Henry Jarvis) Student (1921),[96] Fairclough found himself wedged next to Brill. As a result, Brill later telephoned him to say that he had a vacancy on his staff. Fairclough was appointed in June 1938, to start in September. He also secured a job teaching architects to draw at the London Northern Polytechnic so that 'from complete penury', he was to earn nearly £1,000 a year, and he continued to teach at Kingston until he was called up for war service in 1942. Thus was set also his future career as a teacher. Brill had 'been of enormous help'.[97] Fairclough and his wife were equally fortunate with their landlords in London and remained at 32 Cathcart Road until it was bombed in 1940.

Two important plates remained to be completed on Fairclough's return to London in 1937, *Traghetto* (25) and *Palma Cathedral* (26). In the catalogue of his plates Fairclough has recorded the number of states and the number of proofs of each. As those states remain in his possession and are not in either public or private collections it was decided not to record them in detail. One example has been chosen so that the stages in the evolution of the plate, which is what states are, can be charted. The choice has fallen on the lovely *Traghetto* (25), redolent of Venice which, as has been noted, Fairclough first visited in the summer of 1935. He was to return in 1961, and thereafter it was to provide more subjects for his needle than anywhere else. On his first visit 'there were no vaporetti, no motor taxis, just gondolas and nothing else, gondolas with lights on the prow and the water like glass. Venice is reflections and you can't have reflections any more because of the ripples which come through to the Grand Canal from the Giudecca, even when the Grand Canal is closed to traffic.'[98] Years later, driving West along Ullswater, he found its stillness, and reflections 'rapturous', as they used to be in Venice.

Traghetto (25)

State I: two proofs. The plate measured $7\frac{3}{4} \times 9\frac{1}{2}$ inches. In the first proof, the landing stage projects further to the left, leaving what Fairclough has described as 'a hole in the composition'. In the second, touched proof he tried to fill the 'hole' by putting in the stern of another gondola, drawn in ink, but he decided to reduce the size of the plate.

State II: two proofs. The plate has been reduced to $7\frac{1}{4} \times 8\frac{3}{8}$ inches.
The reduction intensifies the composition. It has eliminated part of the landing stage on the left, together with the two mooring posts, and the slight reduction in height means that four of the remaining mooring posts reach to the top of the plate, providing the vertical accent. The lateral accent is given by the landing stage and railing, the graining and detail of which change little from the first to the last state. The prows of the four gondolas on the right have been shaded and the water darkened below the two nearer to the centre of the composition.

State III: two proofs.
There is further work on the left of the plate: the shading in the water is taken down from the two posts on the extreme left to the landing stage, the definition and shading of the water has been extended between the two posts and the gondola on the left. The two seahorses on each side of that gondola have been shaded and darkened, as has the metal blade on the prow. Previously left white, it has been neatly shaded in with parallel lines. These additions, if relatively small, are certainly in the interest of tonal harmony of the plate and further its sense of completion. In the second, touched proof, the artist has added a gondolier's hat lying on the staging to the lower right of centre, and has also added

in ink eighteen birds at the top, between the posts.

State IV: two proofs.

The additions on the touched third state have been engraved, the birds at the top and the gondolier's hat at the bottom of the plate.

State V: two proofs.

The only discernible difference from the fourth state is in the addition of minor flecks in the centre of the pom-pom of the gondolier's hat. On one of the two proofs, Harold J L Wright has inscribed '*A Pub^d. edition of | (40 proofs) 1937*'.[99] From this it would appear that the published state was the same as the fifth and therefore the final one.

It is only by going into such details as those described above, and as can be seen in Campbell Dodgson's descriptions of Austin's prints, that the careful work of the etcher and engraver can be understood and his final achievement fully appreciated.[100] Even so there may be those who prefer earlier to finished states. It is also evidence of Fairclough's care and exemplary thoroughness that he has retained the proofs of the states of his plates. The later evolution of *Traghetto* (25), and of *El Kantara, Toledo* (23), *Palma Cathedral* (26) and *Magdalen College, Oxford* (33), which were reworked in drypoint, will be considered below.

When Fairclough was about to leave England on active service in 1945, he decided to take some plates to Frank Welch so that his wife 'might have some stock to sell if anything happened to me'. The plates which he selected were *Spanish Beggar* (24), *Traghetto* (25), and *The Large Cart, Rothenburg* (28). Welch got him to sign blank sheets of paper on to which he would then print the plates. One of these proofs has survived in the artist's collection and bears out his observation that Welch 'wanted to print much too powerfully but he couldn't do much with engravings'. Welch's proof is noticeably darker and more heavily inked than those made by Fairclough himself.[101]

In discussing Fairclough's prints, mention has been made of the influence of his teacher and friend, Bob Austin. *Palma Cathedral* (26), as has been argued before,[102] while inviting comparison with Austin's own etching of the subject ten years earlier, shows the comparison to be to Fairclough's advantage. With *El Kantara, Toledo* (23) and the slightly larger *Palma Cathedral* (26) Fairclough comes into his own and his work reaches maturity. Austin's wife, Ada Harrison, described the cathedral as 'one of the loveliest churches in Europe … it enjoys a building's cardinal felicities: it belongs to an admirable period, it stands on a perfectly natural site, and no compulsion, either of vainglory or too numerous population, caused it to be made too large'.[103] 'The church itself, by the true architectural virtues of proportion, light and line is exquisite …'[104] and Fairclough has portrayed it thus as a result of his visit in March 1936. He has captured the beauty of the natural site. He has tackled 'the flying buttresses and rose windows, all that intricate architectural tracery head on, with the awkward angles and challenging juxtapositions of the nearby buildings and light and shade' in a way which rivals if not excels that of his teacher.[105] In *Fine Prints of the Year* for 1938, Campbell Dodgson wrote: '*Palma Cathedral* (Pl.13) by William (sic) Fairclough[106] is an elaborate and accurate etching, consistently carried out in closely laid and carefully bitten lines, of which the total effect is a little dull. The reproduction exaggerates some of the darker passages, especially the tracery of the rose windows.'[107] The epithet 'dull' rankled with Fairclough until 1970 and beyond, as will be seen.

Farriers (27) was engraved over a weekend, using a packet of Senior Service cigarettes as a support for the plate. Fairclough took it to Harold Wright at Colnaghi's (see note 99) with other subjects from which Wright selected six and published a prospectus in June 1938. The editions were to be forty proofs: *Peasant Conversation* (21) (four and a half guineas (approx. £4.75)); *Traghetto* (25) (three and a half guineas); *Spanish Mule* (20) (three guineas); *Palma Cathedral* (26) (four and a half guineas); *Farriers* (27) (three guineas); and *El Kantara, Toledo* (23) (four and a half guineas). No prints were sold.[108]

On his return journey in 1937, Fairclough had made two drawings near Rothenburg, one of a cart by a roadside and the other of a farm just behind. 'They made a perfect marriage', and the line engraving which resulted is, in his considered view, 'one of the best I've ever done.'[109] As with *Traghetto* (25), *The Large Cart, Rothenburg* (28) started out larger but he had the plate reduced by an old coppersmith in Kingston. The reduction again concentrates the composition, this time on the cart, and 'in went the pigs with smiles on their faces'. These can be compared with Dürer's pigs in *The Prodigal Son* but they are the Lancashire pigs which Fairclough had drawn in 1932, 'put to good effect'. On reflection, Fairclough said that he would change 'the roofage'. 'There's an awful lot of work there', he added, pointing to the downspout on the gutter.[110] 'The relationship of dark to light is just right', was the observation of a fellow etcher who has a proof of it hanging on his staircase.[111] Fairclough has a superb dry proof of the fourth state, cleanly printed like a visiting card. As George Clausen observed: 'I like to print *as clean as possible*. I think the visiting card is the ideal of printing, ie that the plate should give you what you want when wiped clean …'.[112] More recent proofs are warmer in tone. The plate has all the merit of a 'carefully digested composition' combined with the technical accomplishment and brilliance in execution which distinguished Fairclough's two large Spanish etchings.

Draughtsman, Etcher and Teacher: 1938-72
Evelyn Shaw described Fairclough as 'an artist of great sensibility and power' and praised the 'beautiful quality of his drawing.[113] His skill as a draughtsman was also recognised by the Contemporary Art Society which acquired two of his topographical drawings, of Nürnberg and Palermo, which are now in the British Museum.[114]

In the autumn of 1939, Fairclough was engaged by the Honourable Arnold Palmer as one of the artists who would contribute to *Recording Britain*, a scheme which had been sponsored by the Pilgrim Trust and which 'was controlled by a small committee of three: P H Jowett, Principal of the Royal College of Art (successor to Rothenstein); Sir Kenneth Clark (later Lord Clark of Saltwood), Director of the National Gallery (where Palmer had his office); and Sir William Russell Flint, the President of the Royal Watercolour Society,' with Palmer as secretary.[115] The objective was 'to make drawings of places and buildings of characteristic national interest'.[116] *Recording Britain* is 'still oddly unremembered'[117] but 'by the time the scheme was concluded, 1549 drawings had been made by just under one hundred artists, ranging from the already well-established to the hitherto unknown'.[118]

Palmer later wrote to Fairclough: 'I have not the slightest doubt that they (the committee) would give me permission to say now what they thought and said then – that you were just about our most successful "discovery" as a recording artist. As a tribute to your quality as an artist, I think that needs no addition.'[119] Fairclough worked in seven counties, including London. He contributed fifty-eight drawings, notably those of Richmond and Petersham, shared Oxfordshire with Stanley Anderson, and did two drawings in his native Lancashire in August 1940. Thirty-one were reproduced in the four volumes of *Recording Britain* which were published after the war.[120] The price paid was £3 per drawing: 'you were ... always punctual with your commissions, and always producing work which suggested that the scale of remuneration was far higher than it actually was'.[121]

On being asked whether any of the subjects that he had drawn had provided material for prints, Fairclough replied that they had not because they had been of local interest and it had never occurred to him to use them. Being done on the spot, direct on to paper, he had made no preliminary sketches to refer back to once the drawings were handed in.

Also, while many of the houses were handsome, they were private dwellings and did not have the more general appeal of the subjects which Oxford was to provide, as in *Magdalen College, Oxford* (33), *Radcliffe Camera, Oxford* (54), *Magdalen College Tower and Bridge* (58) and *Christ Church, Oxford* (60).[122] In December 1943, the collection of drawings was transferred to the Victoria and Albert Museum and distributed to the various counties whose buildings had been recorded.

The friendly association with Palmer was marked later by the punning bookplate that he did for him, consisting of two palm leaves, in 1949 (35). It was not his first essay in the field of bookplates, as he had done three heraldic ones early in 1939 (30), designed to be coloured by hand, arising out of a series of classes on heraldry given by Charles Henry Vereker. Professor Vereker has written that 'as his work represented almost all the methods of treatment and standards of accuracy which I had been urging the group to adopt, I think I could say that I have never received since that occasion such an encouraging response from a student of a subject of which at first he knew very little'.[123] In 1950 he was to do a fifth bookplate for *The College of St Gregory and St Martin at Wye* (37).

Magdalen College, Oxford (33) of 1940 is Fairclough's largest plate, $16 \times 18\frac{1}{4}$ inches. It resulted from a visit which he paid to Colin Hardie who took him on a tour of the college and up the Founder's Tower. Fairclough undertook an ambitious bird's-eye view of the college, as though he were seated on a taller tower on the south side of the High Street, in the Botanic Garden, looking northwards over the chapel and the hall, the Old Grammar Hall and cloisters, across to the New Buildings. The deer park beyond, and the meadows beside Addison's Walk, lead the eye out to distant country, giving an impression of that 'rural, rural keeping' which Gerard Manley Hopkins celebrated in *Duns Scotus's Oxford*. In this plate there is no trace of 'the base and brickish skirt' nor, apart from the bicycles in the foreground, is there any evidence of the twentieth century. Even the carts are horsedrawn. It is a masterly exercise in the genre pioneered by David Loggan in *Oxonia Depicta* (1665) and revived by Edmund Hort New in the 1920s.[124] The Latin inscription at the base was checked by Hardie, who pointed out that 'NOMEN' should not have an 'S'. The 'S' was removed but the whole line was not burnished out and re-etched, understandably, so that the spacing between 'NOMEN' and 'EJUS', the last two words of the inscription, is wider than between those words that precede them. Hardie also questioned whether the New Buildings did not appear to be too far away, and too small in relation to the college buildings in front. This criticism Fairclough accepted and was to incorporate when he re-worked the plate thirty-five years later. The only other landscape subject of the 1940s Fairclough came on when he was cycling out from the Royal Air Force base at Medmenham where he was stationed in 1943, having been called up, at the age of thirty-four, on 23 January 1942. *Hambleden Orchard* (34) was a respite from the work that he was doing then on the making of models, one of which was of the Mohne Dam being prepared for the Dambusters' raid.

On the strength of these two landscapes (33 and 34) and the work which had preceded them in the 1930s, Fairclough was elected a full member of the Royal Society of Painter-Etchers on 7 February 1946. In the same year, he and his wife bought their house in Kingston-upon-Thames, where they have lived ever since, and moved there with their two children.[125] To start with, Fairclough used the large front bedroom to work in but in 1956 he decided to use the space that could have been a garage at the end of the garden and to build his studio there. The estimate that he received was £1,500 so he decided to build it himself, which, after the solid concrete floor had been laid, he did, at a cost of £450. Simple though it is 'Any person who has had the privilege of visiting Wilfred Fairclough's studio and seen his work will be in no doubt about the stature of this prolific and creative artist. Apart from engraving and etching, he has produced a large number of very fine watercolours and oil paintings.' Pointing out that 'Fairclough must be extremely well organised (and) must have enormous energy', the writer found the studio 'full of businesslike order, the equipment is kept beautifully and in its allotted place. The etching press was specially motorised to his own design and certainly seems a great success. It was converted from a star wheel press.'[126]

'After the war', Fairclough recalled, 'I took some prints (*The Large Cart, Rothenburg* (28), *Das Gänsemännchen, Nürnberg, MCMXXXVIII* (31), *Hambleden Orchard* (34) and some others) to Colnaghi's and was told: 'Mr Fairclough, if you brought the very best print you have ever done you would still go out with it under your arm. There is no sale for prints.'[127] Thus it was that the prospectus for *Magdalen College, Oxford* (33) was issued by B H Blackwell in November 1947, the price being six guineas. Two prints were sold.

In the early 1950s Wilfred Fairclough almost gave up making prints. It was not until 1956 that he produced more than a plate or two a year at most. The revival of interest in prints came from the initiative of the Honourable Robert Erskine who opened his St George's Gallery in Cork Street in 1954, bringing over work from Paris, including that of S W Hayter and Anthony Gross.[128]

In 1955, Fairclough made his first exercise in a rewarding field for subjects, *Miss Hattie Jacques, Players' Theatre* (42). Such a theatrical subject appears very early in his career in *The Wings, Blackburn Theatre Royal* of 1932 (*List*, 2). At a concert, at the opera, or in the theatre, while the time for sketching is limited, there are none of the problems which he was to experience in Rome and Venice.[129] In (42), *Bedford Box, Covent Garden* (51) of 1957 and *Covent Garden, Wings* (56) of 1959, the contrast between light and dark, between black and white, the dramatic quality of scene and subject, look back to the etchings of music-halls by Sickert. In the same vein, *Jacques String Orchestra, Hampton Court* (52), moderated by the daylight coming into the Orangery on the left, looks forward to the group of subjects inspired by music in Venice which were begun in 1971. Local subjects he found in the yard of Bert Crowther at Syon in Middlesex, which contained an amazing accumulation of sculpture and wrought iron from bombed sites and demolished houses, as in *Angel and Bell* (46), *The Stoic* (48), *Cherubs and Trophies* (53) and *Wilderness* (66).

The year 1957 was unusually full as can be seen from the catalogue. Seven plates were produced whereas there were none in 1958. The reason for this is that the Royal Society of Painter-Etchers held their usual exhibition in February and March at which Fairclough showed *Covent Garden, Grand Tier* (47), *The Stoic* (48) and *Two Ladies on a Beach* (49). It was then decided to hold the next exhibition over the Christmas period, in December 1957 and January 1958, in the hope, which proved vain, of increasing the number of sales. Fairclough therefore produced *Gaiety Theatre* (50), *Bedford Box, Covent Garden* (51), *Jacques String Orchestra, Hampton Court* (52) and *Cherubs and Trophies* (53) for that second exhibition. Apart from the showing in January of that year, there was no exhibition in 1958, and the Society returned to its usual exhibition practice in 1959. *Gaiety Theatre* (50) was a commission from the English Electric Company which Fairclough received through the advertising company J Walter Thompson, and it recalls the skill which Fairclough had put into *Recording Britain*. The theatre, which stood on the corner of the Aldwych and the Strand, was about to be pulled down. In the process he drew the interior, and a part of the circle bar, a carved pediment, ended up in his studio. Unusually he did not print the edition himself but left that to Harry Welch. As the English Electric Company took delivery of the plate he signed and dated it on the plate to identify the artist. The scrupulous observation of the topographical artist is to be seen in the precise delineation of the two contrasted street lights, that on the right recalling the Edwardian baroque glory of the theatre which now survives only in the etching.

In 1961, at the age of fifty-four, and after fifteen years of professional work in teaching, Fairclough received a Leverhulme Research Award which enabled him to revisit Italy. It was 'the return to Europe'.[130] He had to fit the journey into the summer vacation and the heat that he experienced would have weakened the resolve of a much younger man. Fairclough persevered, keeping a *Journal* of his tour in which he punctiliously noted what he saw.[131] He was a very thorough sightseer in Florence, Rome and Venice. The *Journal* also gives a valuable insight into the practising artist's and teacher's mind. It is clear how much importance he attaches to order, as already noted in his own studio, and the proper way in which work should be approached:

It interests me to see *how* people work and wherever I go and see these works or people working who really know their job I am continually impressed by the order in which they work. By order I mean real working order. Things done at the right time in the right place and to the right degree.[132]

On his visit to the Scuola della Decorazione e Incisione in Florence, he made detailed notes on the pottery, 'very orderly and well laid out', and he had a keen eye for ceramics, noting the tiled floors in the Palazzo Venezia[133] and visiting the museum at Faenza.[134] In the Palazzo Pitti he speculated on

What makes one picture different from another? All the patience and conscientious work can be taken and done and yet the result is nothing. A technical treatment but nothing to move or strike a chord. Art cannot be taught. Drawing and painting can be taught and so the tools created and sharpened but unless these are in the hands of an artist they are nothing at all or very little.

He noticed the 'inlaid tables – shells, very beautiful and well-designed. Discipline and necessity of craft controlling design'.[135] On his return to Rome he wrote that 'The biggest change since I was here is the enormous increase in motor traffic. Cars are parked in every nook and cranny.'[136] The Piazza del Popolo, where he hoped to sketch, 'is a vast sea of parked cars'. It was 'almost impossible to draw' as he could not see the ground.

After the traffic in Rome, and the noise in Arezzo and Perugia, it was a relief to reach Venice: 'How quiet it is, no motor cars, no Vespas, no wheels at all'.[137] In addition to going to see the exhibition devoted to Carlo Crivelli, falling under the spell of Carpaccio, visiting Padua to see the frescoes by Giotto in the Eremitani ('they really do ring the bell with great glory'), praising the ceilings by Tiepolo in the

Ca' Rezzonico, and being impressed by Van Dyck's *Ages of Man* in Vicenza, in a broad catholic sweep of appreciation with no Ruskinian exclusions, he drew. Because of the blinding sunlight, he had to get out in the mornings. The references to his work are numerous: 'Out after breakfast very early to see and draw the fish market' (18 August); 'Drew all morning. Drawing takes longer here because half the time the thing you are drawing is obscured by crowds of people having their photographs taken' (20 August);[138] 'Worked all day' (21 August); 'Drew till my eyeballs dropped out' (22 August);[139] 'Finished some work from the top of the campanile' and '11 pm went up the campanile. Full moon and clear sky. It was all quite out of this world' (26 August).[140] It had been from his first visit to Venice in 1935 that *Traghetto* (25) had resulted. From this, and subsequent, visits well over forty plates were to follow. 'This was the completion of the best journey I've ever made apart from minor irritations in Paris. I've refreshed my mind on things seen before and seen things I did not know existed.'[141]

It was a sabbatical crammed into eight and a half weeks. The years ahead were to be more demanding professionally, with his appointment as Principal of the Kingston College of Art the following year, in 1962, and as Assistant Director of the Kingston Polytechnic and Head of the Division of Design from 1970 until his retirement in 1972. Yet the stimulus of that journey and the work that resulted from 'the return to Europe' have marked the rest of his creative life.

As a teacher his last years at Kingston were certainly onerous. His appointment as Principal coincided with a complete reorganisation of art education, central examinations giving way to recognition of the schools by the Council for National Academic Awards. Such recognition gave autonomy to the schools, allowing them to conduct their own assessments of student's work over a period of three years. This change meant the complete restructuring of the School of Art into four schools, Fine Art, Graphics, Design and Fashion, each with a head, side by side with a Department of Liberal Studies. The reorganisation was given vigorous support by the Surrey County Council which authorised the building of a new eight storey addition to the school and the acquisition of extensive annexes.[142]

A Second Career
To call the period after Fairclough's retirement 'A Second Career' might be considered a misnomer because, although he produced few prints in the 1940s, and none in 1951 and 1952, he worked on copper or zinc throughout the 1950s and 1960s. However, an analysis of the catalogue reveals that it is a fitting description. He did 31 plates in the 1930s,

excluding those on the *List*, and a further 48 in the following thirty-two years, a total of 79 up to 1972. In the eighteen years since 1972 he has produced 60 more. These figures reveal what a high proportion of his work, well over a third, and his best, has been achieved in old age. As Henry Rushbury told him when they met on holiday at Instow in Devonshire in 1957, 'It is hard work to get up there. It is harder still to stay there'.[143] Working at that level, Fairclough is proud to maintain that he is objective about his work and that had there been any falling off in it, he would have stopped. It remains to be seen of what this outstanding degree of production consists and how it was achieved.

Two years before he retired, Fairclough took up the plate of *Palma Cathedral* (26) of which Campbell Dodgson had written that 'the total effect is a little dull'. 'No man of any self-respect can retreat before the charge of being a bore. The accusation is so grave, so wounding and so fundamental that a retreat might easily become a rout.'[144] Frederic Warburg's words perfectly describe Fairclough's feelings which he expressed at his lecture with typical frankness: 'This rankled for years – I didn't like being a bore so when the time was ripe I tore into it with drypoint'.[145] The reworked *Palma Cathedral* has changed from the soft greys of (26) to the richly toned (75). It is a new subject meriting its new number in the catalogue. He was also to tear into three other plates from his early period. (75) was followed in 1974 by its fellow Spanish subject, *El Kantara, Toledo* (23, now 83) which has come out even darker, and, in 1975, by *Magdalen College, Oxford* (33), similarly reworked in drypoint, and now (90). In the last, Fairclough has made good the criticism which Colin Hardie had raised in 1940. He has burnished out the New Buildings and re-etched them. He has increased their size by a fifth, widening them on the right, raising their height, and he loses the left part of the range behind the plane tree which was then gone over with drypoint. The overall treatment has altered the mood of the light, summery landscape; it has obscured the intricate work on the roofing slates but has improved the architectural balance of the whole. He also reduced the size of the plate, removing the inscription from the base.

These 'before and afters' reached their climax in *Traghetto* (25) which became, in 1981, *Traghetto del Giglio* (105). Where the first three plates were reworked, with the alteration noted on *Magdalen College, Oxford* (90), *Traghetto* (25) was transformed. First 'the birds went' and, in their place, are the buildings and the campo on the other side of the Grand Canal. Moored gondolas, and one crossing over, are added as well. In the first state of *Traghetto del Giglio* (105), of which there are two proofs, drypoint has been added to the two gondolas on the left, the gondolier's hat has been etched and darkened, and, in the second state, the gondolas on the right have also been worked over in drypoint. Closing the composition at the top, rather than the reworking of the plate, has made a new subject of it and one which is entirely balanced and harmonious. The transformation is astonishing, such is the difference between the 'before and after'. It is worth mentioning that *The Large Cart, Rothenburg* (28) has not been torn into or transformed, but allowed to remain as it was in 1938. *Traghetto del Giglio* has become one of the evocatively atmospheric views of Venice that are found in Fairclough's later work. It was preceded by *Venice, Night* (88) of 1975, and *Venice, Palazzo Dario* (92) of the following year, which are almost a pair. The lustrously dark night skies are separated, by the illuminated façades of the palazzi, from the dark groups of gondolas in the foreground. Both these etchings rival in their intensity and variety those of Venice by Whistler and McBey. *Venice from the Lido* (104) shows domes and campaniles in silhouette. Fairclough has captured the feeling of Venice in the rain, and it often rains in Venice, in *Venice, Two by Two* (103) and *Venice, Two to One* (112), titles which refer to the umbrellas which are also in evidence in *Venice, Storm* (111) of 1983. In all three subjects he has combined aquatint with etching, creating a texture which is admirably suited to the atmosphere. In (111) Fairclough's mature way of laying the subject on the plate has now become so natural that no trace of influence from Austin's practice can be detected. The crossing of the diagonals in the composition, the varied texture, are united with what is almost a trademark of Fairclough's late prints, a brilliant, patient and precise rendering of such details as the ironwork and railings in the context of the setting which they do much to enhance.

Nearly all of the prints of the last eighteen years, with the exception of the atmospheric views of Venice, have been of figurative subjects, either single figures alone (80, 89, 93, 95, 99, 102, 106, 116 and 118), or in groups in restaurant interiors (84, 86, 97, 109, 121 and 123) or in relation to music (76, 78, 81, 87, 91, 94, 98, 101, 119 and 136). Since 1982 Lucerne has alternated with Venice in providing townscapes with figures and market scenes (107, 113, 114, 117, 120, 125, 127, 128 and 131) and, since 1985, Fairclough has drawn on subjects inspired by the Carnival in Venice (122, 123, 124, 126, 129, 130, 132, 133, 134, 137 and 138).

The reworking of the four early plates runs parallel, chronologically and tonally, with the musical subjects which began in 1971 with *S Giorgio Maggiore, I Virtuosi di Roma* (76). One of their characteristics is the contrast of dark against light. These subjects are taken from concerts or performances of which the precursor was *Jacques String Orchestra, Hampton Court* (52), with the musicians, their bows and music stands. In Venice, Fairclough discovered and enjoyed the music of Monteverdi, Cavalli and Vivaldi, performances of which he combines with an architectural setting. In *S Giorgio Maggiore, I Virtuosi di Roma* (76) the concert takes place in Andrea Palladio's masterpiece of sacred architecture, the interior of which Fairclough described as 'really severe but in no way empty. Very cool and lovely.'[146] All these Venetian musical subjects share an awareness of the whole ambience, place, architecture, music and light, creating not only an unusual richness and warmth in the atmosphere but also the dynamic tension which is found in Fairclough's later etchings.

In 1972 he returned to London for *Covent Garden, Orchestra Pit* (78), an ambitious over-view in which the white scores of the music throw into contrast the players and the range of boxes beyond, looking back to Sickert as in *Bedford Box, Covent Garden* (51) and *Covent Garden, Wings* (56).[147] The next year he went back to Venice for Vivaldi's *Juditha Triumphans, Scuola Grande di San Rocco* (81) where the orchestra had to pit its virtuosity against that of Tintoretto. Violins, double basses, music stands again, 'cello, harpsichord or piano, singers and conductor, were all observed in one single performance. In the case of *I Musici Cantori, Rehearsal, Bergamo* (87) of 1975 he was able to complete the drawing during the rehearsal and to make the portraits of the musicians during the performance. The stone balustrade, and the reredos of the Virgin and Child behind the players, give the subject a firm setting. Of *Venice, Mefistofele Fantasia* (91) of 1976, the music composed, as the wrought-iron notice on the left makes clear, by Boito, Fairclough wrote:

It is the second version of it I have done. The first essay was very large, soft ground in colour and was a total disaster by any count, … deserves total destruction but I have not yet got round to the point of execution [it has since been carried out]. The second version is a different kettle of fish. It was originally to have been just the band blowing away but, in riffling through some drawings, I had the great misfortune to come across a drawing of S Marco done in 1935 from almost the same spot. It was the same size and scale as the band and the two studies fitted together as if made for each other. So there I was, landed not just with the difficulties of the musicians but with all the knobs of S M plus the Clock Tower and a bit of the Doge's Palace. The floodlighting is all invented the like of which San Marco has never seen. All of which increased the work by two weeks and complicated the job enormously.[148]

There was another complication in that he got the bell of the French horn in the wrong position. When this was pointed out to him by one of the horn players at Covent Garden, he felt obliged to correct it which he did with scraper, charcoal and burnisher.

Also set out of doors, if informally, is *Venice, Regatta Band Rehearsal* (94) of 1977, with many figures done from the steps of Santa Maria della Salute. It was when he was working on this plate that Fairclough, holding his breath to keep his hand steady, had to go to hospital with angina. 'The part in the upper right of the plate went in later', a difference which is just noticeable when it is pointed out (149). *Venice, La Fenice, Solo Violin* (98) of 1979, when he had recovered, was done in the theatre which he had first visited in 1961, and found 'pretty and feminine'.[150] The solo violin was Salvatore Accardo, 'the page turner was a complete invention of my own. She developed into quite a character,' remarked Fairclough. *Venice, Vivaldi, Chiesa di Santa Maria della Pietà* (101) of 1980 has a strongly architectural setting. The church was that of the choir of nuns for whom Vivaldi composed. It has also beeen described as 'one of the most elegant and beautiful sacred buildings of the eighteenth century in Venice'.[151] The group of musicians is enhanced by the noble tabernacle behind them, and by the perfectly rendered altar rail, and the archangels, Michael and Gabriel, flanked by St Peter and St Mark. The sculpture is the work of Morlaiter, Marchiori and Gai, a perfect complement to the composer. Taking the Venetian musical subjects together it is hard to think of another series which so richly combines setting and subject, so much work and attention to architectural and musical detail, forming a splendid tribute to Venice. Later Fairclough was to return to this type of subject in *Venice, Light Music* (119) in 1985 and *Piazza San Marco, Light Music* (136) in 1989.

The technical brilliance which distinguishes Fairclough's work is to be found in the groups done in restaurants and in the subjects inspired by the Carnival. Celebrating his recovery, 1979 was marked by three redoubtable successes: *Venice, Lunch at Torcello* (97), *Venice, La Fenice, Solo Violin* (98, already mentioned), and *Venice, The Rose and the Writ* (99), a skilful view of a French writer combined with chairs and elements of still life. The numinous quality of Torcello combines with the details of the tablecloths, vases of flowers, the scrolling on the backs of the chairs, and the slatted roof. The framing of the subject, and its placing on the plate, even to the round dish in the foreground, echoing the gondolier's hat, are masterly, as they are in its pair of 1982, *Venice, Torcello Afternoon* (109). The light in both is muted daylight, filtered, thrown up by or caught in table cloths, or refracted from the jackets of the waiters, while in *Burano Wedding, Il Gatto Nero* (121) of 1985 the daylight, which was diffused by the curtains at the back of the restaurant, is combined

with the artificial light from the overhead chandeliers, which
was golden. These subjects, as Fairclough has said, 'are all
to do with light'.[152]

This essay has been concerned with the career and prints
of Wilfred Fairclough himself to the exclusion of all but the
briefest references to his marriage, and to his wife, Joan
Vernon-Cryer, herself a successful watercolourist. *Family
Reunion* (100) of 1980 belongs with the restaurant subjects.
The assembled family are, from left to right, the artist; Celia
Fairclough, born in 1945, who lives and works in Toronto,
Canada; Lisa Fairclough, the elder grandchild, born in
1970; her sister Jo Fairclough, born in 1971; Joan Vernon-
Cryer; their son, (Christopher) Michael Fairclough, born in
1940, who studied at the Kingston School of Art from 1957
to 1961, and won the Rome Scholarship in Engraving in
1964; and his wife, Mary (Cecilia) Malenoir, his exact contemporary at Kingston, and his successor in the Rome
Scholarship the following year. Gathered round the Christmas turkey, wearing their paper hats, are four practising
artists and three holders of the Rome Scholarship in Engraving.[153] The convivial subject was first caught by the flash-
light of the camera before it was transferred to etching and
aquatint.

It has been seen how hard Fairclough worked as a
draughtsman in Venice. He later recalled:

This leads me to the way I work. Until the past five or seven years
(up to the late seventies that is) I've always worked on the spot,
whether indoors or outdoors, I have worked in the presence of the
subject. Nowadays, with advancing years, drawing outdoors is very
uncomfortable, and it's very exhausting, and can be extremely
unpleasant. It's all right in St Mark's Square where there are plenty
of people about, but, in other places, there are groups of hooligans
who are only too delighted to find an old gentleman quietly drawing, and bullyragging him, and trying to steal his equipment …
now I can't do that anymore. So I use a camera … in exactly the
same way as I would drawing on the spot. I am recording all the
different changes, incidents, which are later brought together into
a composition … The point I would personally state is you should
be able to do it without mechanical means.[154]

He also does his own processing and printing. 'My emphasis
is on use – like any other good tool it is and can be abused.'[155]
All the musical subjects were made from drawings done
during one performance when a camera could not be used.

The Etchings of Wilfred Fairclough is concerned with Fairclough as a printmaker. Another book could be written on
the watercolours of Wilfred Fairclough. Just as his draughtsmanship and work on *Recording Britain* were considered
earlier, so some notice should be taken of his work as a
watercolourist, not least because the way in which he sees
those subjects informs those which he depicts in black and

white.[156] For instance, there is the amusing account which
he gave of an occasion in Venice, part of 'the seeing eye':
'… when I see rubbish in the water it's a marvellous colour.
We were marooned once in a flood. Well it wasn't really a
flood but we were in a restaurant and couldn't leave and the
tide took all the vegetables off the market, and the Grand
Canal was absolutely full of lemons, tomatoes, and red peppers
and lettuces – a *marvellous* sight'.[157] The same sense of
delight is also found in a more serious account where the watercolours of J M W Turner were in his mind when he wrote:

We had a good visit to Switzerland and hopefully something will
come out of it – tho' it will take some time. We had a very good
room overlooking the river and wooden bridge (in Lucerne). The
first morning God laid on a Blue Rigi for our entertainment. Didn't
miss a trick, a silver glow in the sky, wreath of mist and ducks flying
off the still water. He repeated the performance on the last morning
before we left. A good deal of Turner's imagination was in getting
out before dawn and painting what he saw in front of him. That
is the time of magic and it is all over in a very few minutes, after
that the day is more humdrum until the evening when a different
magic happens. We also had a Red Rigi on the way back from
Fluelen. So far as I know, no writer on the Red Rigi has ever mentioned that the Rigi is *made* of brown pink rock and even the
slightest touch of the setting sun sets it all alight.[158]

There writes the artist of sensibility, who can detect the
source of 'magic' and recognise it when he sees it.

The visit to Lucerne in 1980 provided a fertile ground for
subjects. The market scenes recalled the sight on the Grand
Canal, stalls laden with vegetables (*Lucerne Market*, 113),
bread and cheese (117), flowers (128) and even cacti (120).
The fish market, with its arches, and fountain dated 1926,
provided the subjects for *Onlookers* (125) and *Lucerne Pike*
(127):

'I have had a pretty busy time especially just lately getting prints
ready for the RE. The two I normally send turned into three when
a very large Pike (fish) raised its head and said 'If you don't do me,
I will haunt you'. As ill luck would have it, I had a piece of copper
just the right size so I had no excuse and had to 'do it'. Joan doesn't
like it much, says she thinks it is going to bite her. The other two
plates are of *Lucerne Fishmarket* (125) (where I found the pike) and
the second a Venice Carnival, a figure in a cloud of white tulle
(126). Work that one out in black and white with a needle! The
show opens this week.[159]

All the subjects in Lucerne are distinguished by a framework
which is firm without being insistent or overbearing. It is so
well conceived that it may be overlooked in the activity that
is going on. For instance, in *Lucerne Market, Bread and
Cheese* (117) in which the pots of jam in the foreground with
their transparent paper covers are beautifully drawn, the
composition is enclosed by the building on the left and the

roof over the stall, which has been worked in aquatint, while on the right is the coping of the wall and the railing going back in perspective. It is a reminder of what can also be seen in the two musical subjects, *Lucerne, Selected Duets* (107), in the careful delineation of the iron railings, and in the paving stones of *Lucerne, Solo Flute and Flags* (114). In his figurative subjects Fairclough rises to the challenge of rendering the whole of the environment, eliciting a mood and a sense of place as distinctively in Lucerne as he does in Venice.

There is a personal factor which accounts for the way in which Fairclough has been able to produce such a consistent body of work in the last eighteen years. As Charles Bartlett observed, he must be 'extremely well organised' and have 'enormous energy'.[160] Of the organisation there can be no doubt, as has been seen in his admiration for, and insistence on, order. His energy has been deliberately and carefully preserved for what he considers to be essential, and that is his work. He writes of 'getting back to the grindstone', of 'shedding', 'all committees gone, no entertaining except for family and very few friends of long standing nor do I go out'. He worked hard in his studio, not so much as the 'rebel' of the Blackburn days but as 'a loner', 'sporting his oak', to keep interruptions at bay: 'At seventy-four I have to accept an energy conservation policy so that I can continue to produce drawings and prints'.[161] For the same reason he has been reluctant to undertake commissions but did so in Cumberland in 1981:

The weather improved on Tuesday and I managed a very good day indeed. Kirkstone Pass, Ullswater, Aira Force, round to Martindale and Sandwick. Hopefully got a lot of information and notes so something may come of the trip – that is a hope not a promise.[162]

There was no shortage of energy in the seventy-four year old to accomplish so much in the day. What came of it was a watercolour of Aira Force which was turned into the etching *Ullswater, Aira Force* (110) in 1982. As he sketched the fall from below, he recalled that it 'is the Great Reichenbach Falls in miniature. Amazing'.[163]

It was in 1985 that Fairclough embarked on the series of subjects inspired by the Carnival in Venice. *Venice Carnival, Make Up I* (122) was a subject glimpsed by the artist in the cloakroom of the Hotel Danieli. It is notable for 'its lovely velvety blacks so typical of his work at its best' and it is those tones which distinguish these latest works contrasted with the figures in 'white tulle'.[164] The 'lovely velvety blacks' are to be found in *Venice Carnival, Paris in Venice* (123), which is also a restaurant group, *Venice Carnival, Masks* (124), with its background of San Marco and the campanile, and in *Venice Carnial, Make Up II* (133). 'The cloud of white tulle'

which was realised in *Venice Carnival, Nozze* (126), assisted by the use of aquatint, is to be found in the most recent of all these Venetian subjects, *Venice Carnival, Secrets* (137), which unites whites, resonant blacks and aquatint and provides the subject for the limited edition of *The Etchings of Wilfred Fairclough*.

Fairclough's description of how he approaches each plate helps in the appreciation of how the subjects have been achieved:

'As you see from the drawings, the studies of these prints are done in a formal way, because when I am drawing, all I'm looking for is information – I don't want anything else – I want information, which I can take into the studio and work on and eventually refine into a composition which I then put onto a plate, because I find that if you take a design too far you've exhausted all your energies. So you must always keep something to keep you alive, something you've got to invent completely anew on the plate – in this way you are kept alert.

When you consider that before you have your final print, there are your studies, there's your preliminary drawing, there's the tracing, there's the needling of the plate, there's the biting of the plate, and then there's the printing itself. That's six stages, between the initial image and the final print, and in any one of them it can die on its feet. So to avoid this, I try to keep the thing on the boil right to the end. It needs concentration.[165]

Concentration, energy, liveliness and refinement are all there, as is the technical skill by which the subjects are realised. 'Superb technique and conscientiousness don't always make good art ... Technique should be the servant not the end product',[166] recalls Fairclough's thoughts in the Palazzo Pitti.

Wilfred Fairclough has disclaimed 'trying to express some inner soul' in his work,[167] but his individuality, what he has to give as a human being, is inescapable. That individuality might be defined as the spiritual quality of each human being. In Fairclough's work, whether it is in the cool grey prints of the 1930s, or the tonally rich etchings since 1972, there runs throughout his personality, 'shrewdly and humourously observant', as Colin Hardie recognised.[168] If there remains an elusive element, a subtlety, which may escape analysis, that is the essence of the artist and the man, the individual contribution which transcends his technical skill and the 'draughtsmanship of a master printmaker'.[169] The best tribute to the man and his achievements in black and white are words which he may have read sixty years ago by that fellow practitioner, E S Lumsden: 'To be a great etcher a man must be peculiarly sane and yet sensitive and alive'.[170]

Acknowledgements

To the gratitude expressed in the Foreword for his invitation
to contribute to *The Etchings of Wilfred Fairclough*, a further
ample measure must now be added for the artist's patience
in answering questions and for reading and amending the
account of his work. Thanks are also due to those organisa-
tions which contain the information and related material
which has been checked in the course of its compilation. For
their kind assistance and for the readiness with which they
have made their facilities available warm thanks are due to
Mrs Eunice Martin, Dr Bernadette Nelson and Dr J J L
Whiteley in the Ashmolean Museum; Mr Nicholas Turner
and Miss Hilary Williams in the British Museum; the
General Secretary of the British School at Rome, Ms Ann
Marie Tighe, to whom additional thanks are due for permis-
sion to quote from the archives in her care relating to
Wilfred Fairclough's tenure of the Rome Scholarship in
Engraving from 1934 to 1937; and Emma Rossiter, archivist
of the Royal College of Art. In addition to the helpfulness
found in libraries and print rooms it is a pleasure to acknow-
ledge that encountered in the University of Durham, from
Professor Richard A Chapman, and in the University of
Oxford, from the college secretary at New College, and Mrs
C J Hopkins, the assistant archivist at Trinity College.

I am also very grateful to Mr Michael Blaker RE, the editor
of *The Printmakers' Journal*, for his willing consent to the
frequent use which has been made of material published
therein; Mr Colin Clark; Mr C G Hardie, for his permission
to quote from his letters and reports; Mr Brian North Lee;
Mrs Anne Stevens, for her invariable assistance; Professor
C H Vereker, for his recollections of 1939; and Mr Stephen
Wildman, Deputy Keeper of Prints and Drawings at the Birmingham City Museum and Art Gallery, for the use of quo-
tations which are acknowledged in the notes which follow;
nor should the contribution of Michael Fairclough be omit-
ted, because it was he who persuaded his father to cooperate
in the production of the book.

IAN LOWE

Notes

1 *The Journal of the Royal Society of Painter-Etchers and Engravers*, No.6, 1984, *The Wilfred Fairclough lecture at the R.E.*, p.4-6. The lecture was given on 1 March 1983 and tape-recorded. The editor, Michael Blaker, has kindly allowed extensive quotation from that lecture and also from the one given by Ian Lowe on 27 June 1987 to mark the artist's eightieth birthday in the now-named *The Printmakers' Journal*, No.10, 1989, p.15-18. Subsequent references below will be abbreviated to *Journal*.

2 E S Lumsden, *The Art of Etching A complete and fully illustrated description of etching, dry-point soft-ground etching aquatint and their allied arts, together with the technical notes upon their own work by many of the leading etchers of the present time*, Seeley, Service and Co, London 1925, p325.

3 The biographical information in the essay is based on interviews with the artist, referred to hereafter as verbal information, on letters between Wilfred Fairclough and Ian Lowe since 1976, to which dated references will be found in the notes which follow, and the two lectures printed in *Journal* (1 above).

4 On Edward Biggs see *List of unpublished plates*, No.6, p.112, hereafter referred to as *List*.

5 *Journal*, 6, 1984, p.4.

6 Lumsden, op.cit.

7 *Prospectus of the Royal College of Art, South Kensington, London, Session 1931-1932*, HMSO, London 1931. Hubert Lindsay Wellington, Hon ARCA, Registrar and Lecturer in Art, 1923-32 (1879-67). See also Christopher Frayling, *The Royal College of Art: One Hundred & Fifty Years of Art and Design*, Barrie and Jenkins, London 1987, p.107.

8 Sir William Rothenstein MA Hon ARCA Kt 1931, Principal 1920-35 (1872-1945). Frayling, op.cit. p.89.

9 Verbal information. Frayling, op.cit. p.107 mentions John Piper's gratitude for Wellington's kindness.

10 *Journal*, 6, 1984, p.5.

11 *List*, 1. The copy is taken from Van Dyck's etching of Philippe Le Roy, baron de Broechem (1596-1679), the first portrait of the subject and from the first state, see Marie Mauquoy-Hendrickx's *L'Iconographie d'Antoine Van Dyck, Catalogue Raisonné*, Bruxelles 1956, p.180, C 1. The quotation is taken from Fairclough's inscription on his proof which was annotated in 1975. R S Austin (see 14) continued the practice in the Engraving School as Professor Alistair Grant records in *150th Anniversary Exhibition Printmaking from the Royal College of Art*, Barbican, London, 4 June – 19 July 1987, p.6.

12 *Prospectus*, op.cit. Alan E Sorrell RWS ARCA, Senior Assistant Instructor of Drawing 1931-39 and 1946-48 (1904-74).

13 Verbal information.

14 *Prospectus*, op.cit. Malcolm Osborne RA RE (later PRE) ARCA (1880-1963); Robert Sargent Austin RE (later PRE) ARWS (later PRWS) ARCA, Hon Secretary to the Faculty of Engraving, British School at Rome from 1926, and see 18 (1895-1973). Francis Dodd ARA ARWS (1874-1949). Henry Rushbury ARA (later RA) RE and see 143 (1889-1968).

15 *Robert Sargent Austin: A Catalogue of Etchings and Engravings*, Robert Douwma Ltd, London, Catalogue 29, November 1986, edited by Peter Black, p.5.

16 Sir Francis Job Short RA PRE (1857-1945).

17 Frayling, op.cit. p.69.

18 *Robert Austin RA PRE RWS 1895-1973 An Exhibition of etchings, engravings, drawings and watercolours*, Ashmolean Museum, Oxford, 16 February–16 March 1980, and Leicestershire Museums, Art Galleries and Record Service 17 January–1 March 1981, edited by Ian Lowe, biographical note, and p.11 for Austin's early etchings which he gave to Short.

19 Frayling, op.cit. p.140. It is incorrect to state that Osborne was 'the last remaining link with the days of Lethaby and Short' because Austin's link with Short remained (see 18 above).

20 On the British School at Rome see below, notes 45 and 46.

21 *Robert Austin*, Ashmolean, op.cit. p.11. Campbell Dodgson, *A Catalogue of Etchings and Engravings by Robert Austin RE 1913-1929*, published by the XXI Gallery, London 1930. Campbell Dodgson CBE Hon RE, Keeper of Prints and Drawings at the British Museum 1912-32, Chairman of the Faculty of Engraving at the British School at Rome, (1929-47), editor of *The Print Collectors' Quarterly* and of *Fine Prints of the Year*, 1936-38 (see 27, and also 46 below) (1867-1948).

22 On Brockhurst see *A Dream of Fair Women: An Exhibition of the Work of Gerald Leslie Brockhurst RA (1890-1978) Painter and Etcher*, Graves Art Gallery, Sheffield 12 December 1986–1 February 1987, Birmingham City Art Gallery, 12 February–29 March 1987, National Portrait Gallery, London, 10 April–31 May 1987, edited by Anne Goodchild.

23 See Harold J L Wright, 'Catalogue of the Etchings of G L Brockhurst ARA RE', *The Print Collectors' Quarterly*, 1935, Vol.22, pp.62-77, no.75, 1932, and see 99.

24 *Journal*, 10, 1989, p.15. Wilfred Fairclough letter to Ian Lowe 13 May 1987.

25 *Journal*, 10, 1989, p.15.

26 ibid.

27 *Fine Prints of the Year An Annual Review of Contemporary Etchings and Engravings*, London and New York 1933, p.3, Pl.11, edited by Malcolm Charles Salaman, Hon RE, from 1923 to 1935 when he was succeeded by Campbell Dodgson (21) (1855-1940).

28 *Journal*, 10, 1989, p.16. Wilfred Fairclough letter to Ian Lowe 13 May 1987.

29 Verbal information.

30 *Journal*, 6, 1984, p.5.

31 *Royal College of Art Distribution of Diplomas on Friday 21 July, 1933*, by the Rt Hon Lord Irwin KG GCSI GCIE, President of the Board of Education.

32 Verbal information.

33 The information quoted here is contained in the file relating to Wilfred Fairclough in the records of the British School at Rome, Regent's College, Inner Circle, Regent's Park, London NW1, where it is to be found in Box 183, and is subsequently referred to thus.

34 *The British School at Rome Exhibition of works submitted in the competitions for the Rome Scholarships of 1934 in mural painting sculpture & engraving*, Imperial Gallery of Art, South Kensington, 20 January–10 February 1934. Fairclough's work was exhibited under No.31 and preceded by that of Joan Hassall (1906-88) and Denise J M L Brown (b.1911).

35 Box 183, op.cit. Austin's reference says almost as much about him as it does abour Fairclough.

36 *Royal Society of Painter-Etchers and Engravers – List of Members and Associates* up to 1982.

37 Box 183, op.cit.

38 Verbal information.

39 *Journal*, 3, 1981, p.4, *Wilfred Fairclough* by C(harles) B(artlett).

40 *Fine Prints of the Year*, op.cit. 1934, p.1.

41 ibid. p.4. pl.18.

42 Campbell Dodgson, op.cit. 59, 64, and 76.

43 *Fine Prints of the Year*, 1934, op.cit. p.4.

44 *The British School at Rome A Note on the School and its Scholarships* by the Honorary General Secretary (Evelyn Shaw, see 68), 1931, p.13-14.

45 *The British School at Rome Exhibition of Works submitted … 1934*, op.cit., unnumbered pages (p.6) lists the Rome Scholars: Job Nixon (1891-1938); for Austin see 14; William Evan Charles Morgan (1903-78); Geoffrey Heath Wedgwood (1900-77); and Edward Bouverie Hoyton (1900-88).

46 *Minutes of the Tenth Meeting of the Council of the British School at Rome*, 1 Lowther Gardens, 15 June 1934, which includes *Report of the Faculty of Engraving*, p.27. On Campbell Dodgson see 21.

47 Stanley Anderson (1884-1966); for R S Austin see 14; Stephen
   Gooden (1892-1955); F Ernest Jackson (1872-1945); Harry Morley
   (1881-1943); Malcolm Osborne, see 14; Henry Rushbury, see 14.
   Rushbury was appointed a member of the Faculty of Engraving in 1929
   and was Chairman from 1947 to 1964. Fairclough was appointed in
   1951 and was Chairman from 1965 to 1973. see 14; and Ian Strang
   (1886-1952).
48 *Minutes of the Tenth Meeting*, op.cit. p.27.
49 ibid.
50 Verbal information.
51 *Minutes of the Tenth Meeting*, op.cit. p.9.
52 Box 183, op.cit.
53 Ellis Kirkham Waterhouse (1905-85), author of *Roman Baroque Painting*, printed for the subscribers to the British School at Rome, London,
   1937, revised edition 1976.
54 Brian Dick Lauder Thomas (1912-89).
55 Box 183, op.cit.
56 Verbal information.
57 Dodgson, op.cit. no.84.
58 Colin Hardie letter to Ian Lowe 2 July 1973.
59 Wilfred Fairclough letter to Ian Lowe 10 September 1985. The relic
   was that of the Circumcision.
60 Box 183, op.cit.
61 Proofs of the two life drawings are in the collection of the British
   School at Rome, Regent's College, London NW1, solander case 22.
62 Lumsden, op.cit. p.332.
63 Box 183, op.cit.
64 *The British School at Rome Report of the Executive Committee*, 1935,
   Report of the Faculty of Engraving, p.19-20.
65 *Report*, ibid. p.1.
66 George Winston Hooper (1910). Murray Macpherson Tod (1909-74).
67 Verbal information.
68 Evelyn Shaw letter to Wilfred Fairclough 12 November 1935. Sir
   Evelyn Campbell Shaw, Honorary General Secretary to the British
   School at Rome, 1912-47, created KCVO 1947 (1882-1974). Alan
   Powers has pointed out that Shaw was 'a vital link between the students
   and the Faculties' in *The Rome Scholarship in 'Decorative' Painting
   1912-1939, British Artists in Italy Rome and Abbey Scholars 1920-
   1980*, Canterbury College of Art, 1985, p.16.
69 Wilfred Fairclough letter to Evelyn Shaw 11 November 1935.
70 ibid.
71 ibid. 8 January 1936.
72 ibid. 16 February 1936.
73 Evelyn Shaw letter to Wilfred Fairclough 27 February 1936.
74 Powers, op.cit.
75 Wilfred Fairclough postcard to Evelyn Shaw 13 March 1936.
76 Wilfred Fairclough letter to Evelyn Shaw 25 March 1936.
77 Verbal information.
78 Wilfred Fairclough letter to Evelyn Shaw 19 April 1936.
79 Box 183, op.cit.
80 See, for example, Basil Gray, *The English Print*, Adam and Charles
   Black, London 1937, p.185, on Austin's 'extraordinary sweetness of
   line' and p.186 where other artists 'have not attained the same balance
   between technique and content which makes Austin's work so
   satisfactory'.
81 David Jones, *In Parenthesis*, Faber and Faber, London 1937, p.149.
82 Stanley Spencer (1891-1959), *Travoys arriving with Wounded at a
   Dressing Station at Smol, Macedonia*, September 1916, oil on canvas,
   180 × 215 cms, Imperial War Museum, London, Catalogue number
   2268.
83 Verbal information.
84 *Minutes of the Eleventh Meeting of the Council of the British School at
   Rome*, 8 July 1937, *Report of the Faculty of Engraving*, p.17.
85 Evelyn Shaw letter to Wilfred Fairclough 22 June 1936.

86 Stephen Wildman, *Two Birmingham Painter-Etchers R. T. Cowern
   (1913-1986) and H. A. Freeth (1912-1986) An Exhibition of Etchings
   and Drawings*, Birmingham Museum and Art Gallery, 7 May–3 July
   1988, p.8.
87 Wilfred Fairclough letter to Ian Lowe 7 September 1986.
88 Wildman, op.cit. p.2.
89 Wilfred Fairclough letter to Ian Lowe 6 October 1980.
90 *Who's Who*, 1982, p.950.
91 Box 183, op.cit. 6 January 1937. Courtenay Arthur Ralegh Radford,
   Director of the British School at Rome 1936-39 (1900).
92 Fairclough has pointed out that 'El Kantara' means 'The Bridge' in
   Moorish so that to add 'Bridge' to the title is tautologous.
93 *Fine Prints of the Year*, 15th Annual issue, edited by Campbell Dodgson, p.4, pl.17.
94 *The British School at Rome Minutes of the Council and Reports of the
   Council and Reports of the Executive Committee and Faculties*, 20 July
   1939, p.23. The fifty-fourth meeting of the Faculty of Engraving took
   place on 13 July 1939. Campbell Dodgson did not sign the minutes
   until 11 March 1946.
95 Reginald Charles Brill (1902-74).
96 Edward William Armstrong (b.1896).
97 Verbal information.
98 ibid.
99 Harold James Lean Wright, Hon RE (1946) (1886-1961). Wright joined
   the print dealers, A Obach, in 1903, and P & D Colnaghi in 1911
   (undated information from A T Eeles). Colnaghi's used to be at 144-
   146 New Bond Street. After the move to 14 Old Bond Street, Wright
   became a partner in the firm. Kenneth Guichard, *British Etchers 1850-
   1940*, Robin Garton, London 1981, second edition, p.37, mentions that
   Wright compiled a list of Fairclough's etchings from 1932-40, which
   did not include 'several tentative earlier works' (see *List*) Fairclough
   recalled that Wright's 'list was compiled at the request of a client whose
   name I never knew. I do not think it was ever published.' (Letter to
   Ian Lowe 22 February 1990).
100 Dodgson, op.cit.
101 Verbal information.
102 *Journal*, 10, 1989, p.16.
103 Ada Harrison, *A Majorcan Holiday*, with drawings by Robert Austin,
    Gerald Howe, London 1927, p.64-5.
104 ibid. p.67.
105 *Journal*, 10, 1989, p.16.
106 Even Campbell Dodgson can nod. 'Wilfred is my only forename as it
    is now called … it is odd that very many people who do not know my
    name always think it is William, it very nearly was!' (Letter to Ian
    Lowe 22 February 1990).
107 *Fine Prints of the Year*, 16th Annual issue, p.4.
108 Verbal information.
109 ibid.
110 ibid.
111 J W Winkelman PRE, 5 October 1989.
112 Lumsden, op.cit. p.334.
113 Box 183, op.cit. Evelyn Shaw letter to Wilfred Fairclough 1 October
    1937.
114 Presented to the British Museum by the Contemporary Art Society,
    1945-12-8-18, 19.
115 The Honourable Arnold Nottage Palmer (1886-1973), letter to Wil-
    fred Fairclough 29 December 1961.
116 *Recording Britain*, vol.I, Oxford University Press, introduction by
    Lord Macmillan, p.v.
117 Wildman, op.cit. p.6. If the proposed exhibition at the Victoria and
    Albert Museum takes place in 1990, the scheme should become better
    known.
118 Arnold Palmer letter to Wilfred Fairclough, op.cit.
119 ibid.

120 *Recording Britain*, four volumes, 1946-49, Oxford University Press.
121 Arnold Palmer letter to Wilfred Fairclough, op.cit.
122 Verbal information.
123 Professor C H Vereker letter to Ian Lowe 9 March 1990.
124 David Loggan (1635-92). Edmund Hort New (1871-1931).
125 See below 153, *Family Reunion* (100).
126 *Journal*, 3, 1981, p.4. *Wilfred Fairclough* by C(harles) B(artlett).
127 Wilfred Fairclough letter to Ian Lowe 6 October 1980.
128 ibid. The second instalment of Ian Lowe's *The History of the RE*, which will cover the period mentioned here, is due to appear in *Journal*, 12, 1991, following *Journal*, 11, 1990, pp.49–53.
129 Wilfred Fairclough's manuscript *Journal* for the period of his Leverhulme Research award remains in his possession. To differentiate it from *Journal*, it is referred to as *MS Journal 1961*. On Rome see p.19 and Venice p.62.
130 Verbal information.
131 *MS Journal 1961*.
132 ibid. p.8.
133 ibid. p.38.
134 ibid, p.73.
135 ibid. p.9.
136 ibid. p.19.
137 ibid. p.56.
138 ibid. p.62.
139 ibid. p.63.
140 ibid. p.66.
141 ibid. p.78.
142 Verbal information.
143 ibid. On Rushbury see *Sir Henry Rushbury RA, RE, RWS A Centenary Exhibition of Drawings and Etchings* selected and catalogued by Stephen Wildman with memoirs by John Ward CBE RA and Trevor Holliday, Birmingham City Museum and Art Gallery, 22 July–10 September 1989, Graves Art Gallery, Sheffield, 14 October–10 November, 1989, and The Fine Art Society, London, 20 November–15 December 1989.
144 Frederic Warburg, *Occupation for a Gentleman*, Hutchinson, London 1959, p.143.
145 *Journal*, 6, 1984, p.5.
146 *MS Journal 1961*, p.59.
147 See also Adrian Bury, *Wilfred Fairclough RE, RWS, ARCA An appreciation* in *The Old Watercolour Society's Club*, The Fiftieth Annual volume, edited by Adrian Bury, 26 Conduit Street, London 1975, p.48, pl.XXII.

148 Wilfred Fairclough letter to Ian Lowe 27 March 1976.
149 Verbal information.
150 *MS Journal 1961*, p.61.
151 Giulio Lorenzetti, *Venice and its Lagoon*, Edizioni Lint, Trieste, reprinted 1975, p.299.
152 Verbal information.
153 *Journal*, 10, 1989, p.18. In addition to the three Rome Scholarships, Wilfred and Joan Fairclough are both ARCAS and members of the RWS. Wilfred, Michael and Mary Fairclough are all full members of the Royal Society of Painter-Etchers and Engravers. Further academic honours include the award of a Royal Academy silver medal to Mary Malenoir in 1962, and Celia Fairclough's degree in French and Italian. Alan Powers, op.cit. p.16, rightly refers to the 'family ties' which were formed through the British School at Rome and fostered by Evelyn Shaw (see 68).
154 *Journal*, 9, 1984, p.6.
155 Wilfred Fairclough letter to Ian Lowe 4 May 1983.
156 On Fairclough as a watercolourist see Adrian Bury, op.cit. pp.41-53.
157 *Journal*, 6, 1984, p.4.
158 Wilfred Fairclough letter to Ian Lowe 6 October 1980. For J M W Turner's watercolour *The Rigi at Sunrise – The Lake of Lucerne ('The Blue Rigi')* see *Early English Watercolour Drawings by the Great Masters*, Special number of *The Studio*, 1919, London, Paris and New York, edited by Geoffrey Holme, p.xvii, pl.28, then in the collection of Walter J H Jones; *Descriptive Catalogue of the Exhibition of Selected Water-Colour Drawings by Artists of the Early English School held at Messrs. Thomas Agnew & Sons Galleries, London, March–April 1919*, and see Andrew Wilton *The Life and Work of J. M. W. Turner*, Academy Editions, London 1979, p.483, no.1524.
159 Wilfred Fairclough letter to Ian Lowe 7 September 1986.
160 *Journal*, 3, 1981, p.4, see 126.
161 Wilfred Fairclough letter to Ian Lowe 12 August 1981.
162 ibid. 30 October 1981.
163 ibid.
164 Joan Fairclough, 24 November 1989.
165 *Journal*, 6, 1984, p.6.
166 Wilfred Fairclough letter to Ian Lowe 16 December 1989.
167 *Journal*, 6, 1984, p.4.
168 see 63.
169 *Journal*, 10, 1989, p.18.
170 Lumsden, op.cit. p.310.

The plates

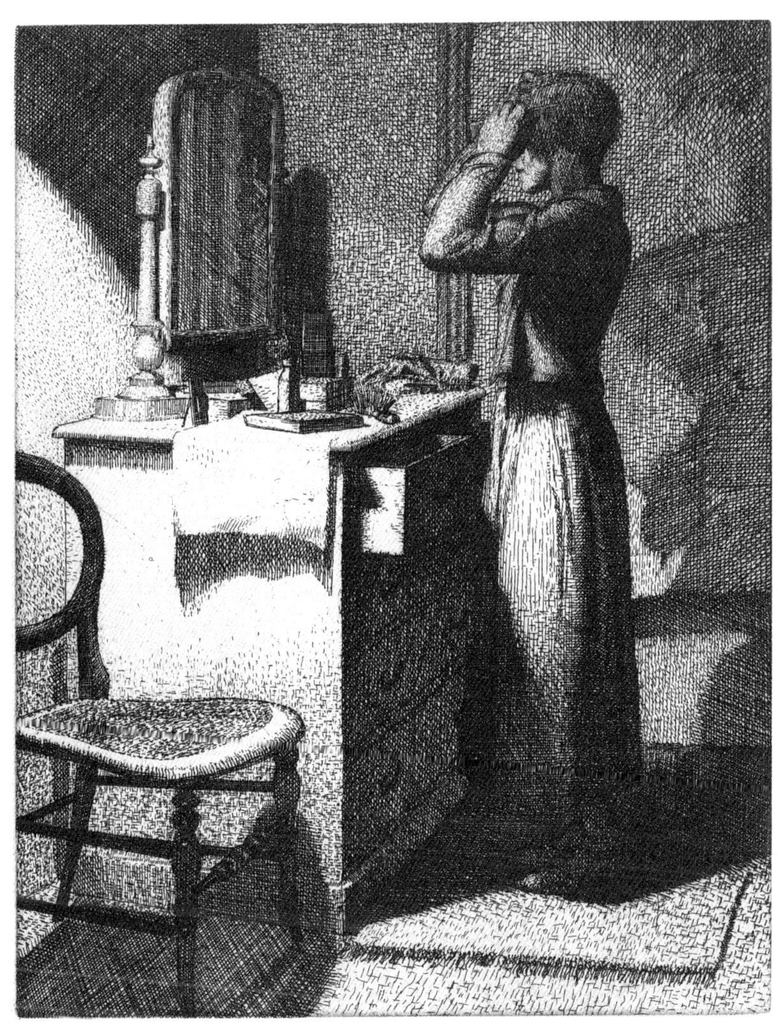

1. Joan Dressing her Hair. 1933. E $7\frac{1}{2} \times 6$ (2)

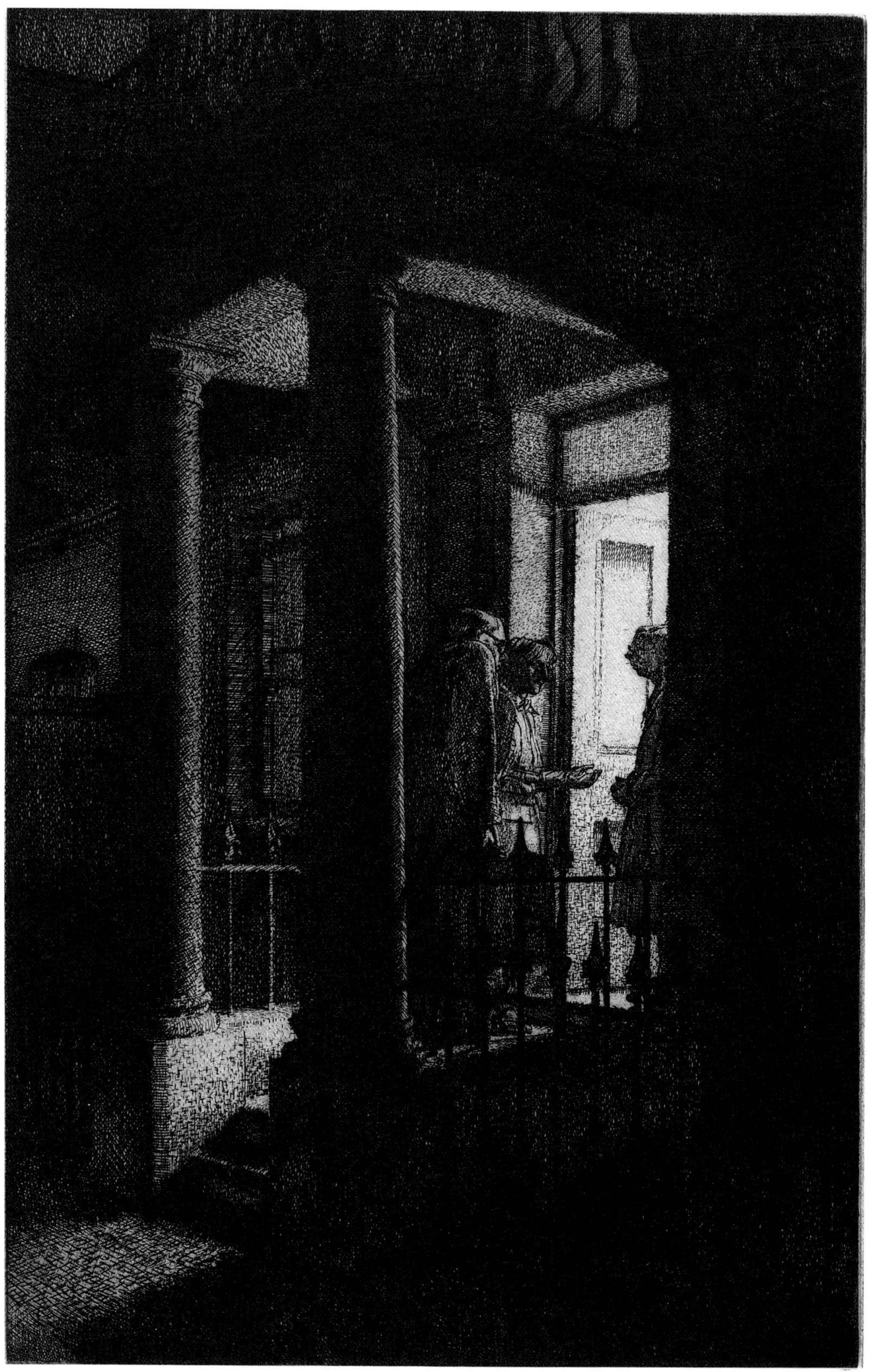

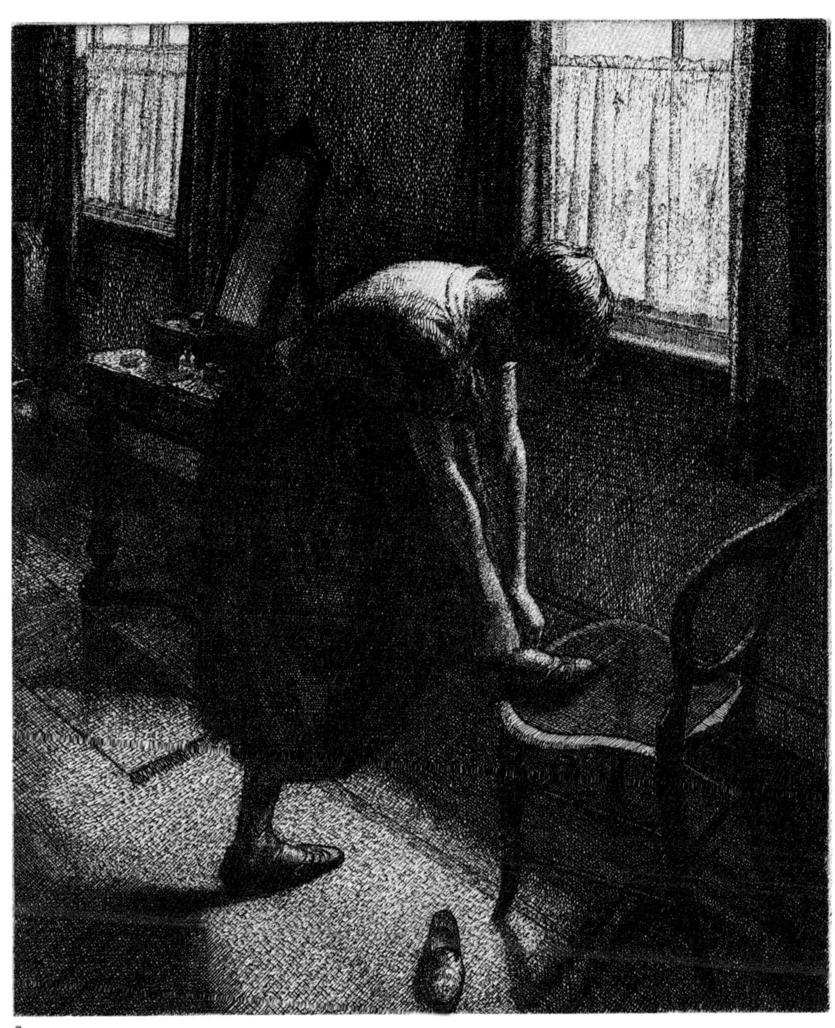

3

2. The Doorway (The Arrival). 1933. E $10 \times 6\frac{1}{2}$ (4)
3. Morning. 1933. E $7\frac{1}{2} \times 6\frac{1}{2}$ (7)

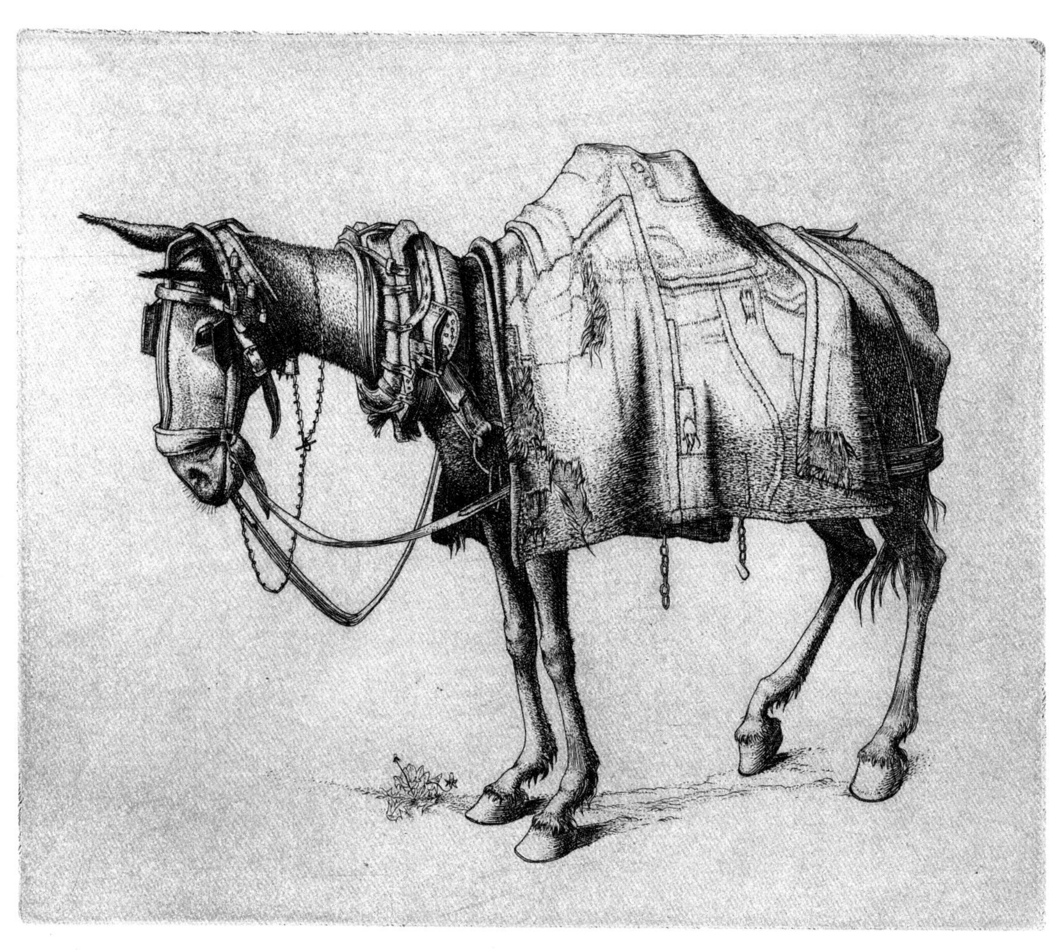

4. The Spanish Mule. 1936. LE $6\frac{3}{4} \times 8$ (20)

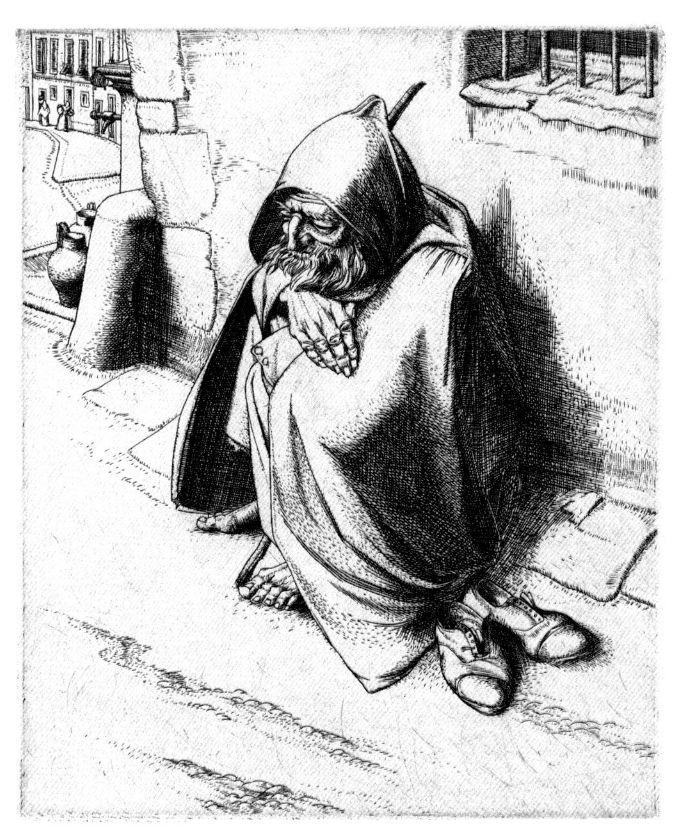

5. The Spanish Beggar. 1937. LE 6 × 5 (24)

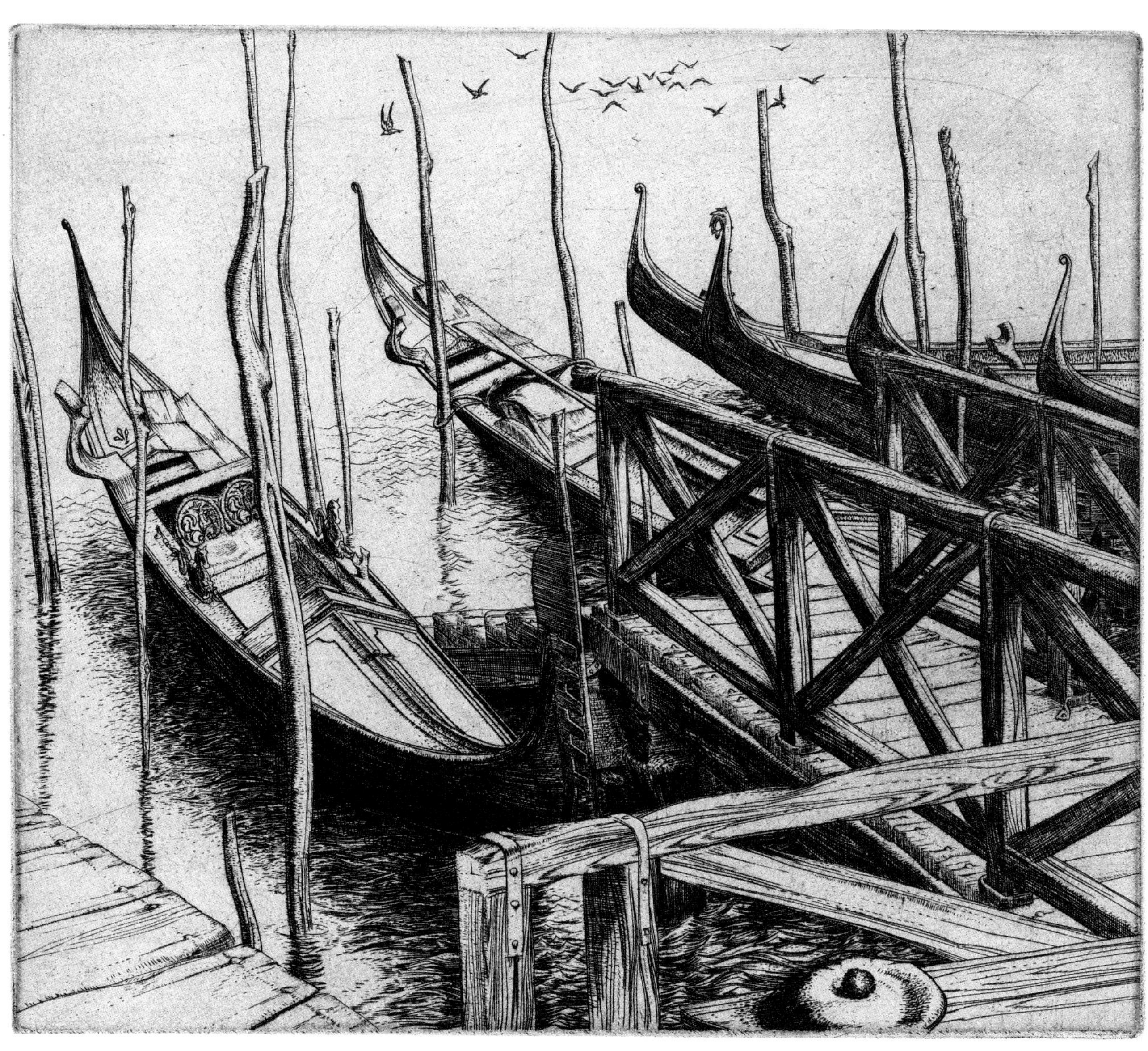

6. Traghetto. 1937. LE $7\frac{1}{4} \times 8\frac{1}{2}$ (25, see also 105)

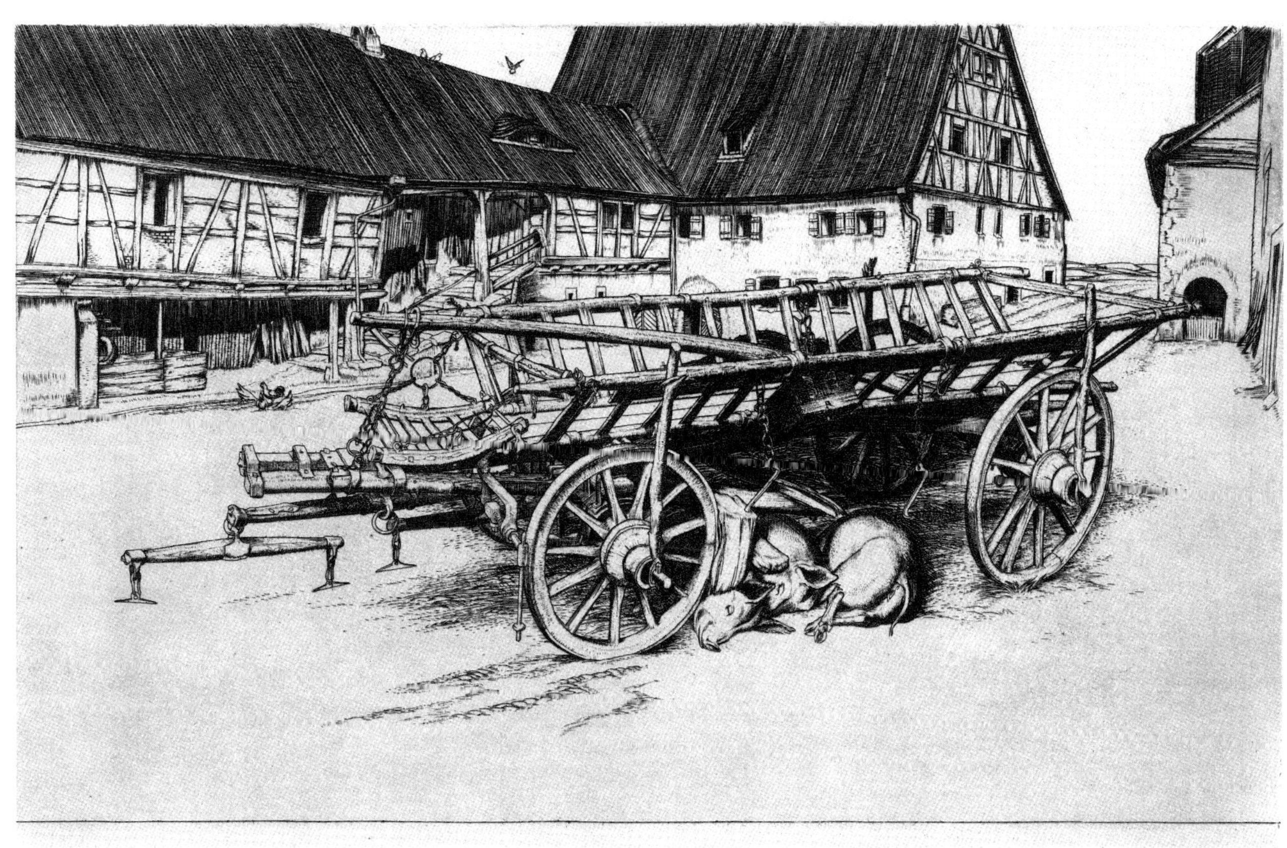

7. The Large Cart, Rothenburg. 1938. LE $8 \times 12\frac{1}{2}$ (28)

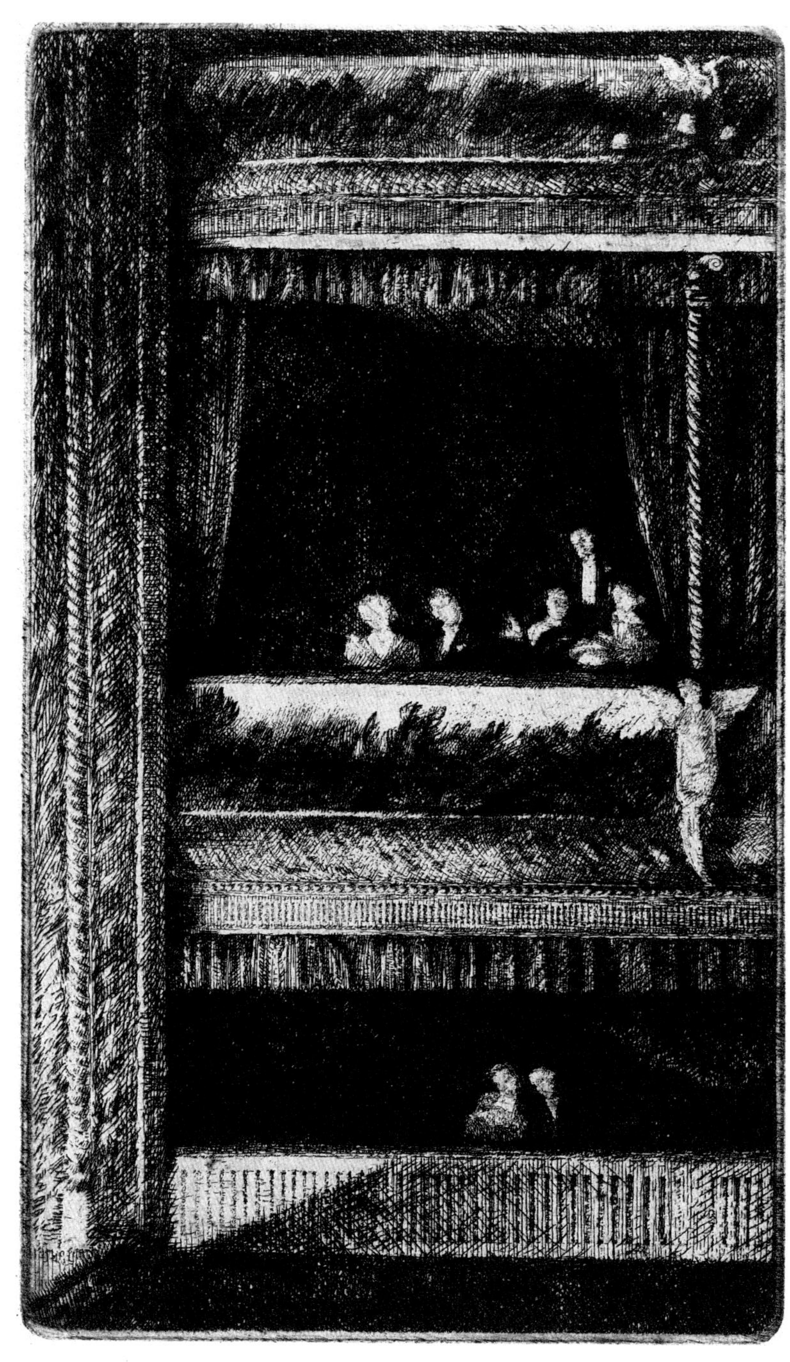

8. Bedford Box, Covent Garden. 1957. E 7 × 4¼ (51)

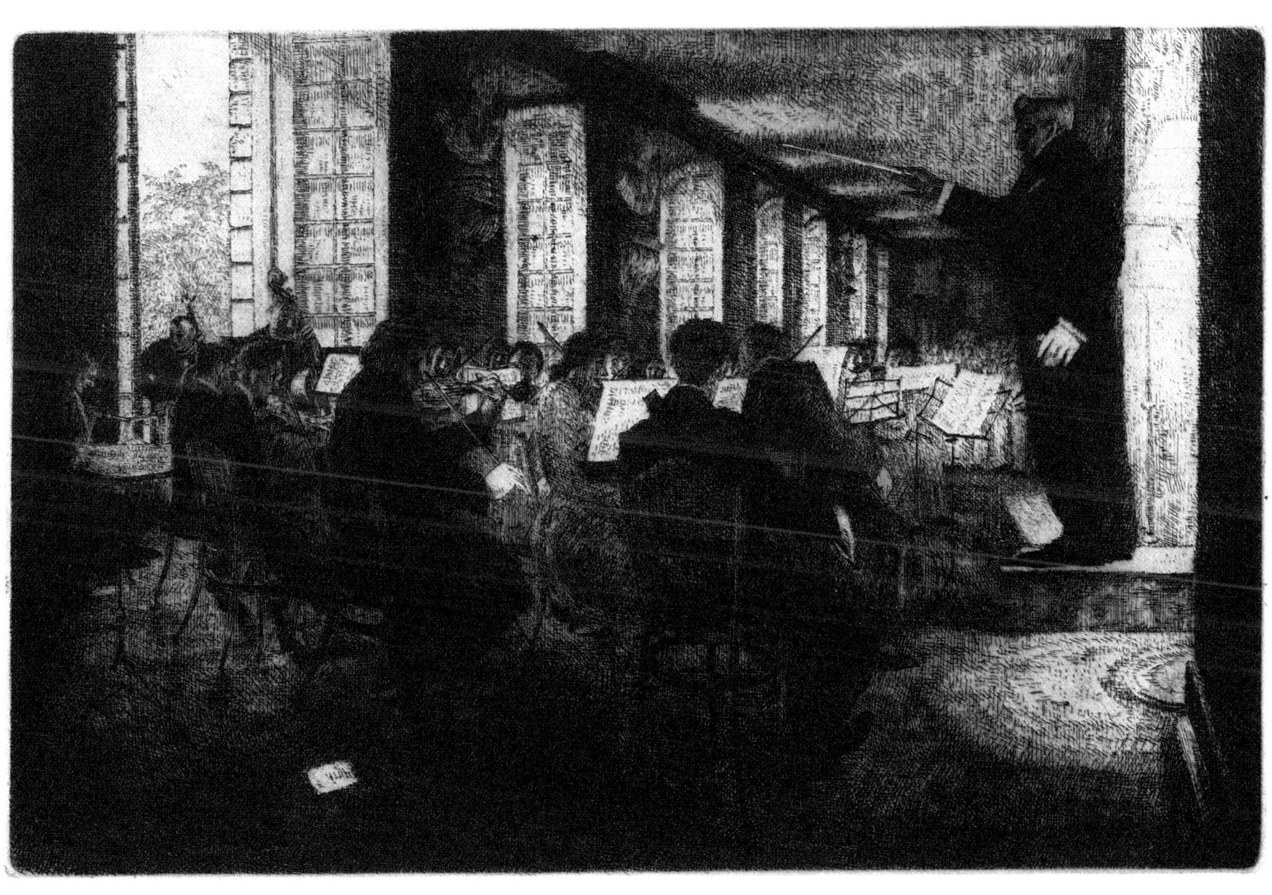

9. Jacques String Orchestra, Hampton Court. 1957. E $6\frac{1}{2} \times 10$ (52)

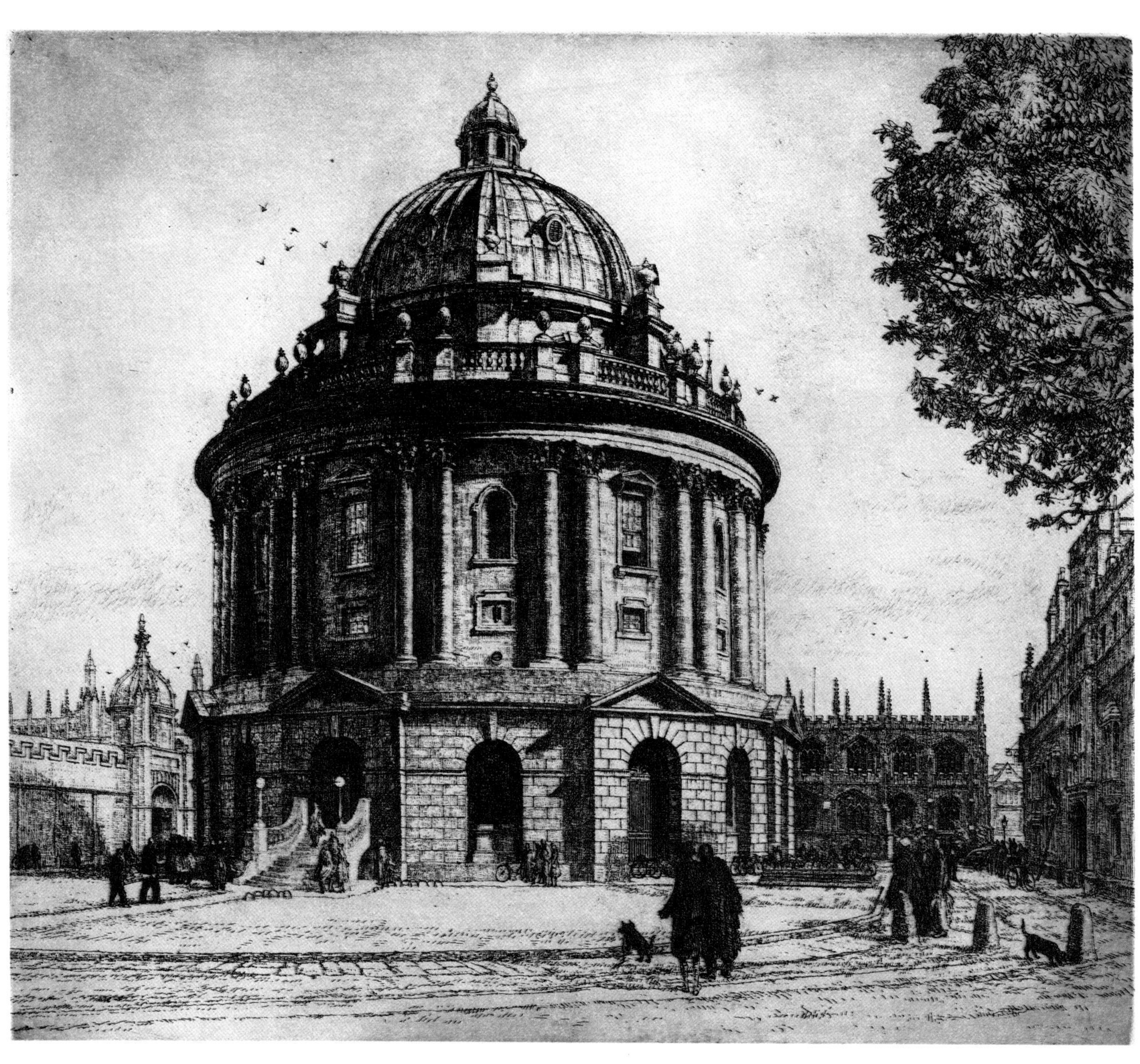

10. Radcliffe Camera, Oxford. 1959. E $11\frac{1}{4} \times 12\frac{1}{4}$ (54)

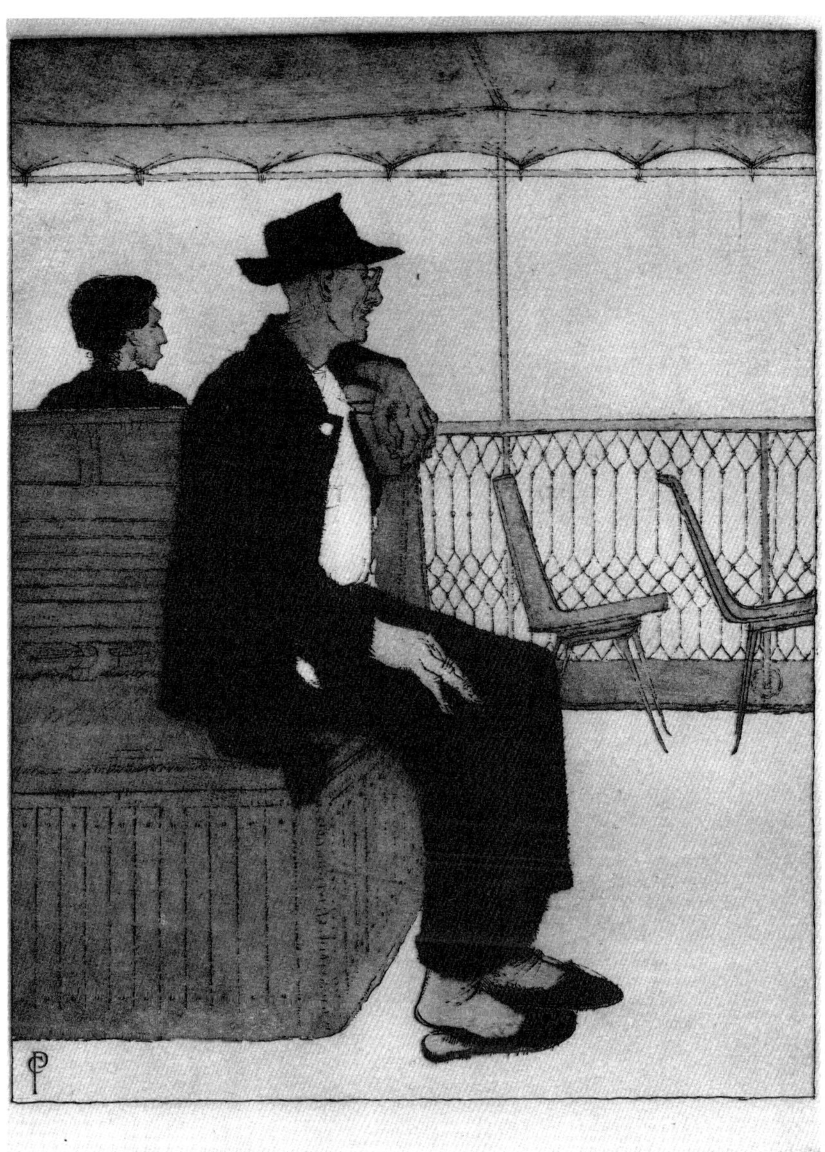

11. Boat to Chioggia. 1964. E/A 12 × 9 (65)

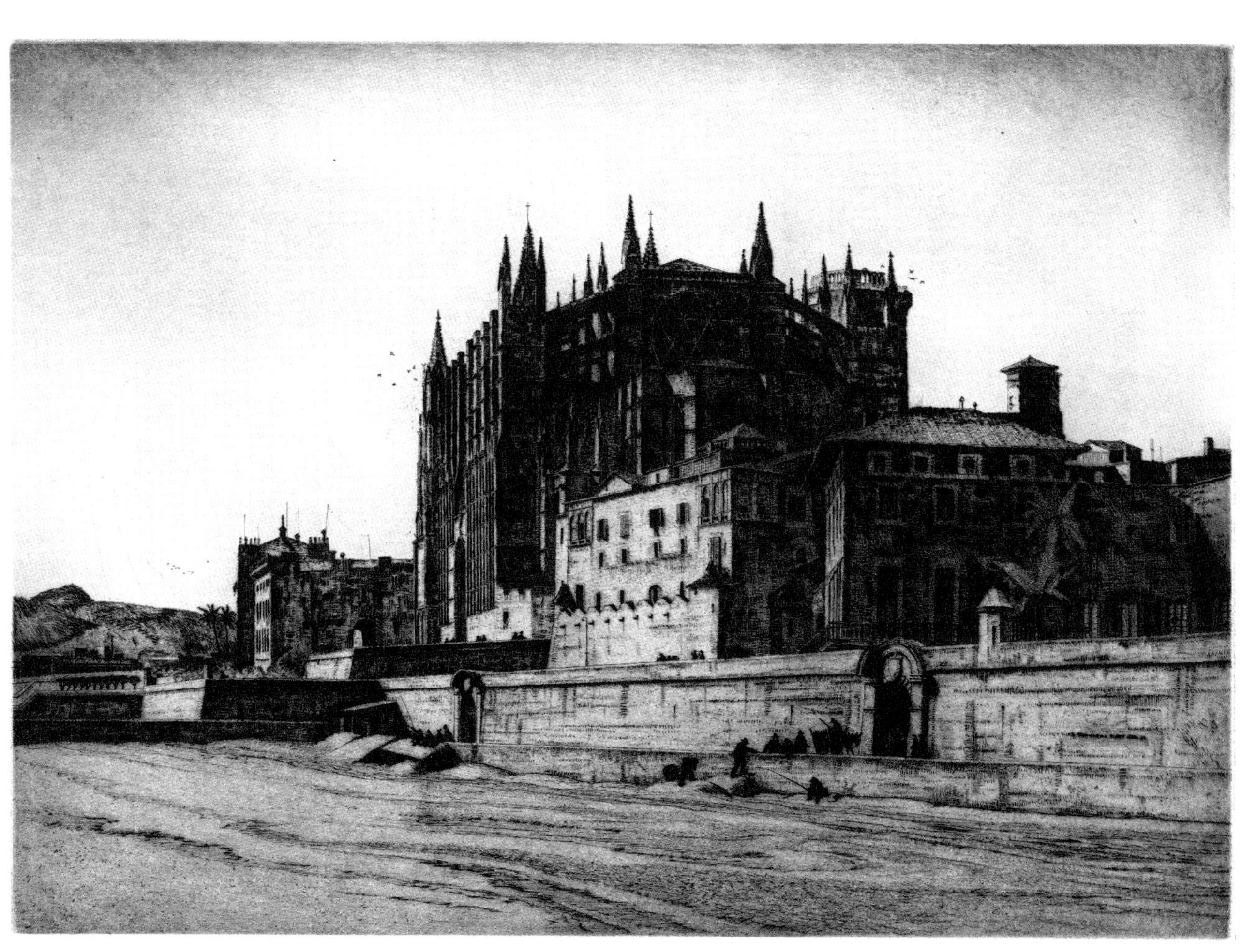

12. Palma Cathedral. 1970. E/D 10 × 14 (75, see also 26)

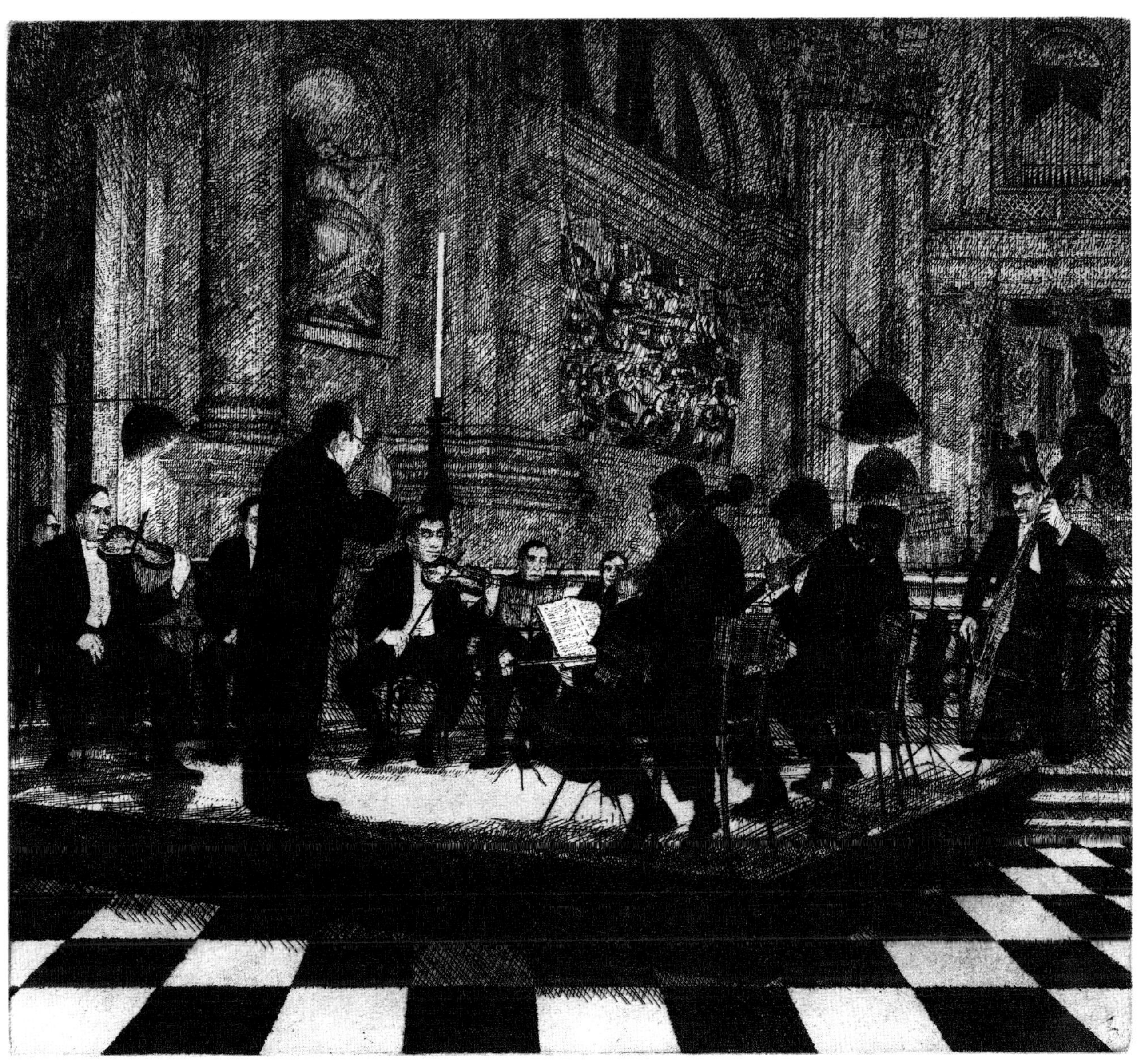

13. S Giorgio Maggiore, I Virtuosi di Roma. 1971. 10 × 11¼ (76)

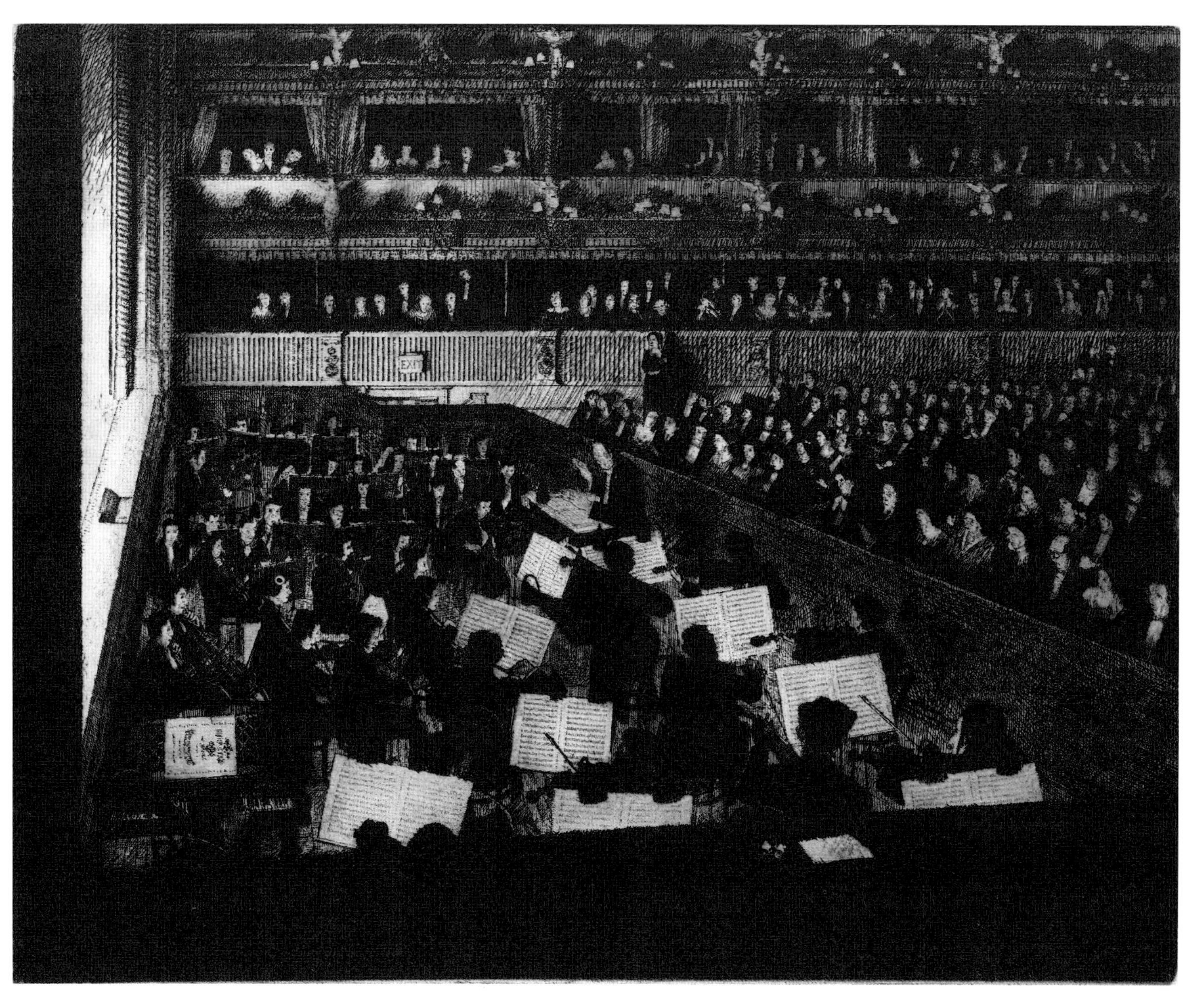

14. Covent Garden, Orchestra Pit. 1972. E $9\frac{3}{4} \times 12\frac{1}{4}$ (78)

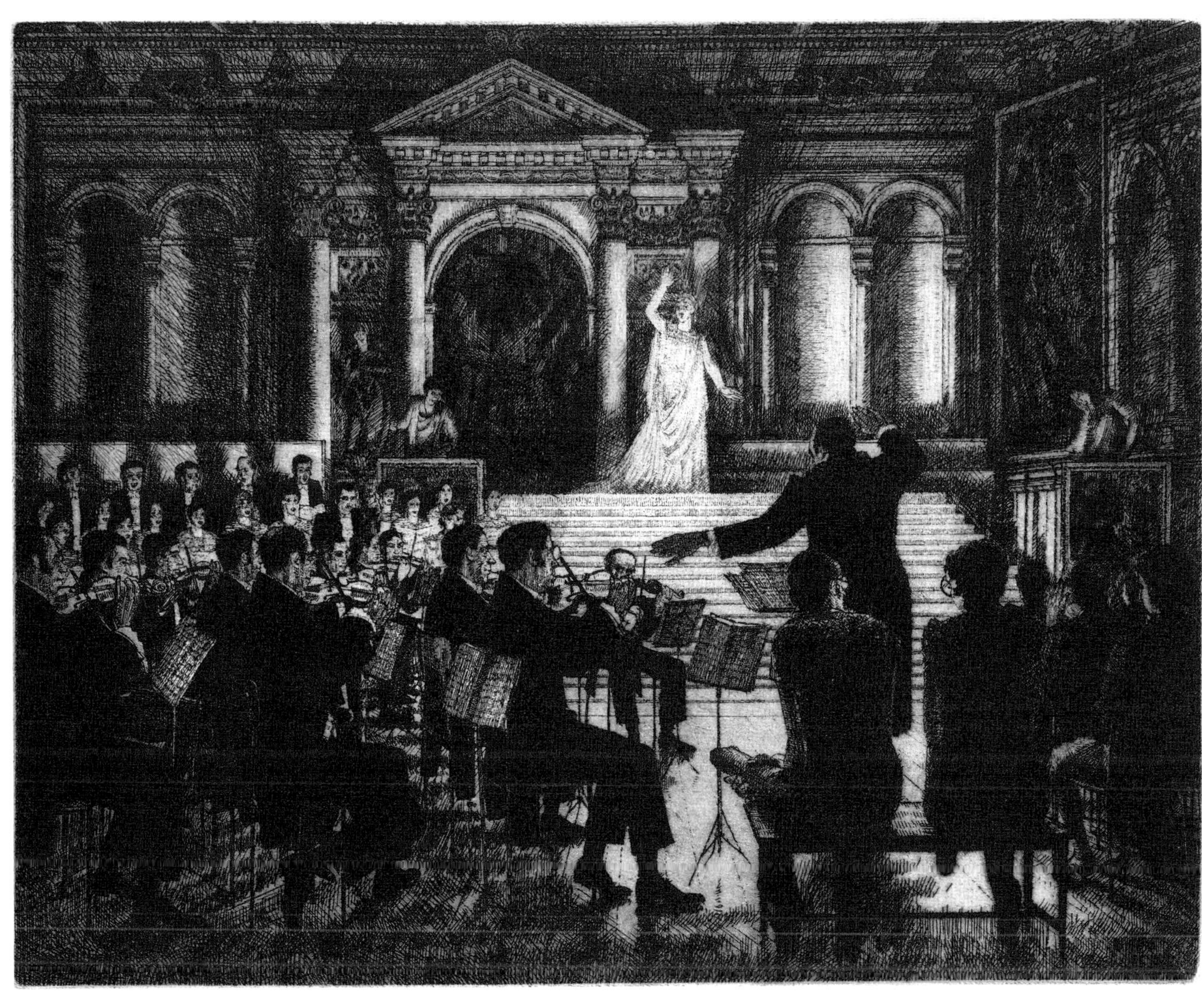

15. Juditha Triumphans, Scuola Grande di San Rocco. 1973. E $9\frac{3}{4} \times 12\frac{1}{4}$ (81)

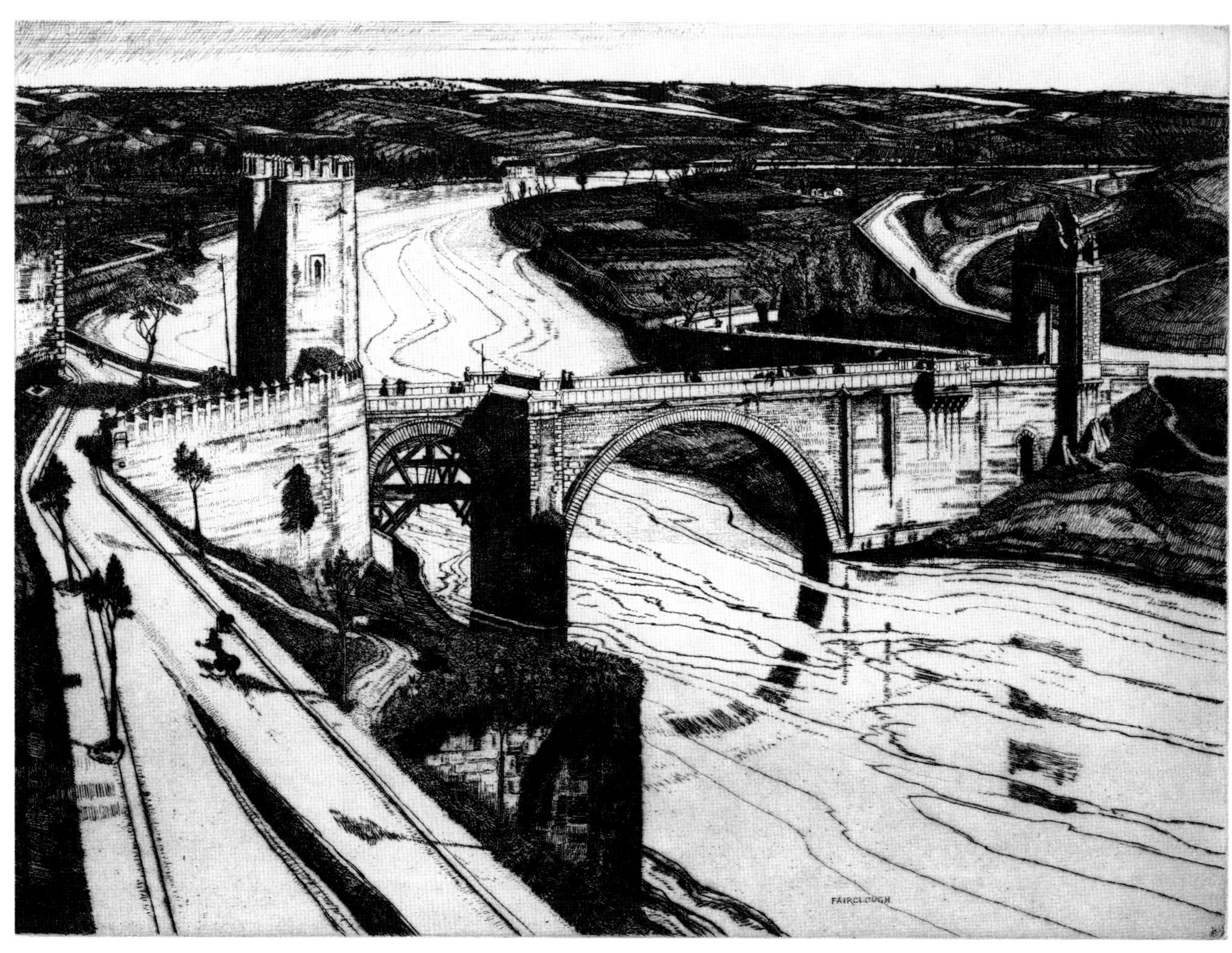

16. El Kantara, Toledo. 1974. E/D $9\frac{3}{4} \times 13$ (83, see also 23)

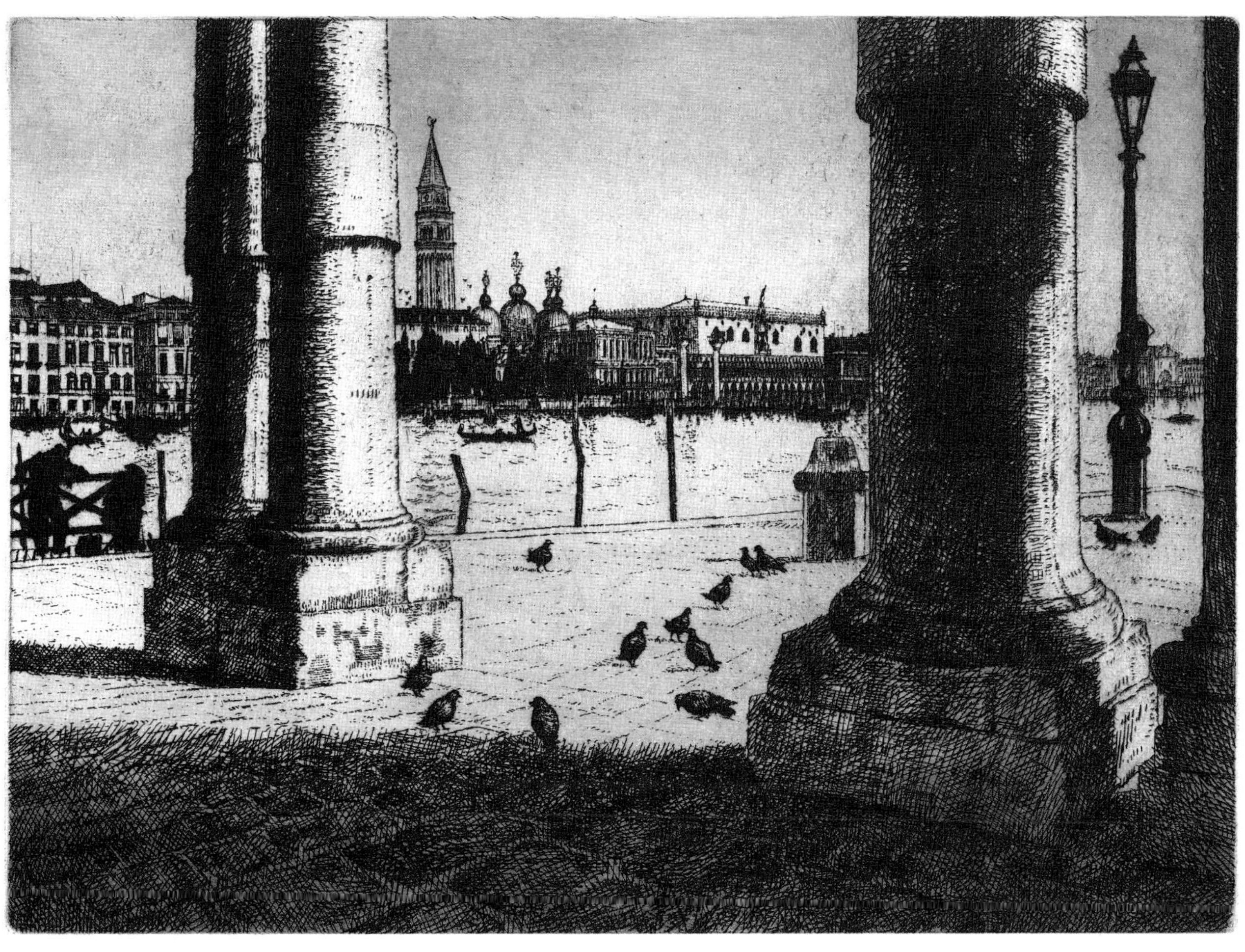

17. Venice from the Dogana. 1974. E 8 × 11 (85)

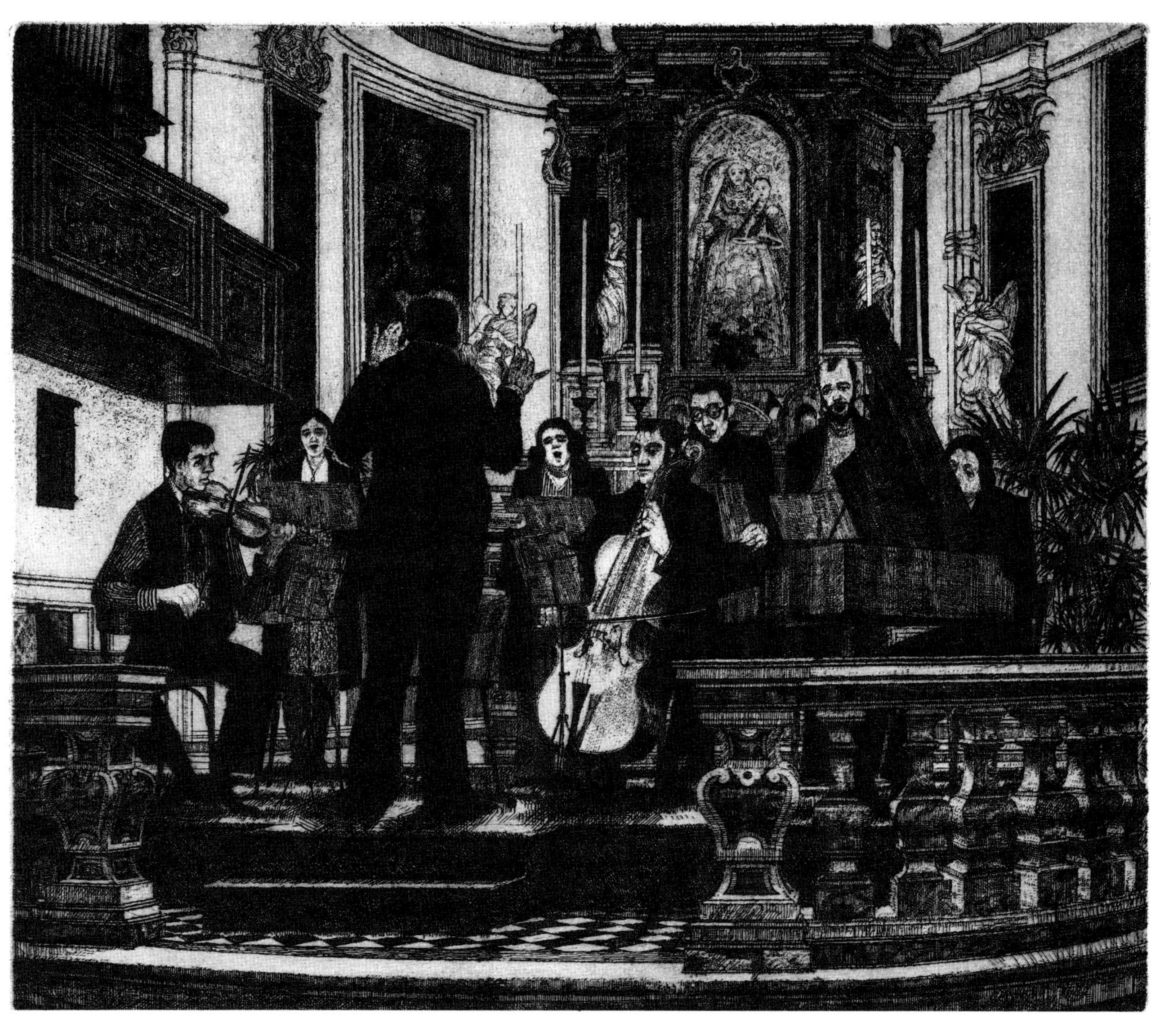

18. I Musici Cantori, Rehearsal, Bergamo. 1975. E 9½ × 11 (87)

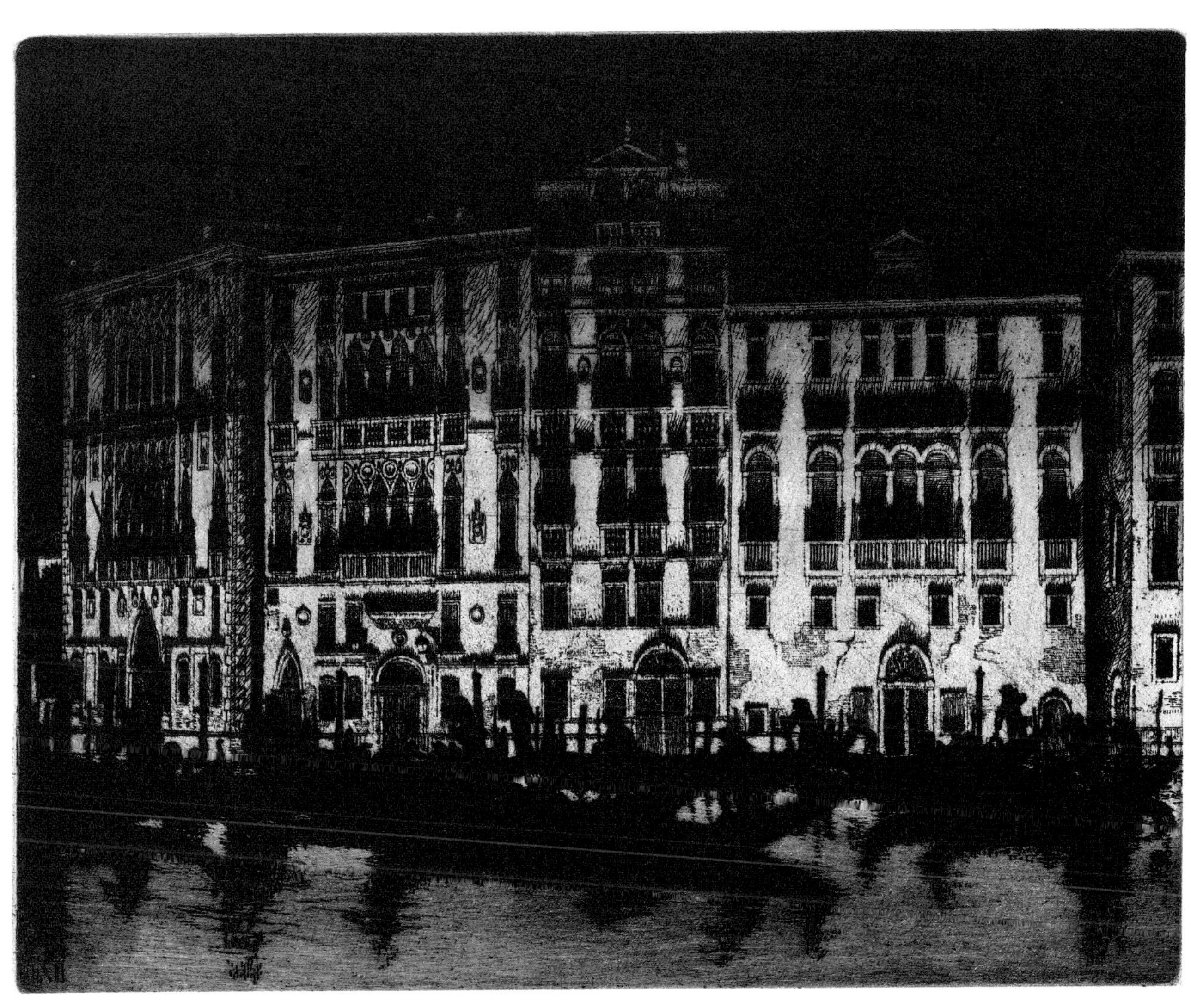

19. Venice, Night. 1975. E 8 × 10 (88)

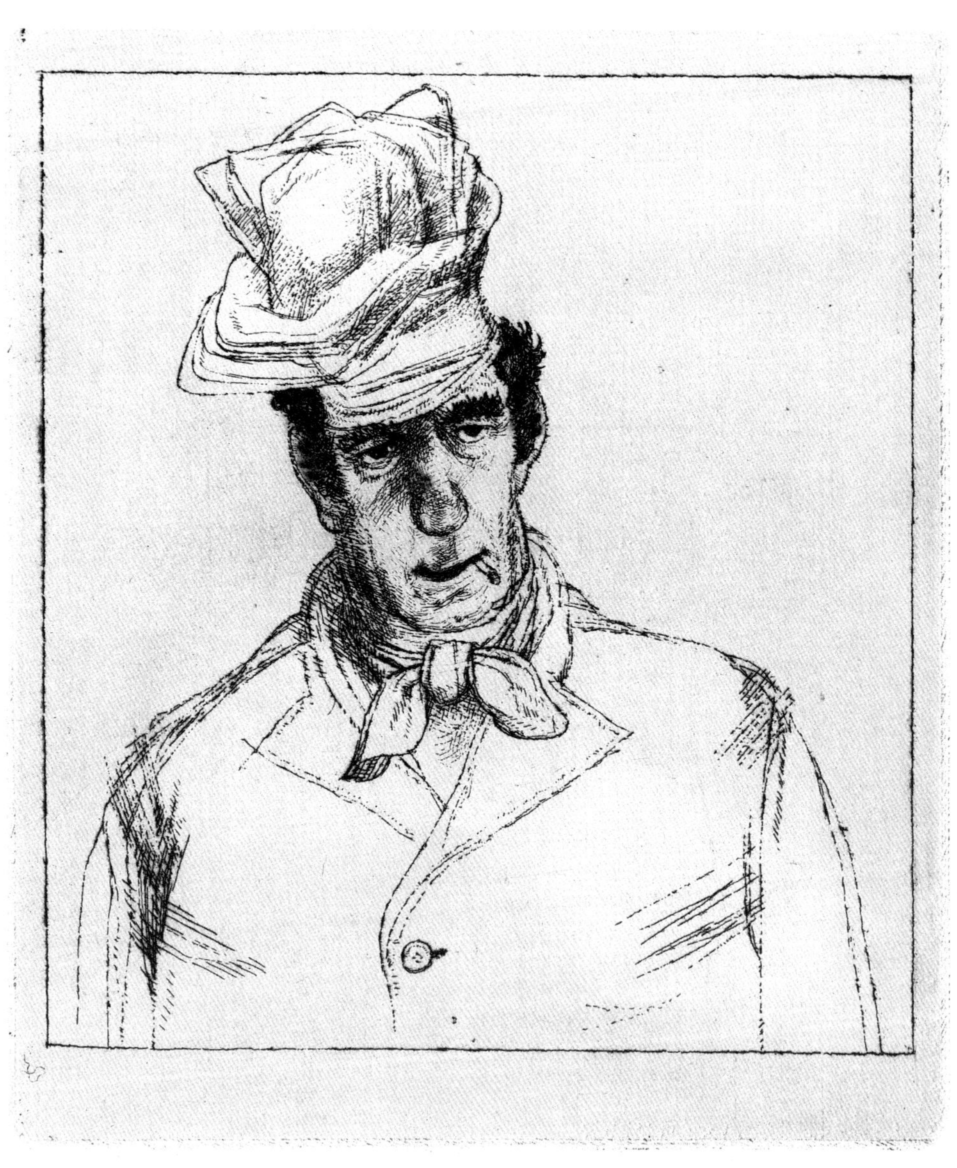

20. The Chef, Bergamo. 1975. E 7 × 6 (89)

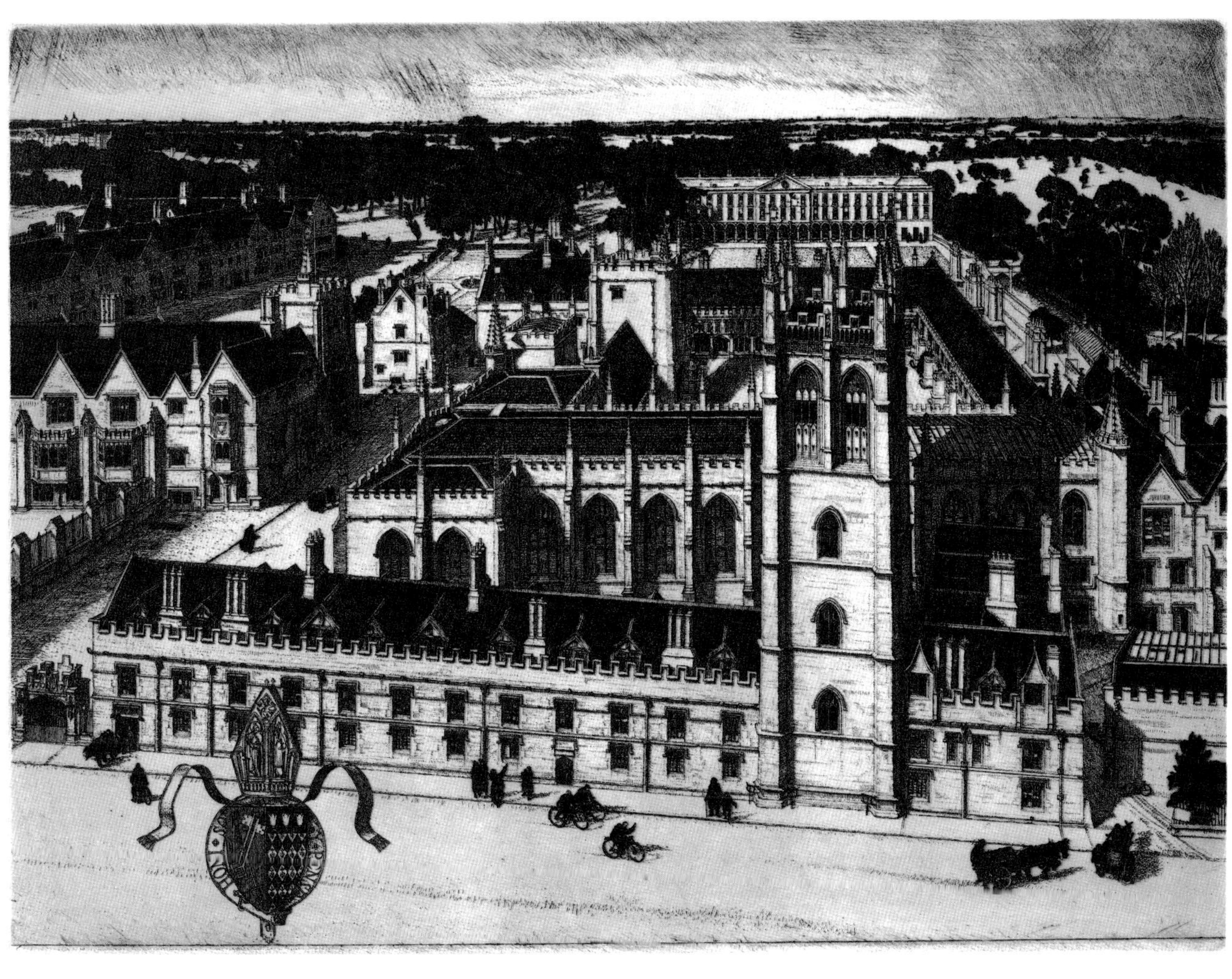

21. Magdalen College, Oxford. 1975. E/D $13\frac{1}{2} \times 18\frac{1}{4}$ (90 see also 33)

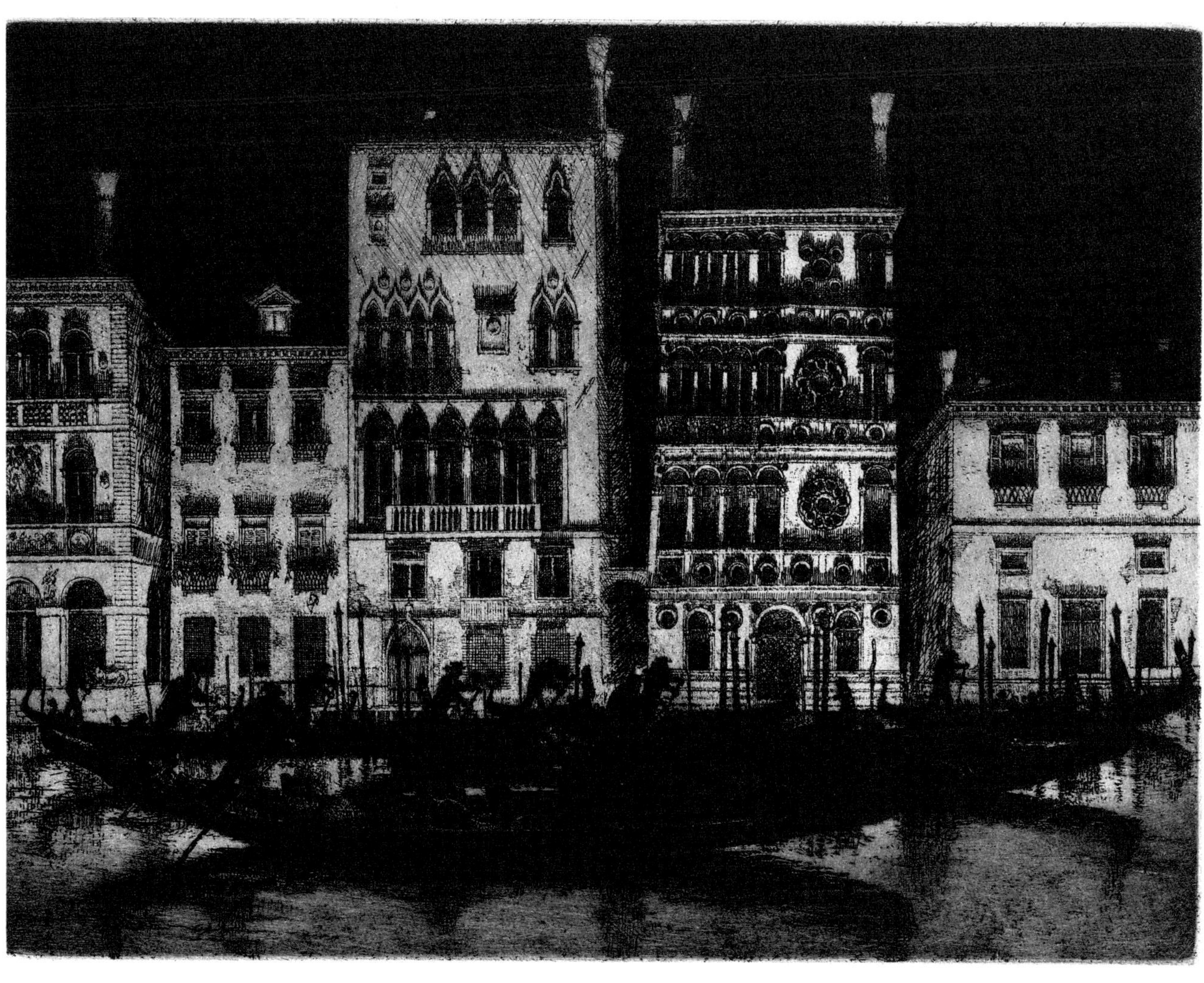

22. Venice, Palazzo Dario. 1976. E 8 × 10¼ (92)

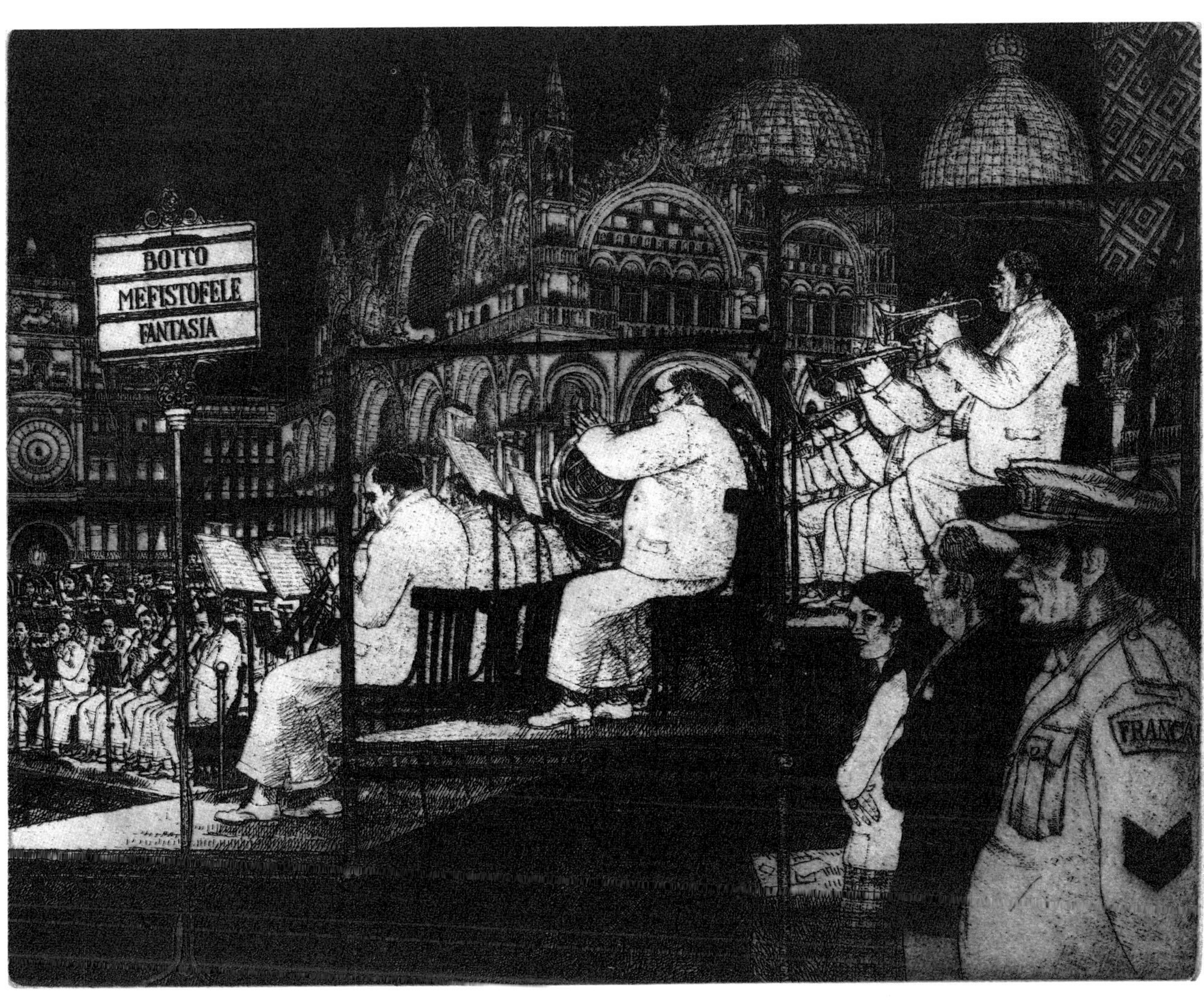

23. Venice, Mefistofele Fantasia 1976. E $9 \times 11\frac{1}{2}$ (91)

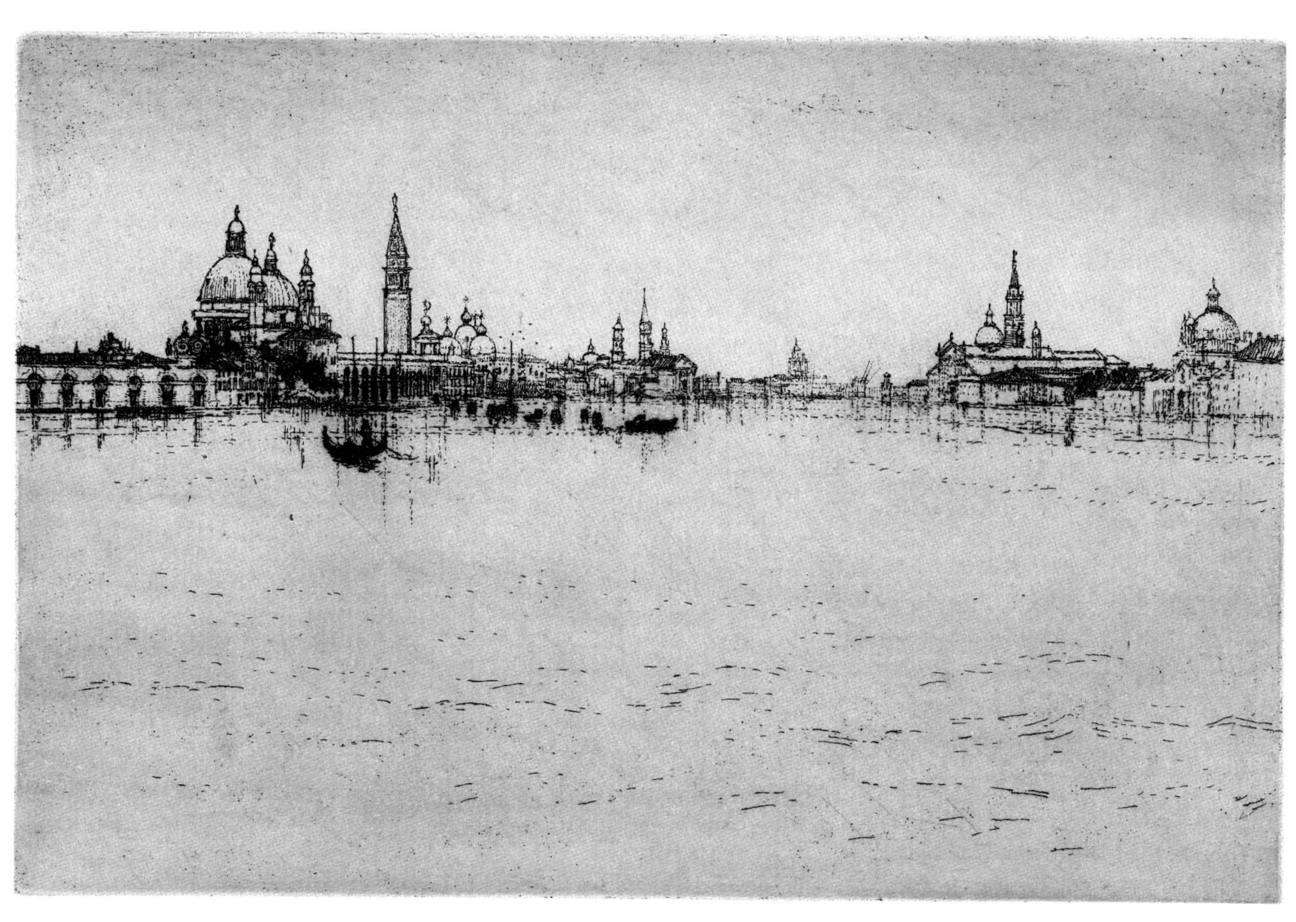

24. Venice from the Giudecca. 1978. E 8 × 12 (96)

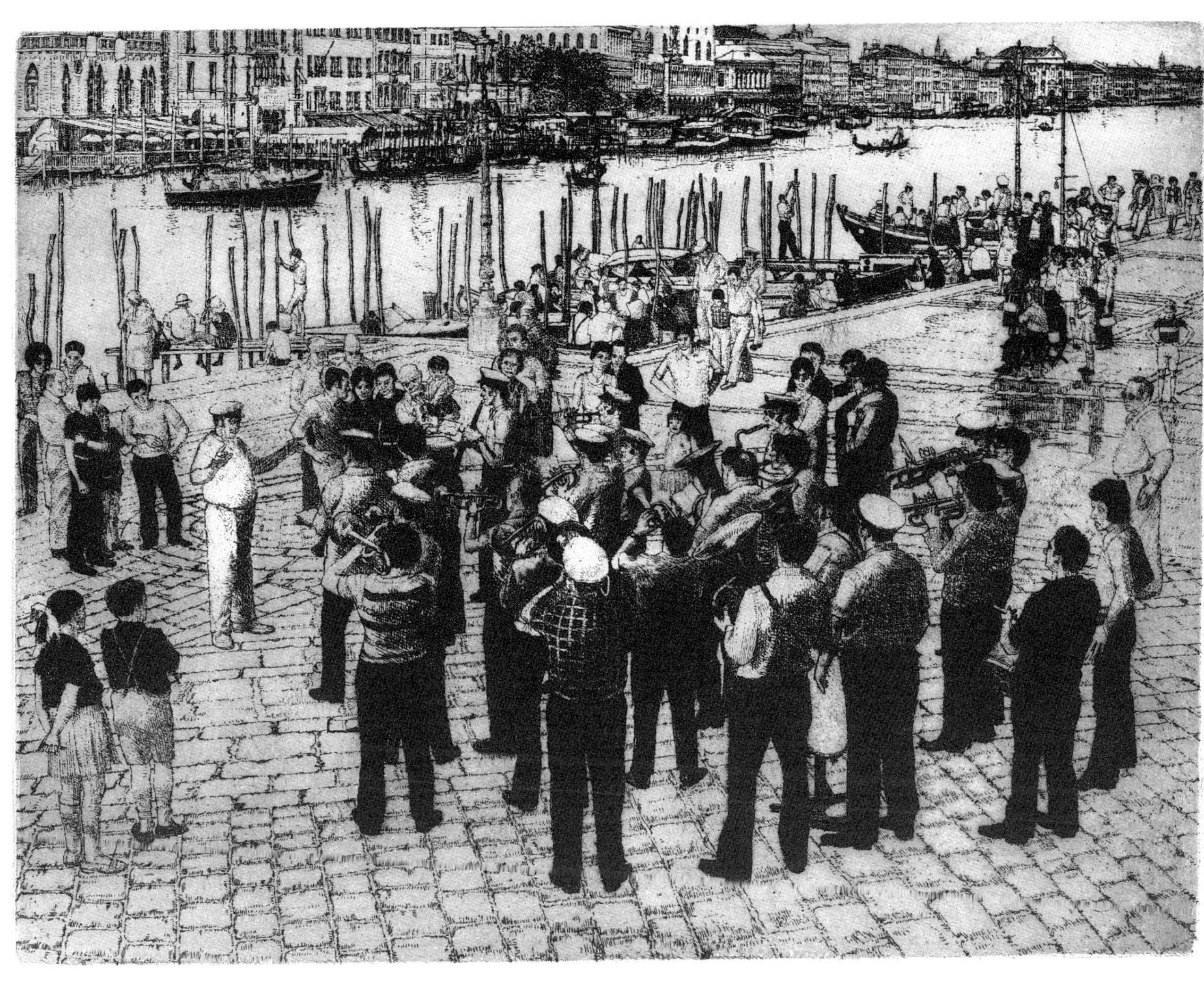

25. Venice, Regatta Band Rehearsal. 1977. E $7\frac{3}{4} \times 10$ (94)

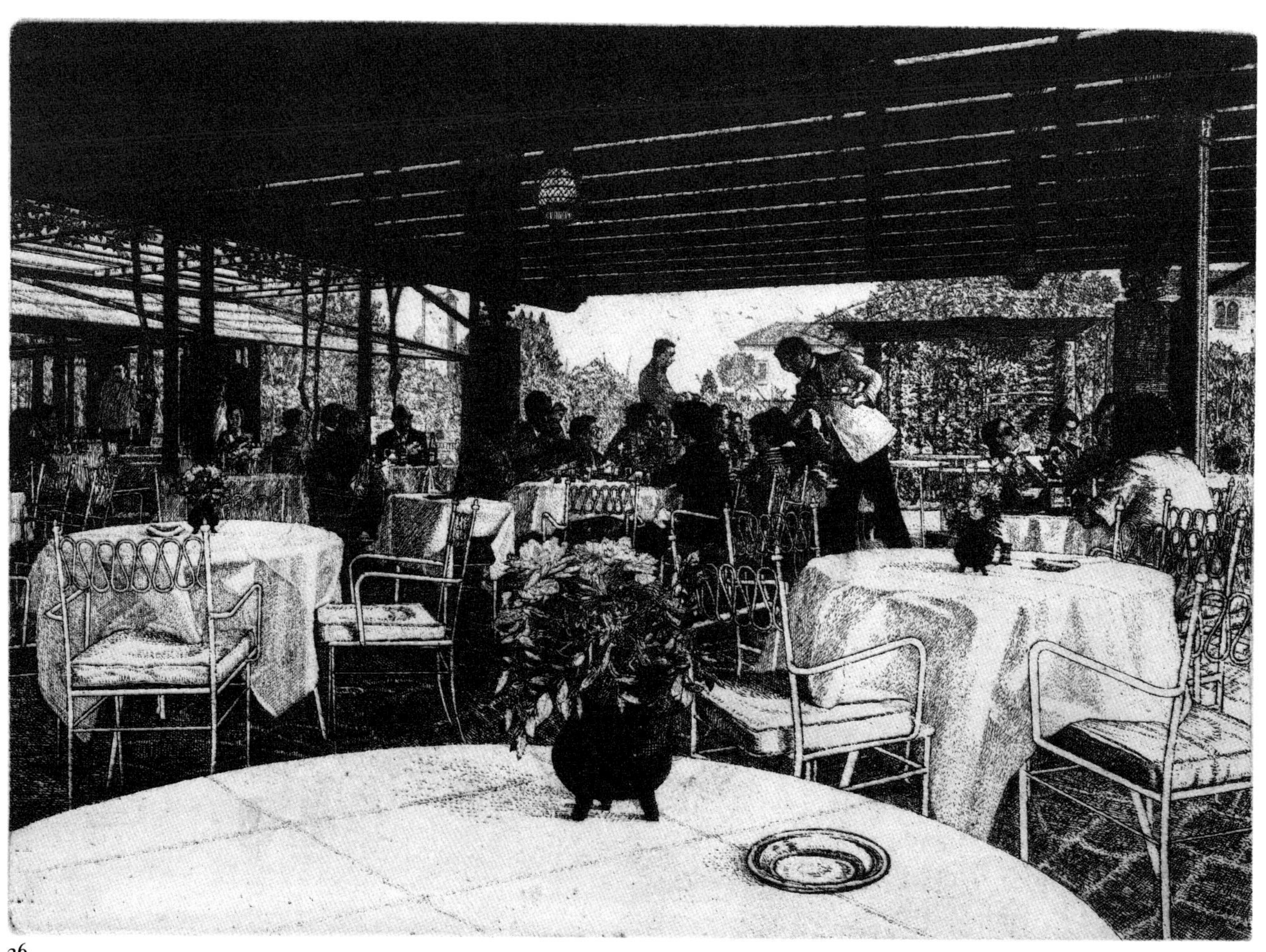

26

26. Venice, Lunch at Torcello. 1979. E $7\frac{1}{2} \times 10\frac{1}{2}$ (97)
27. Venice, The Rose and the Writ. 1979. E/A $9 \times 6\frac{1}{2}$ (99)

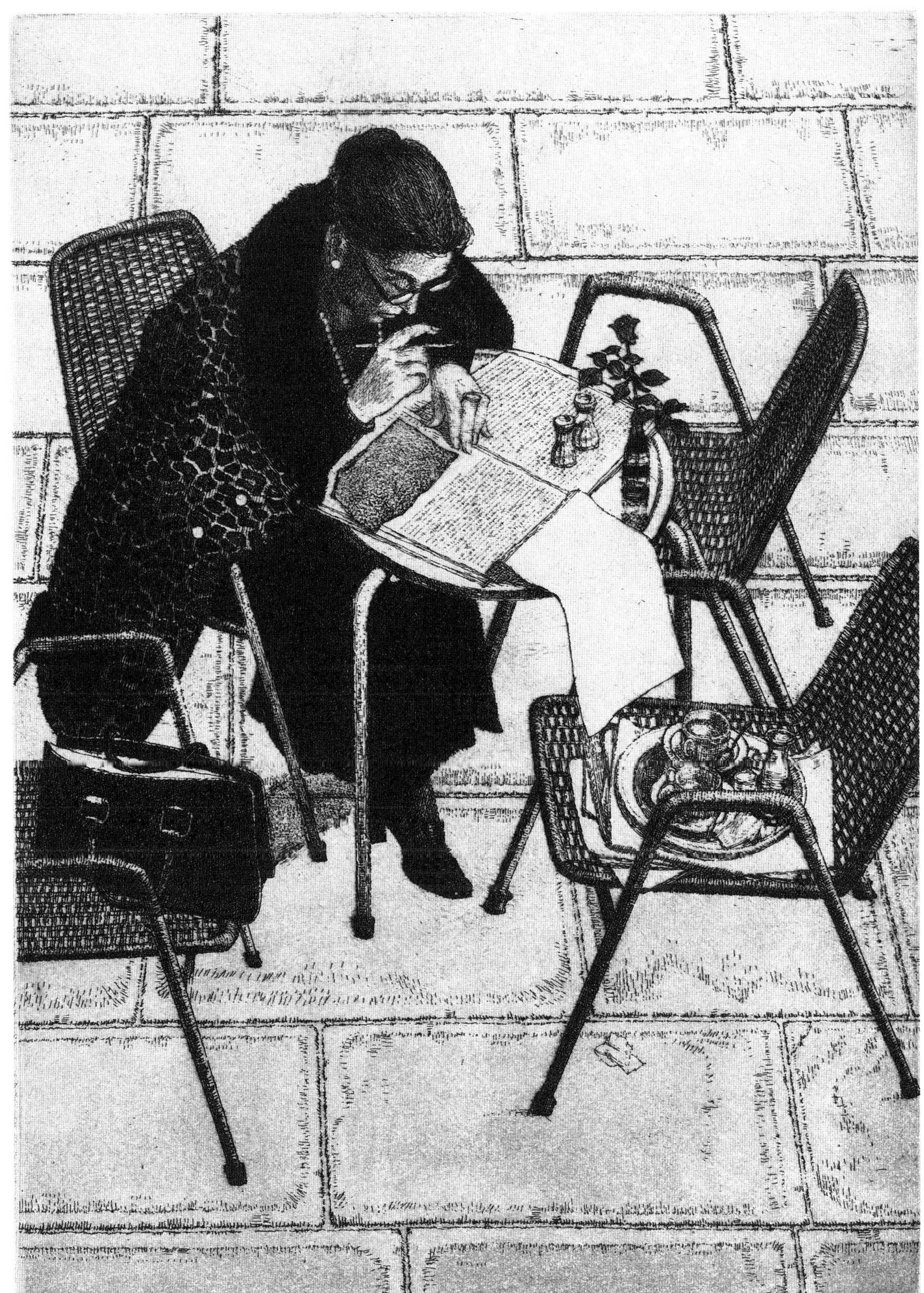

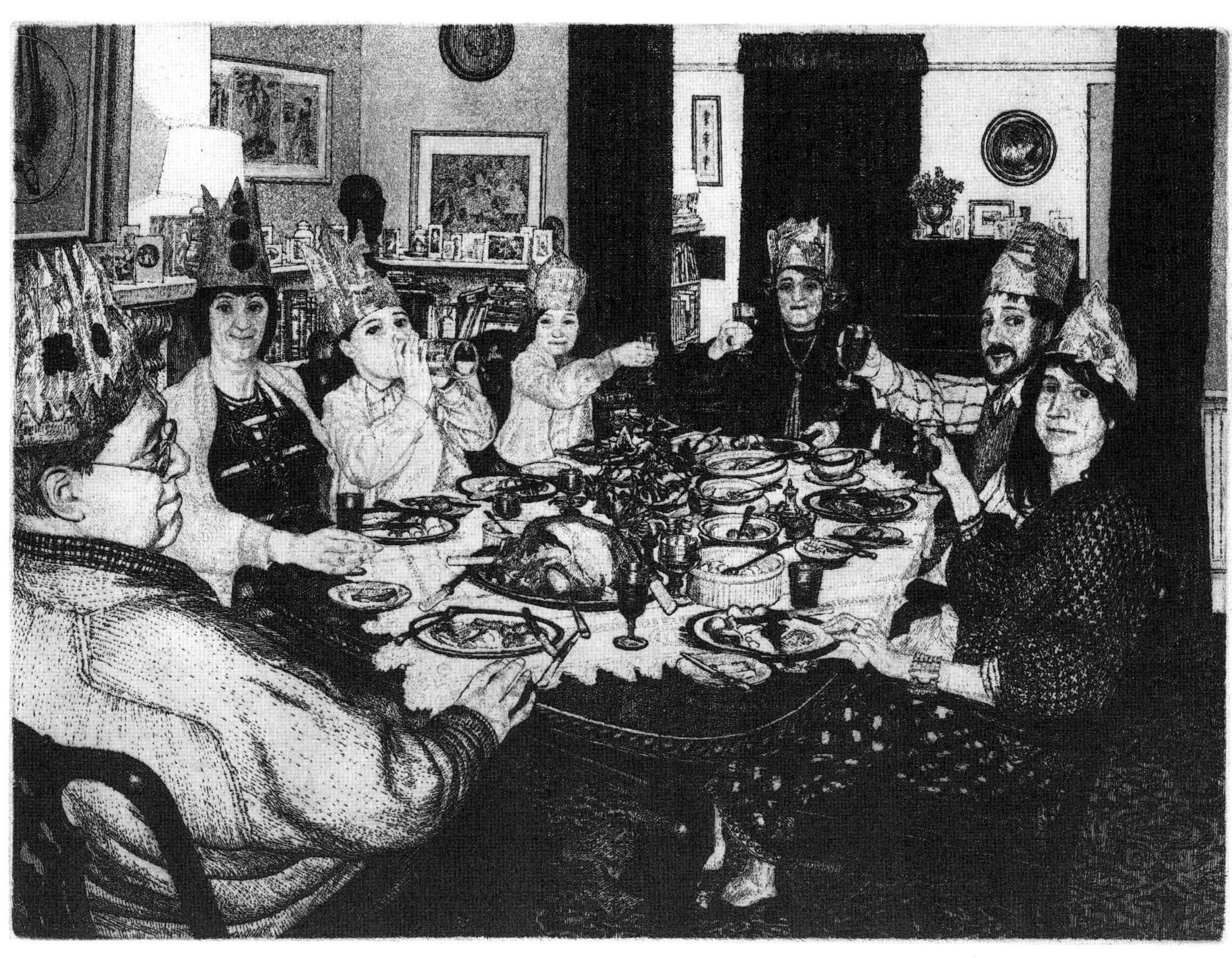

28. Family Reunion. 1980. E/A 8 × 11 (100)

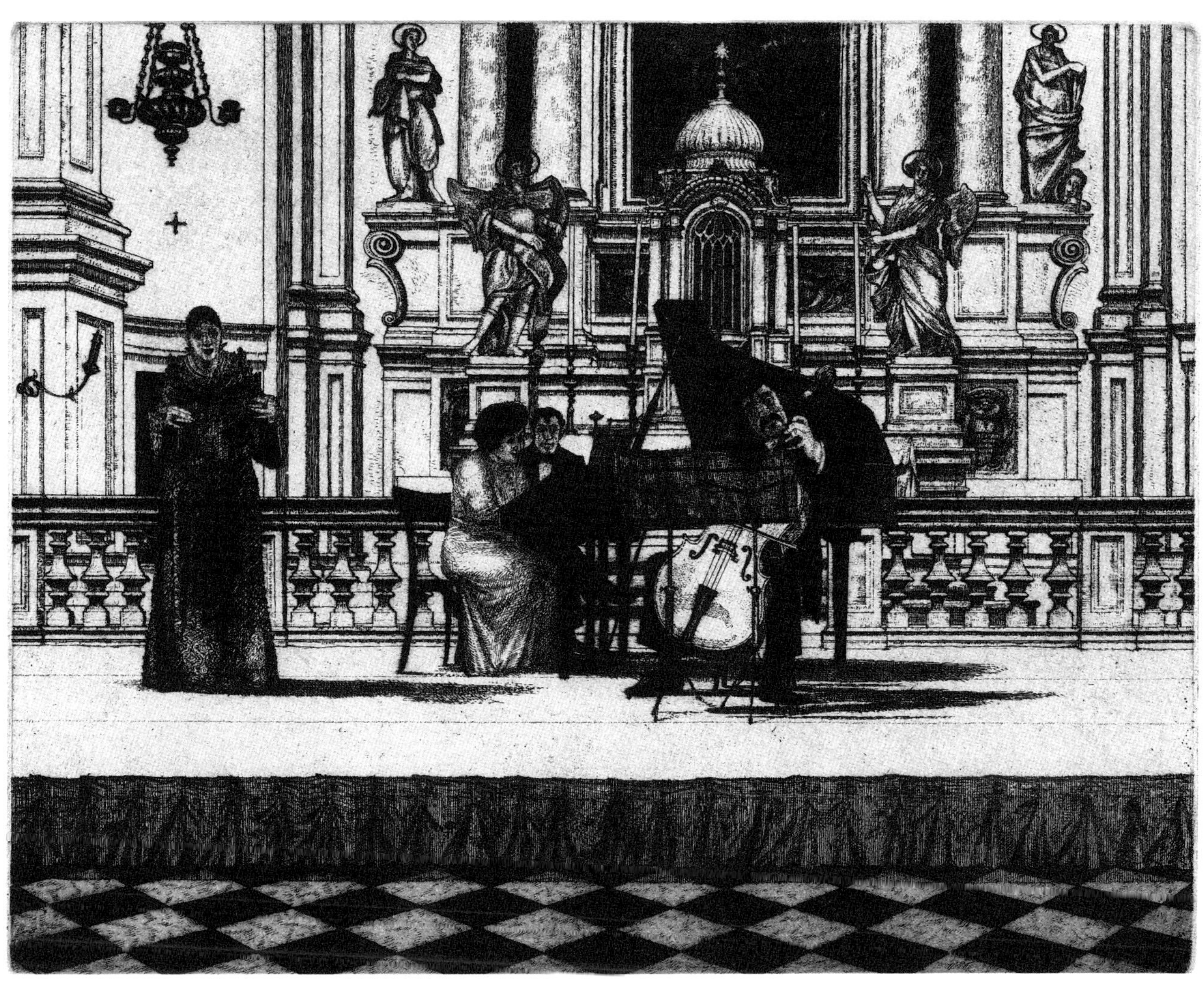

29. Venice, Vivaldi, Chiesa di Santa Maria della Pietà. 1980. E $9 \times 11\frac{1}{2}$ (101)

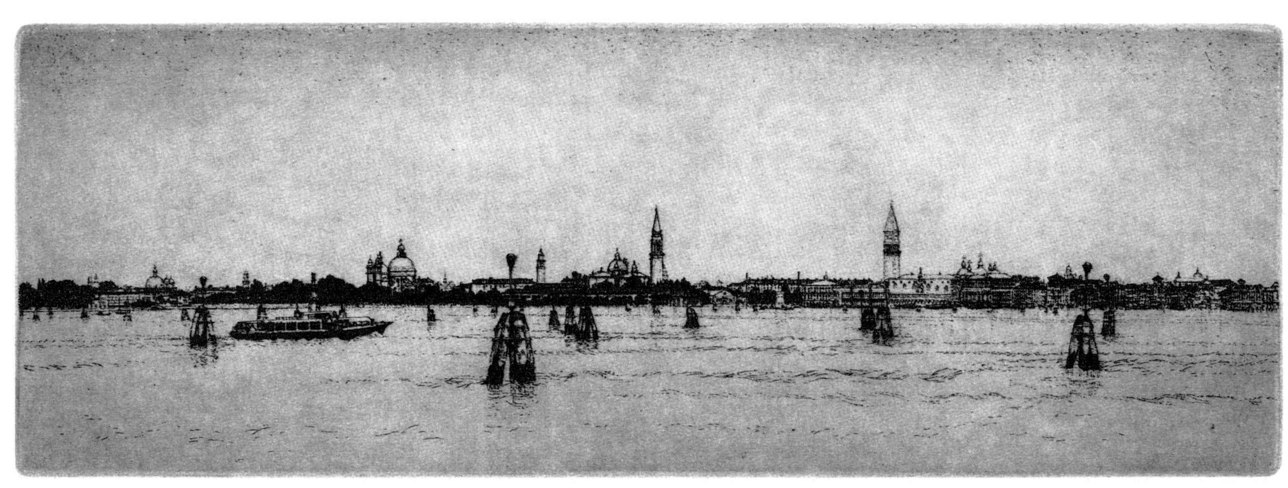

30. Venice from the Lido. 1981. E $4\frac{1}{4} \times 12\frac{1}{4}$ (104)

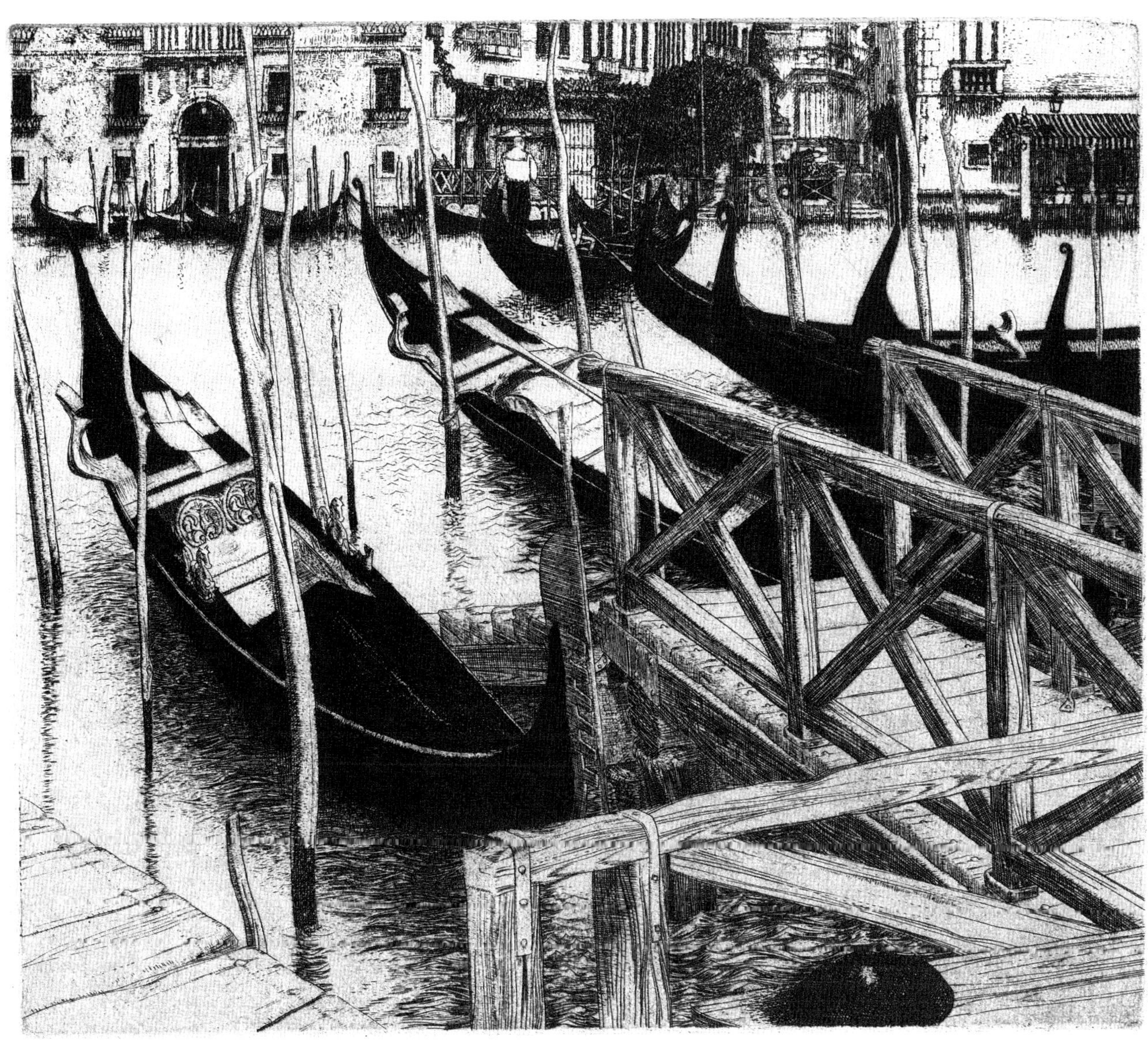

31. Traghetto del Giglio. 1981. LE/E/D $7\frac{1}{4} \times 8\frac{1}{2}$ (105, see also 25)

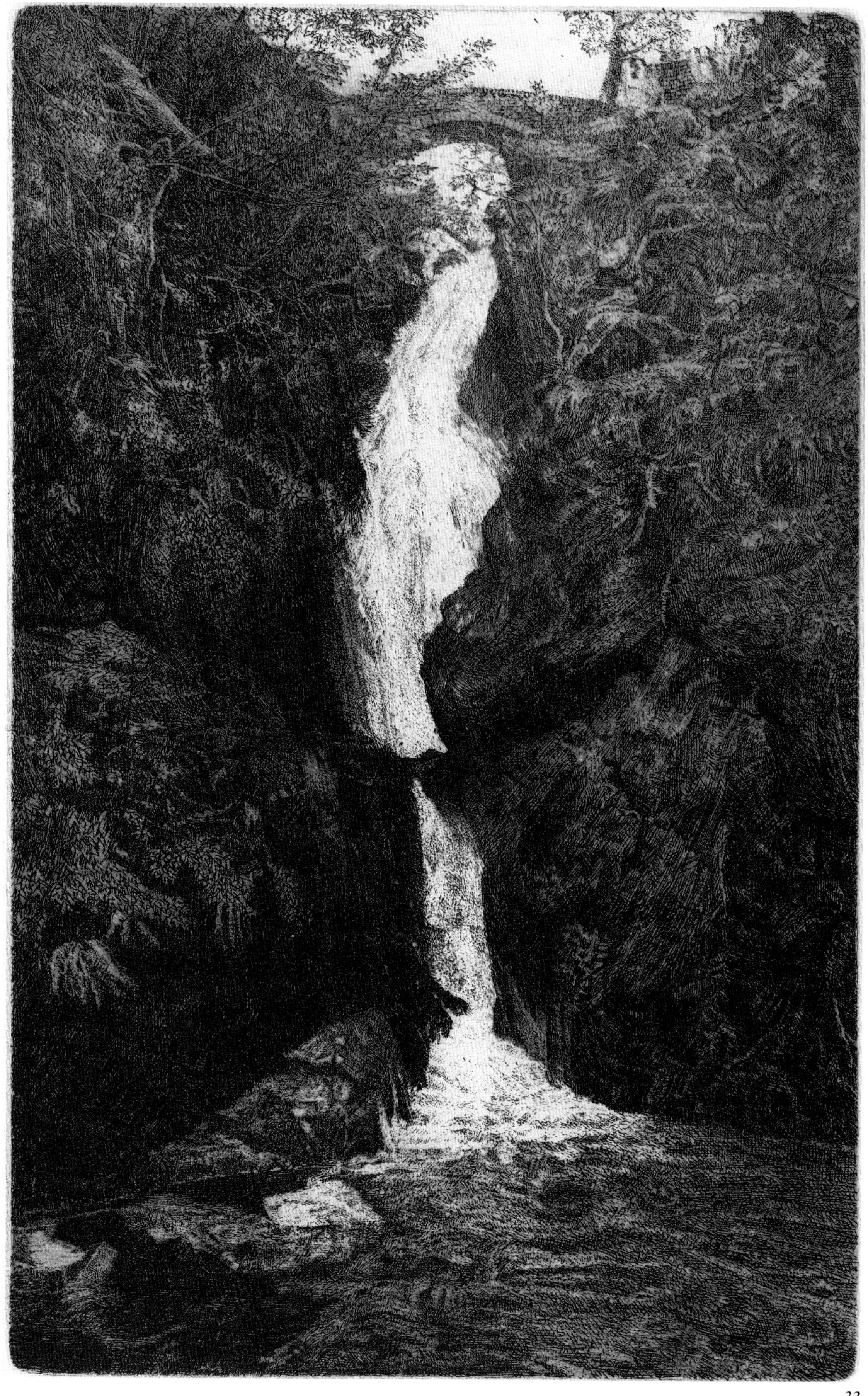

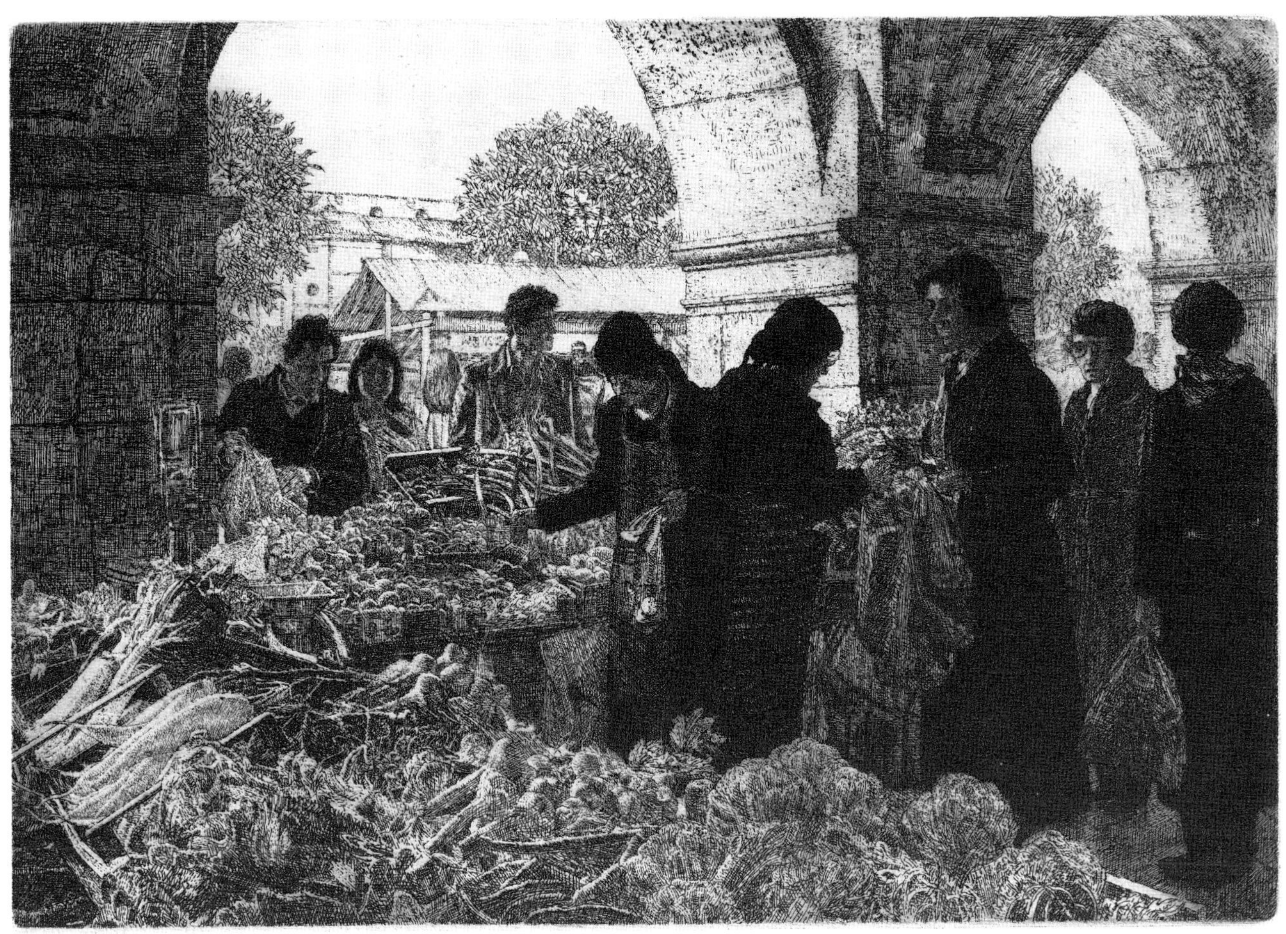

33

32. Ullswater, Aira Force. 1982. E $9\frac{1}{4} \times 6$ (110)
33. Lucerne Market. 1983. E 7×10 (113)

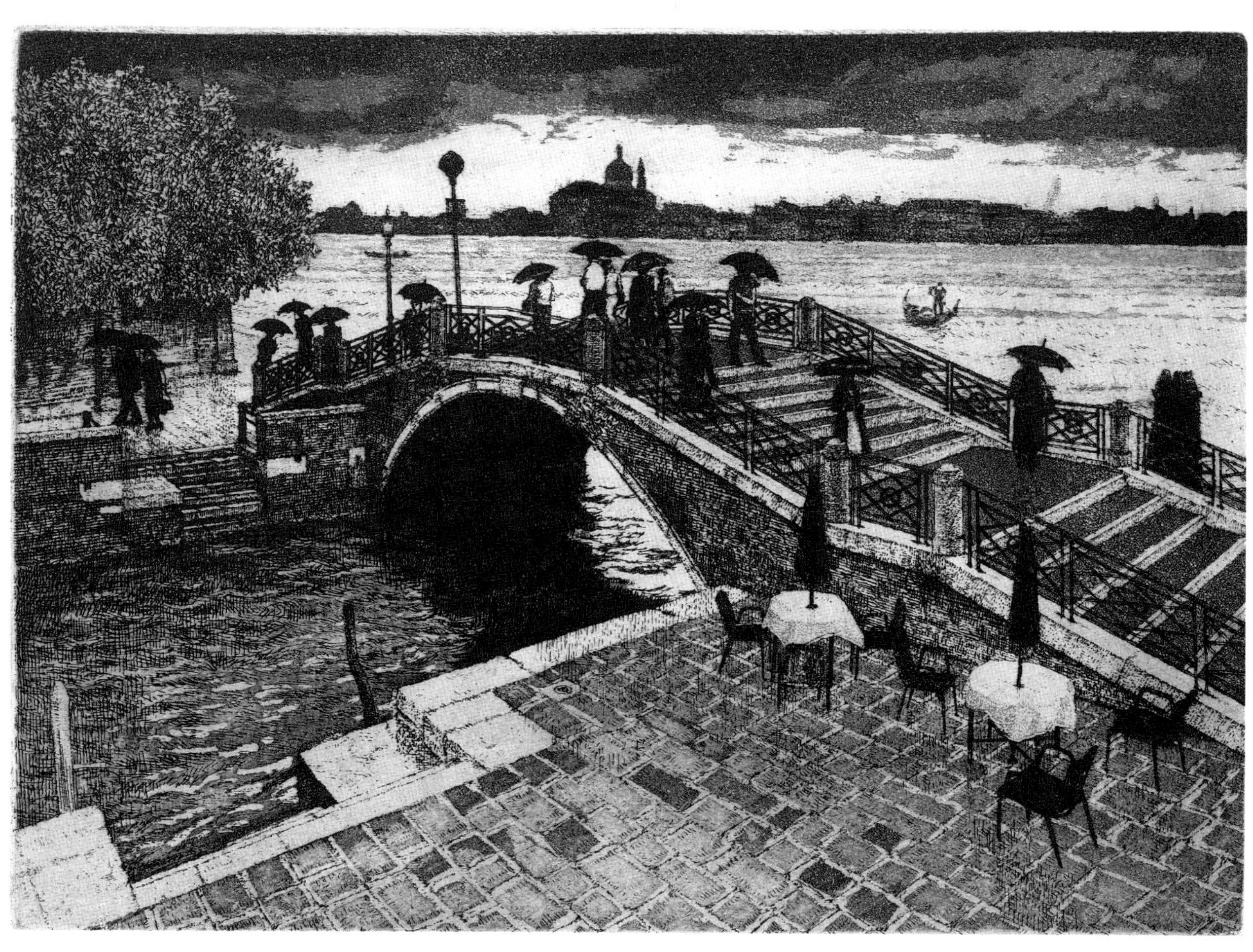

34. Venice, Storm. 1983. E/A 6½ × 9 (111)

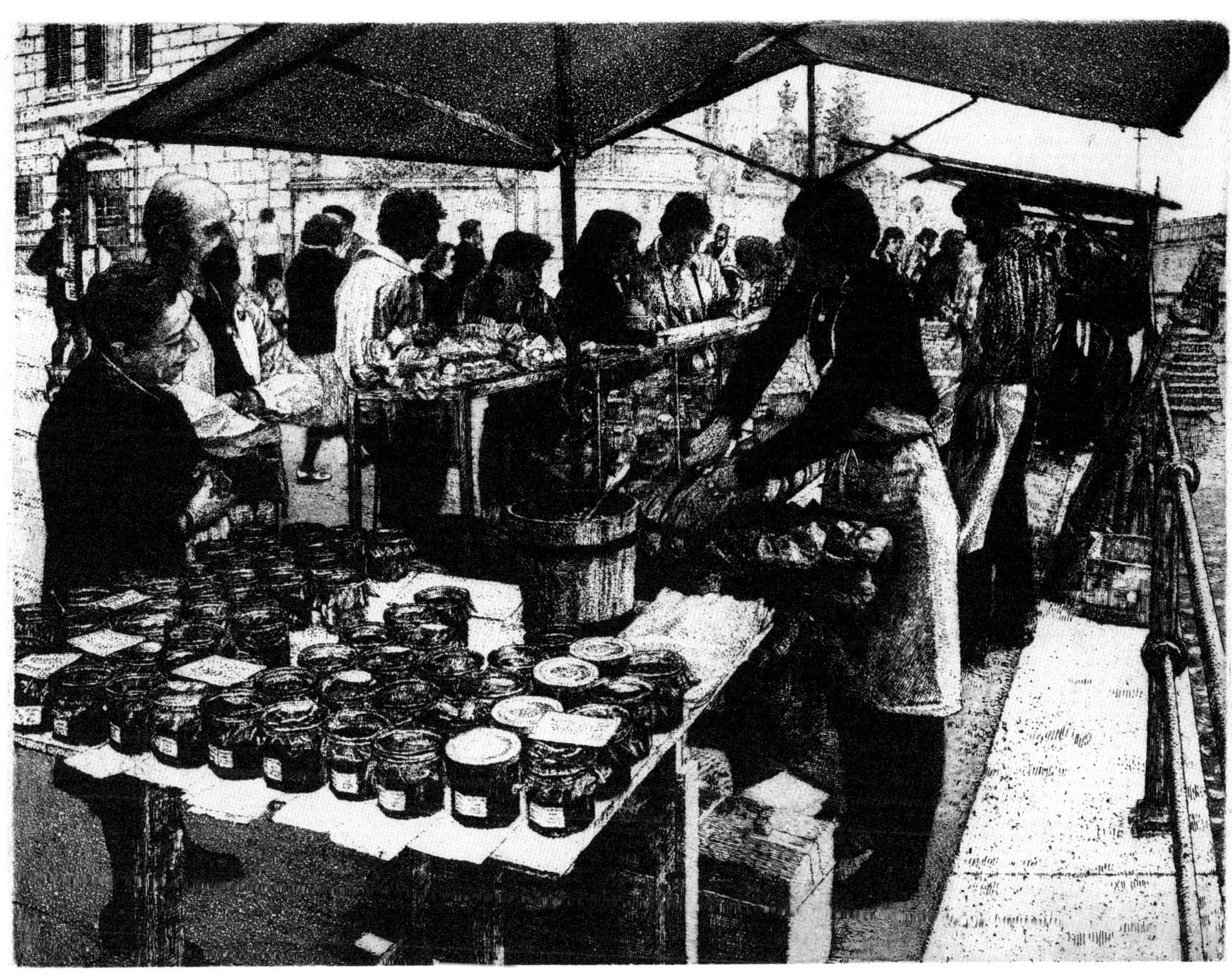

35. Lucerne Market, Bread and Cheese. 1984. E/A $7\frac{1}{2} \times 10$ (117)

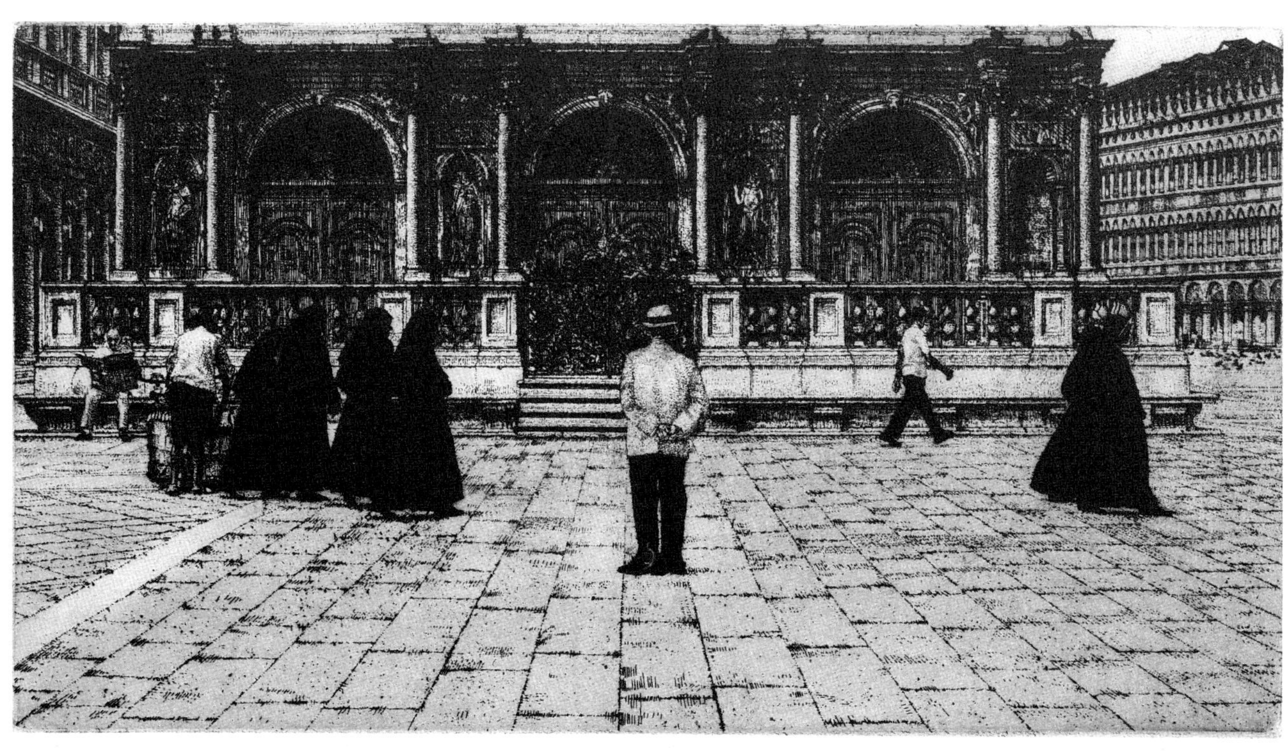

36. Venice, on Parade. 1984. E $5\frac{3}{4} \times 10\frac{1}{2}$ (115)

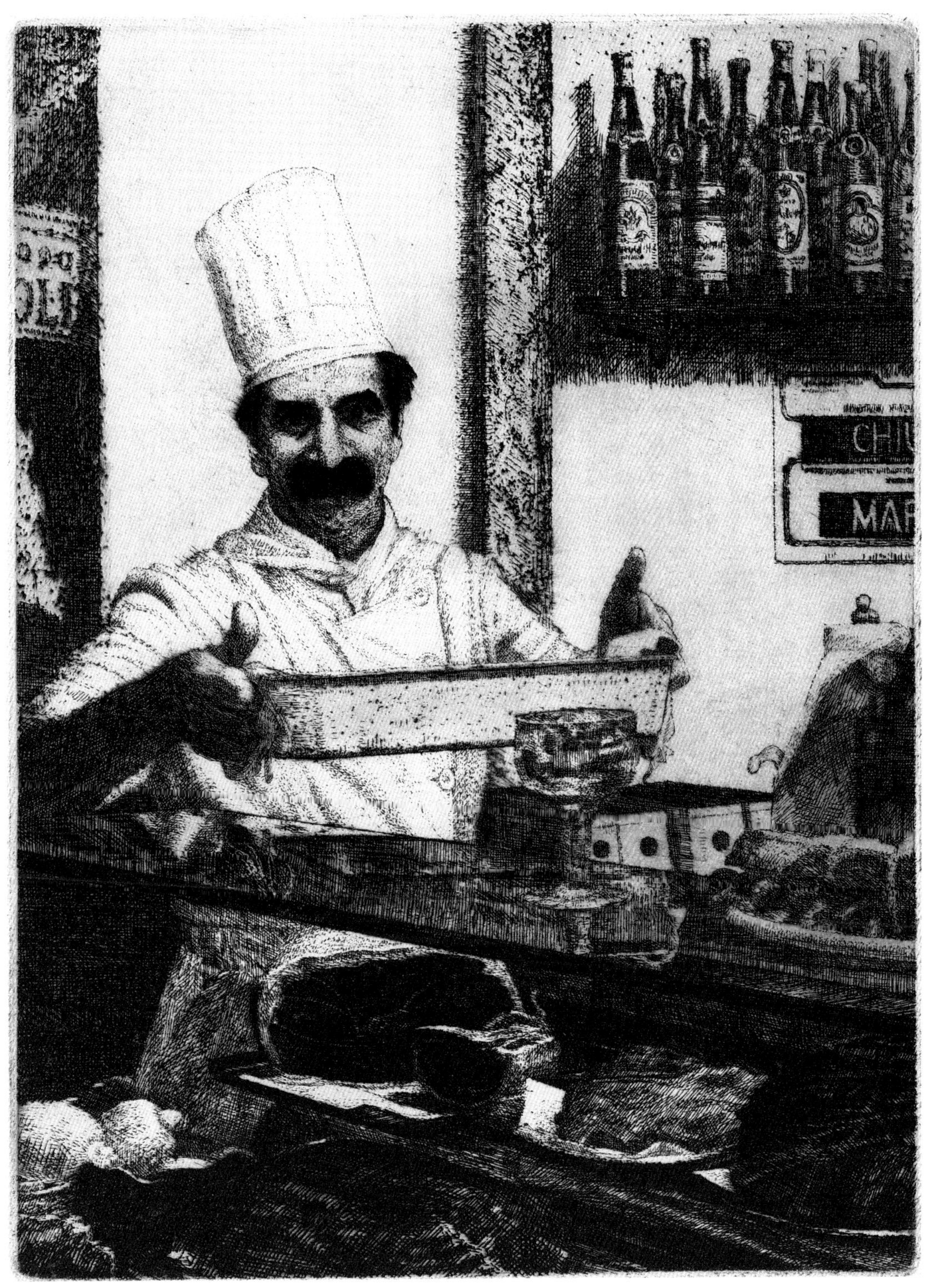

37. Venice, The Chef. 1984. E $7\frac{3}{4} \times 5\frac{3}{4}$ (116)

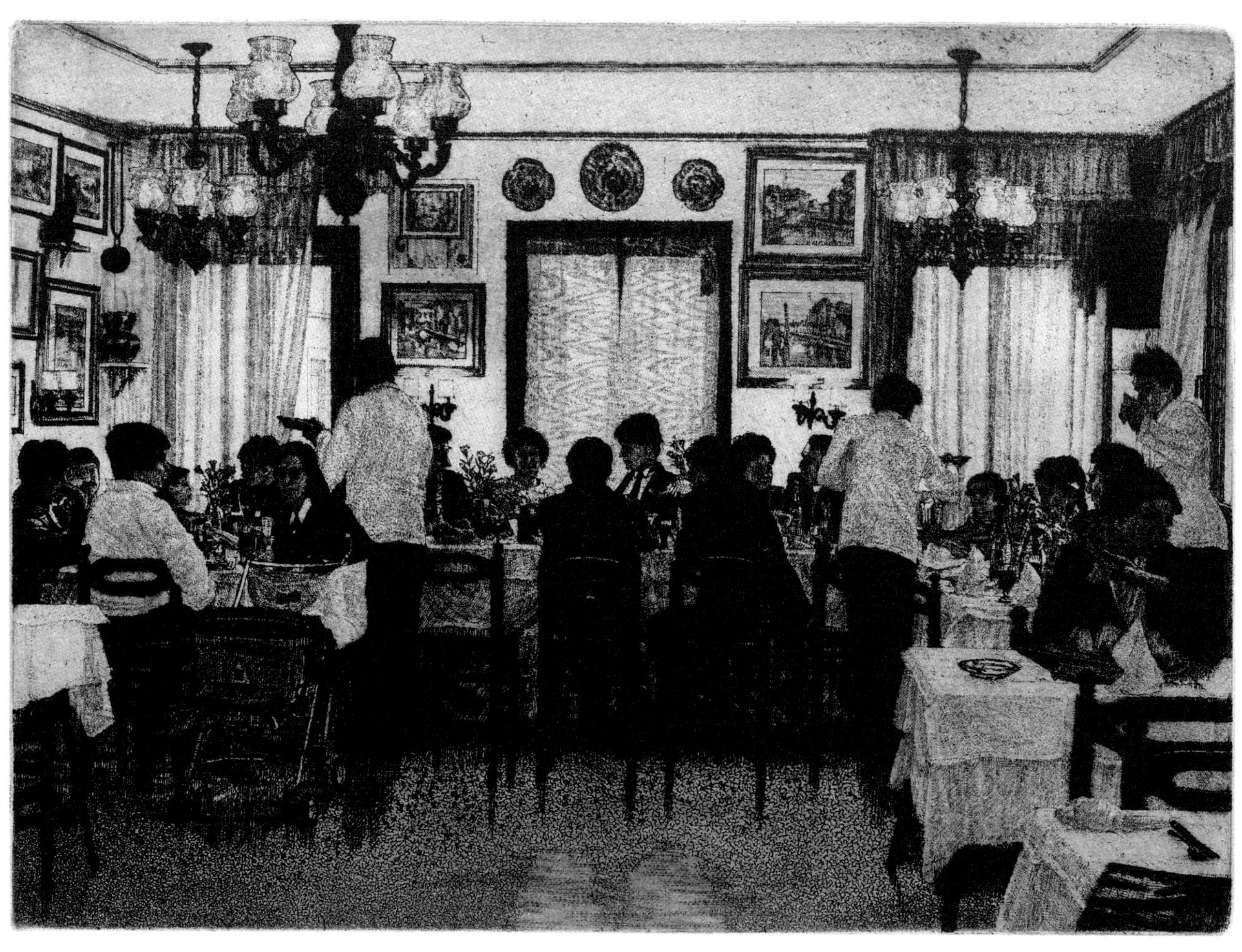

38. Burano Wedding, Il Gatto Nero. 1985. E/A 7¼ × 10 (121)

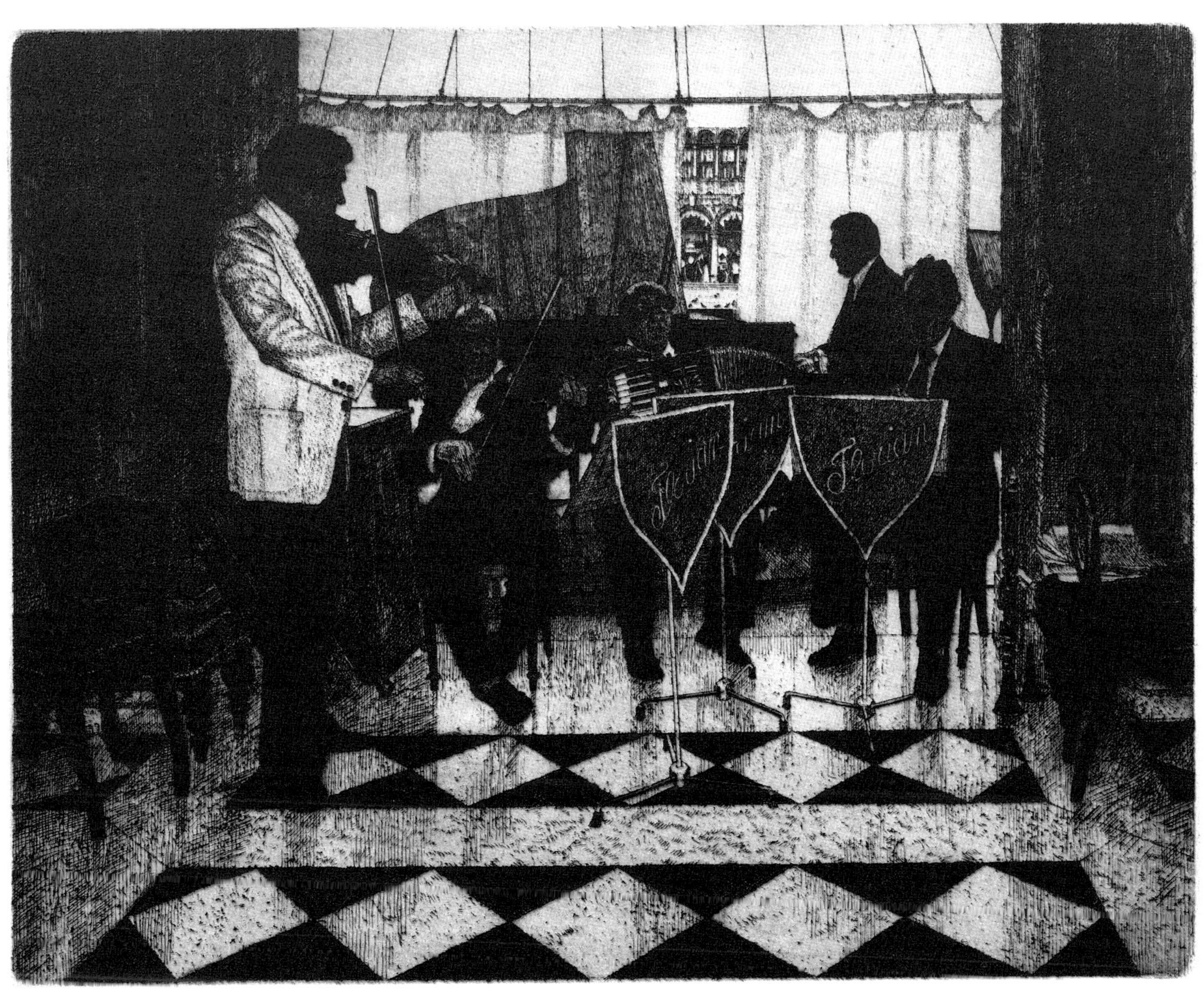

39. Venice, Light Music. 1985. E/D 7 × 9 (119)

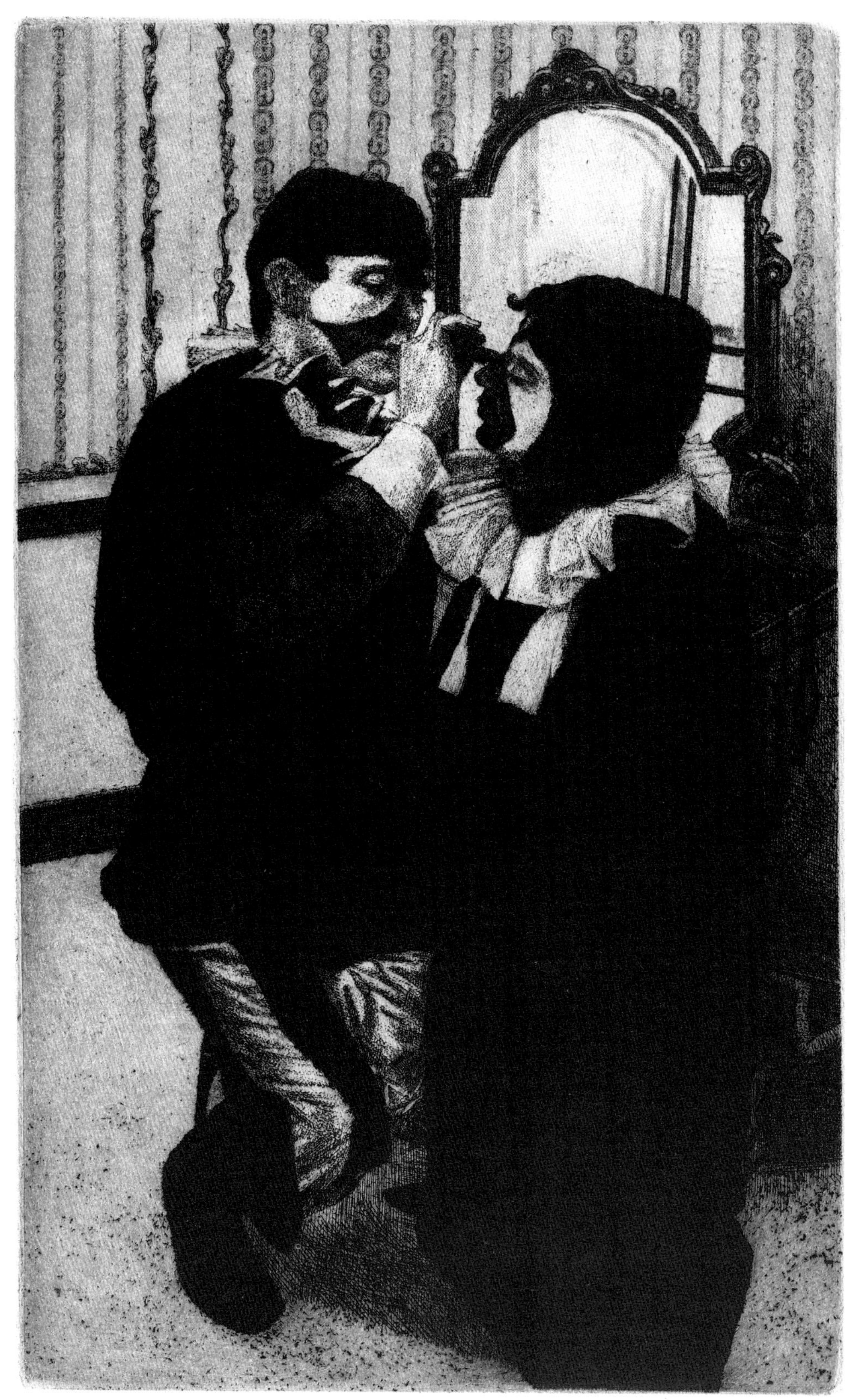

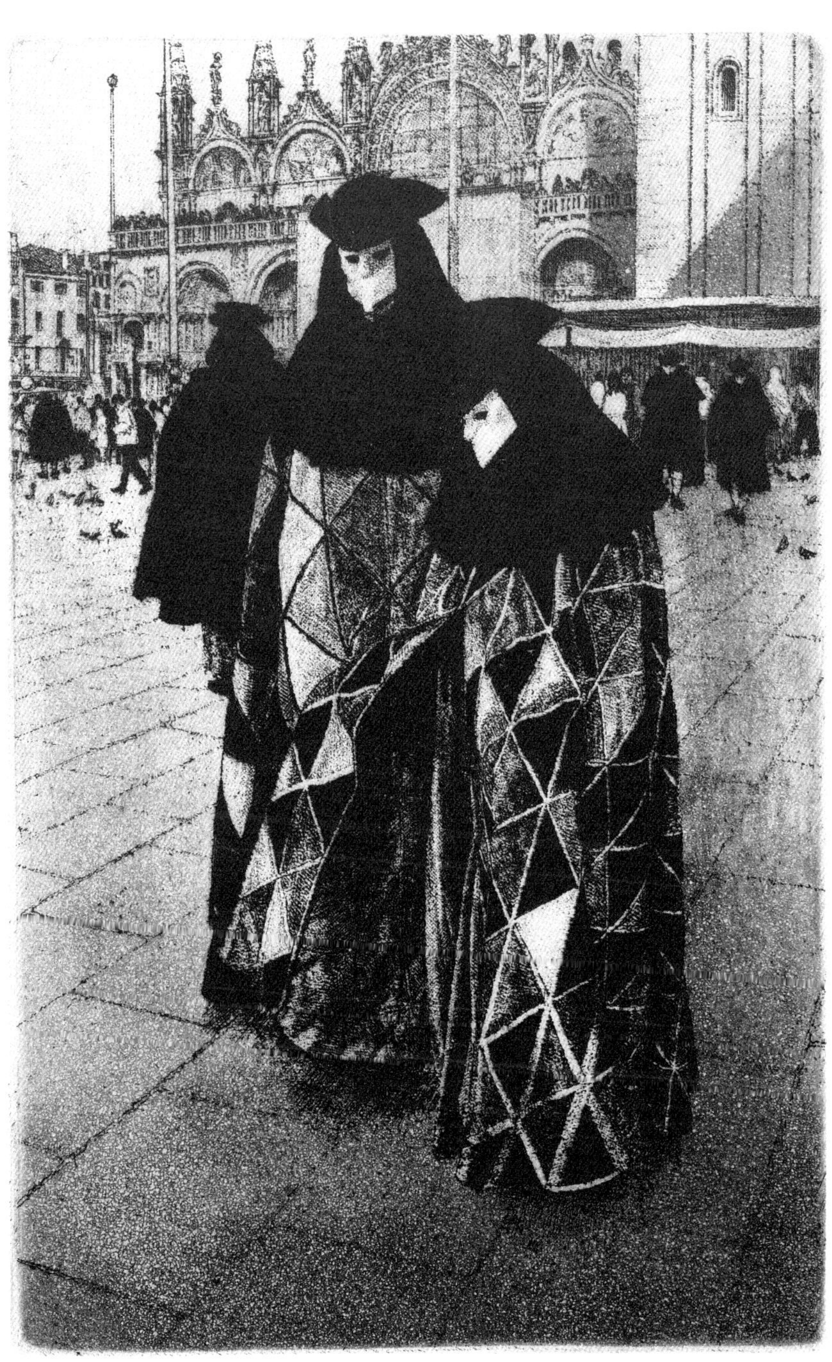

41

40. Venice Carnival, Make Up. I. 1985. E 8½ × 5¼ (122)
41. Venice Carnival, Masks. 1986. E/A 7 × 4½ (124)

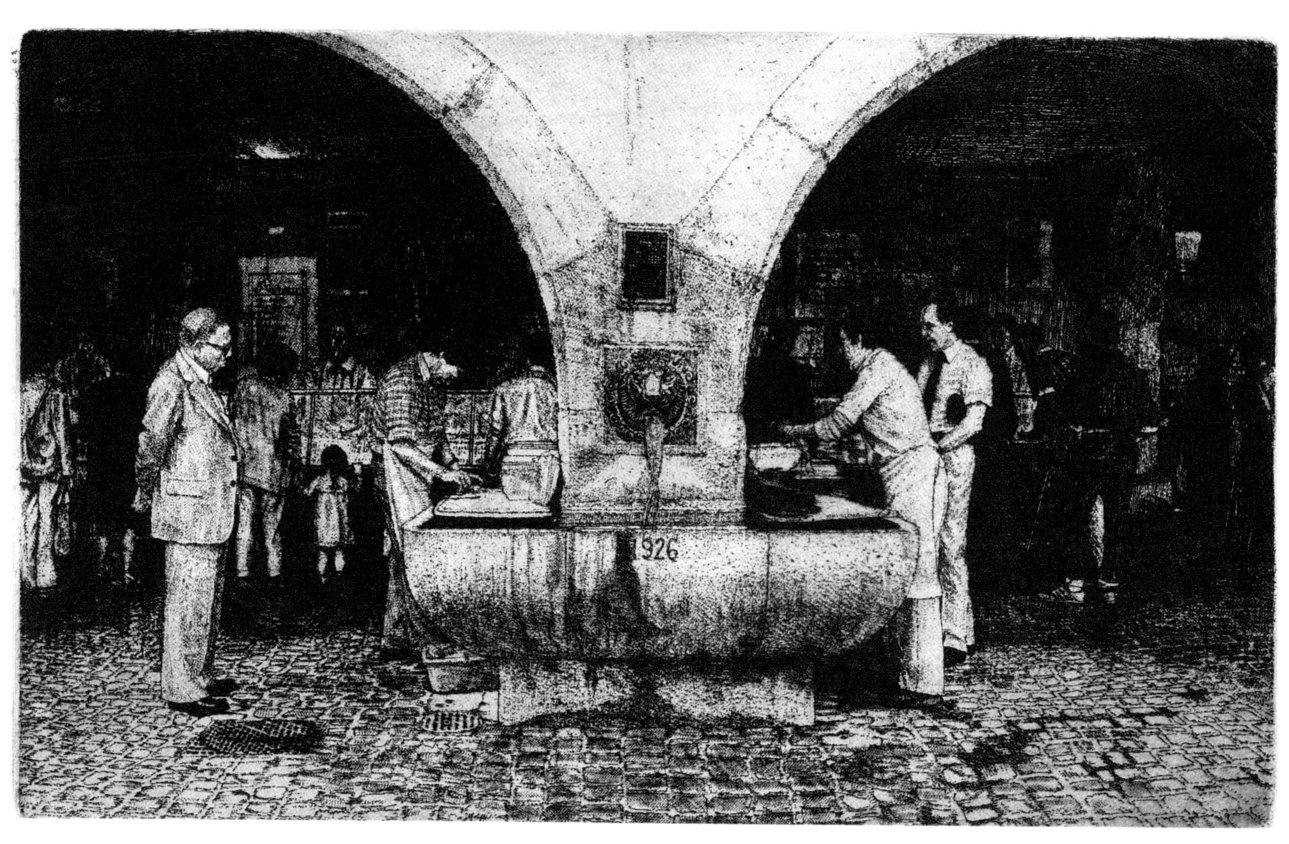

42. Lucerne Fishmarket, Onlookers. 1986. E $5\frac{1}{2} \times 9$ (125)

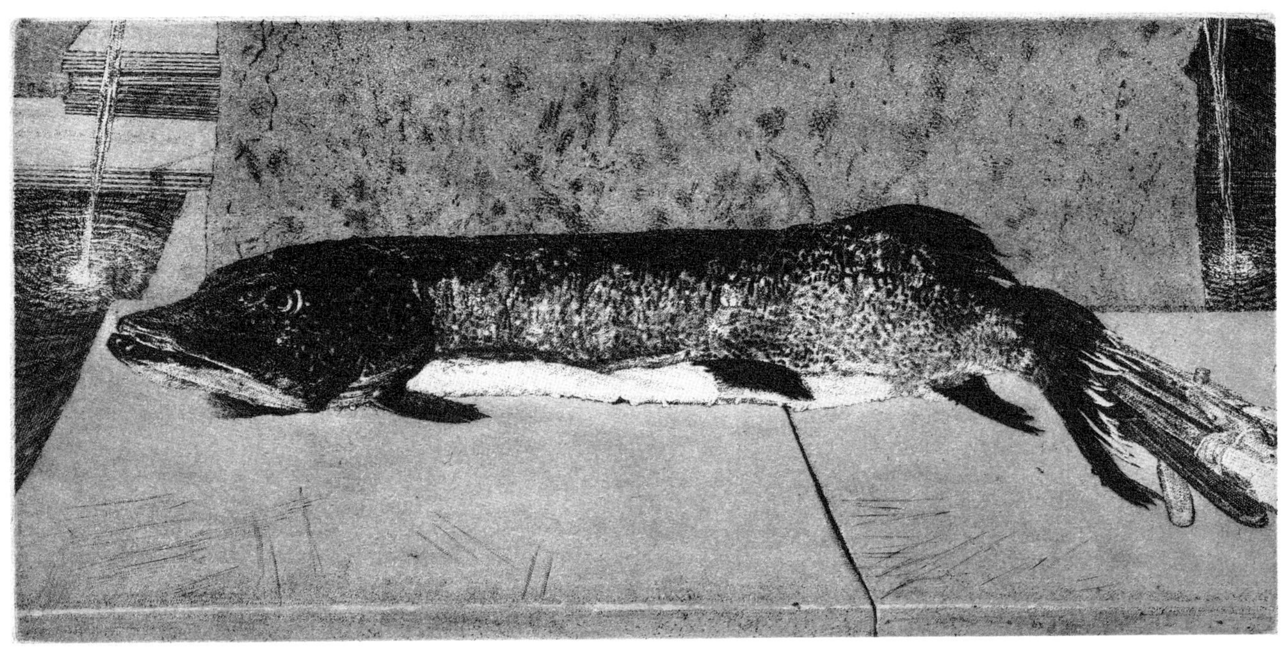

43. Lucerne Pike. 1986. E/A $4\frac{3}{4} \times 10$ (127)

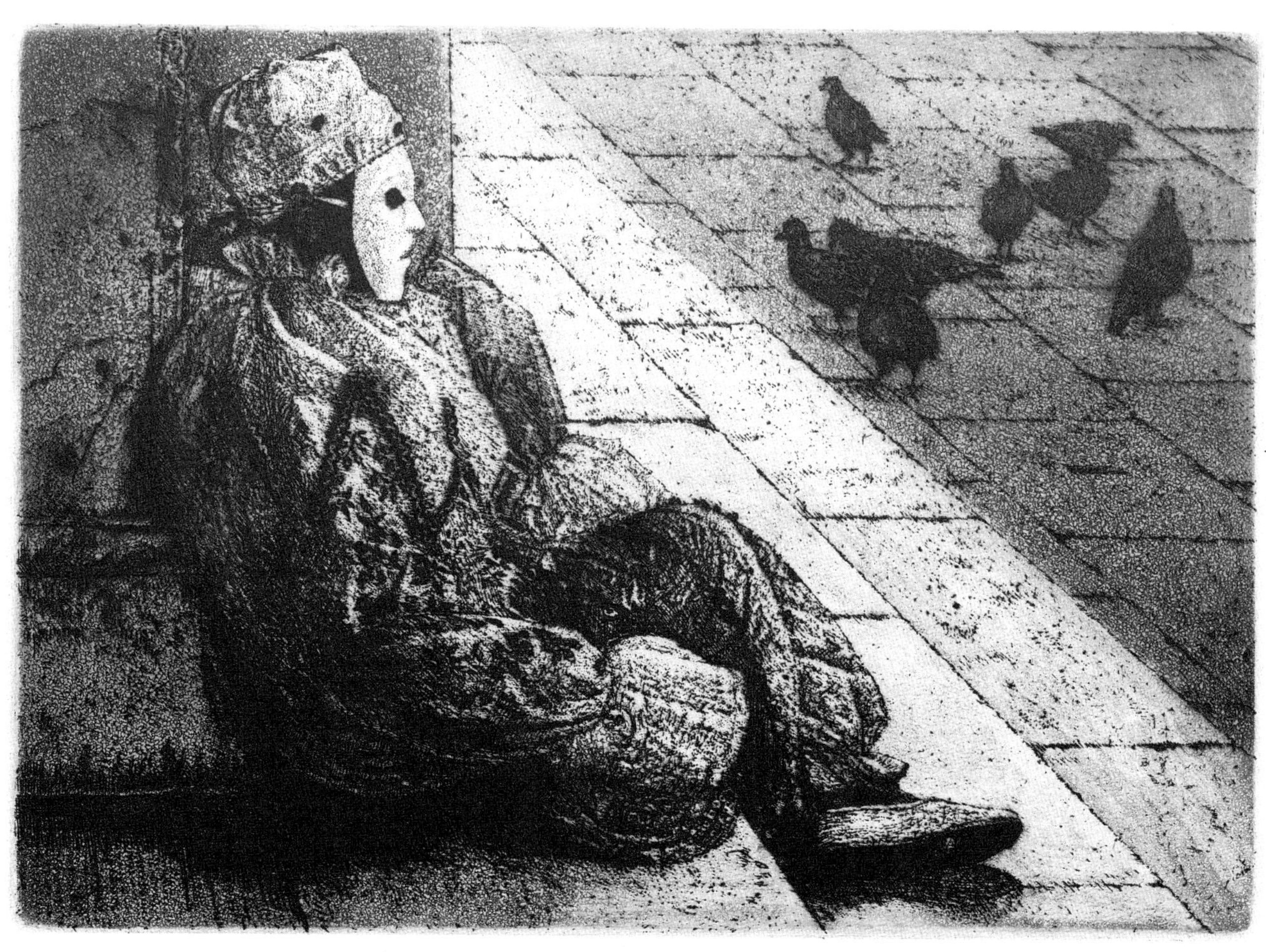

44. Venice Carnival, Clown. 1987. E/A. 5 × 7 (129)

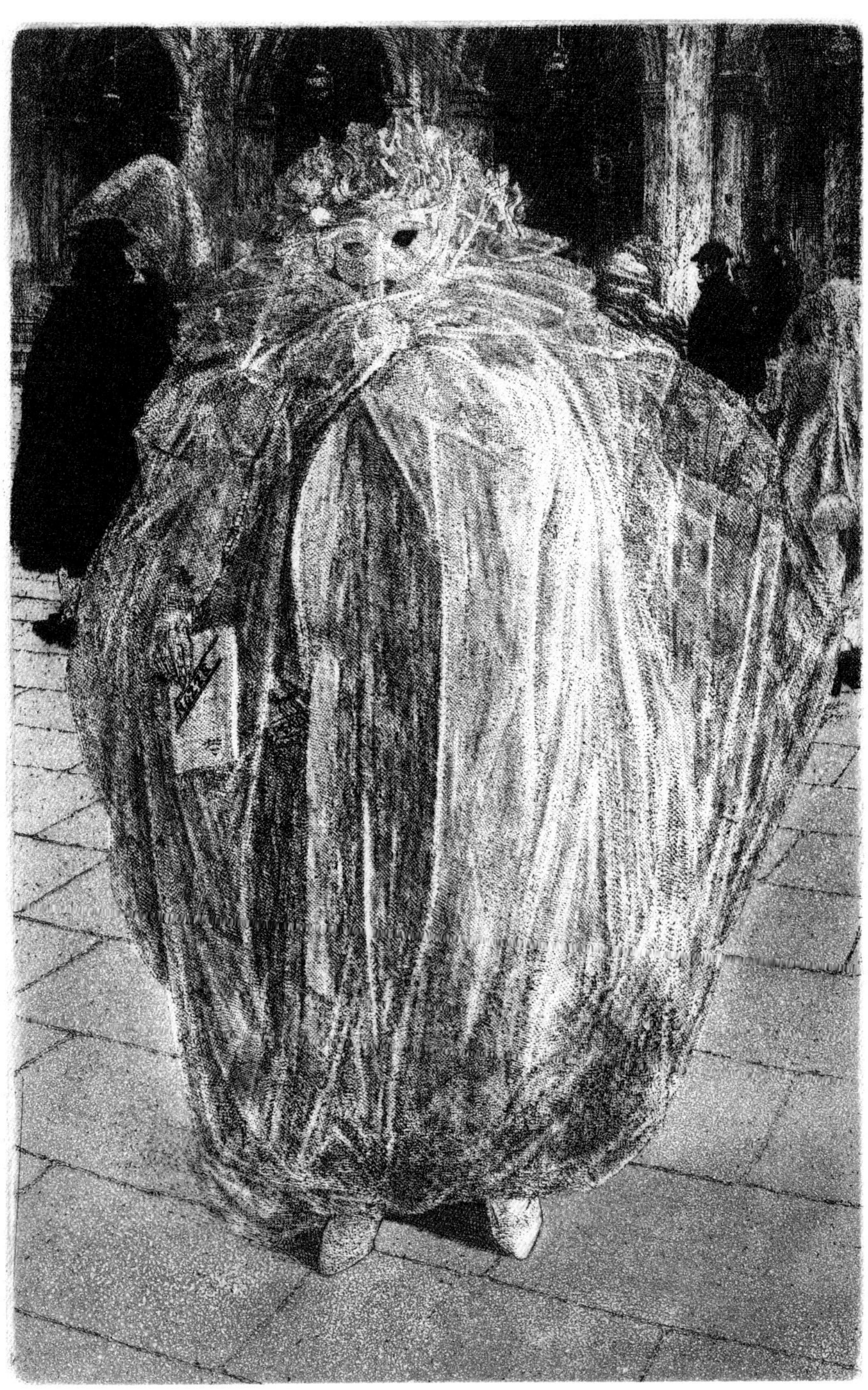

45. Venice Carnival, Nozze. 1986. E/A $7\frac{1}{4} \times 4\frac{3}{4}$ (126)

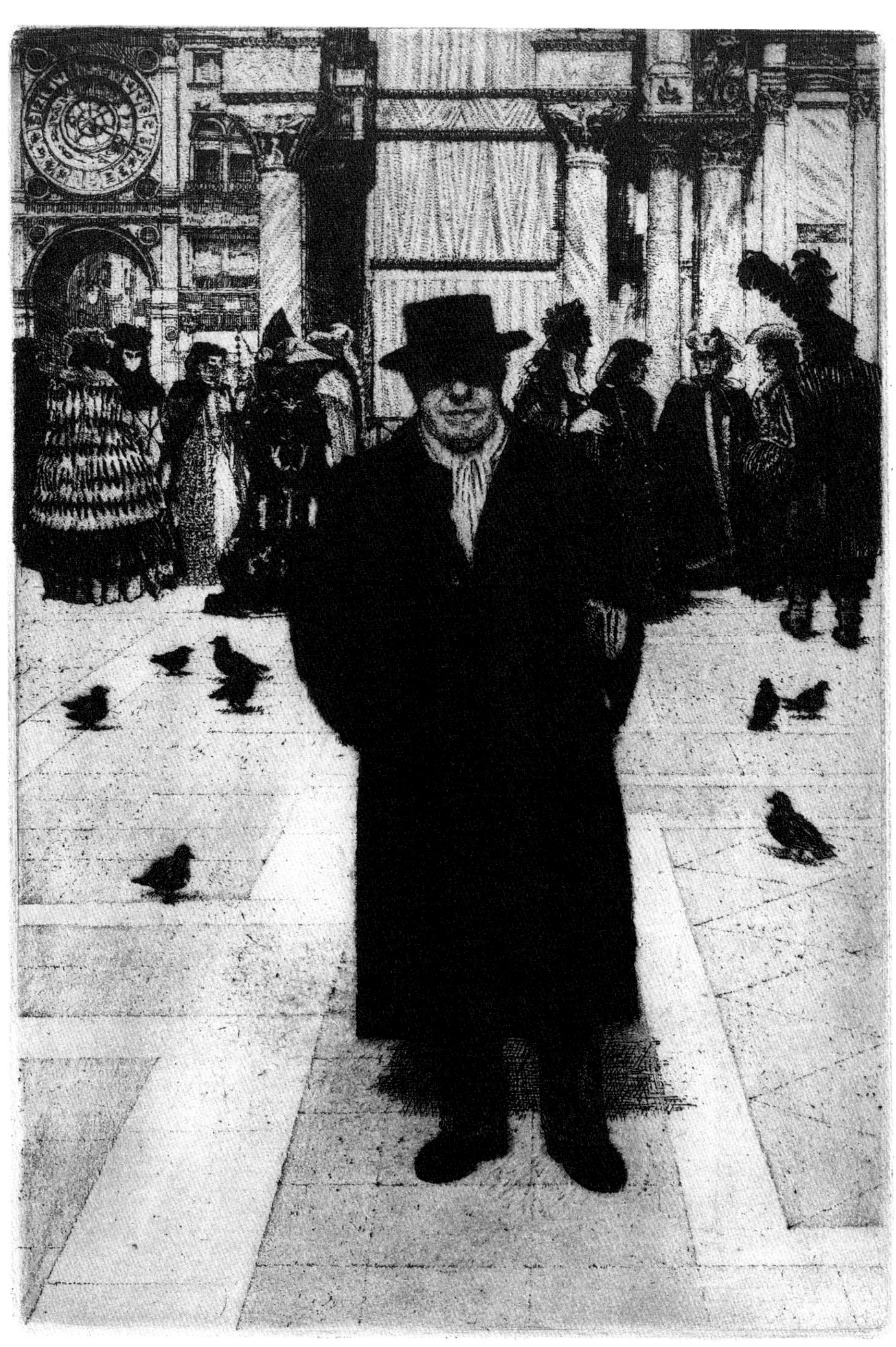

46. Venice Carnival, Man in Black. 1987. E/A $7\frac{1}{4} \times 5$ (130)

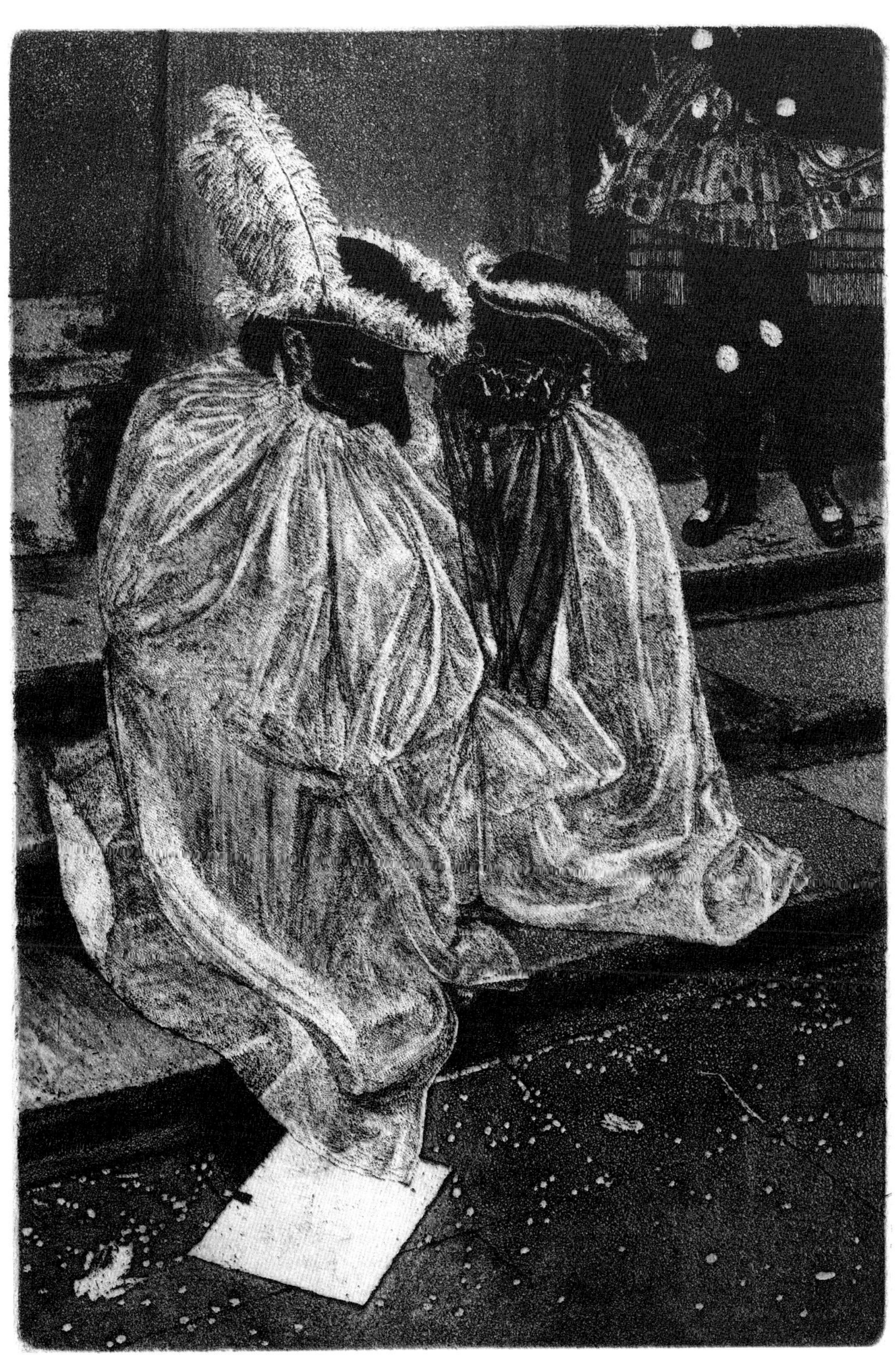

47. Venice Carnival, Secrets. 1989. E/A $7\frac{3}{4} \times 5\frac{1}{4}$ (137)

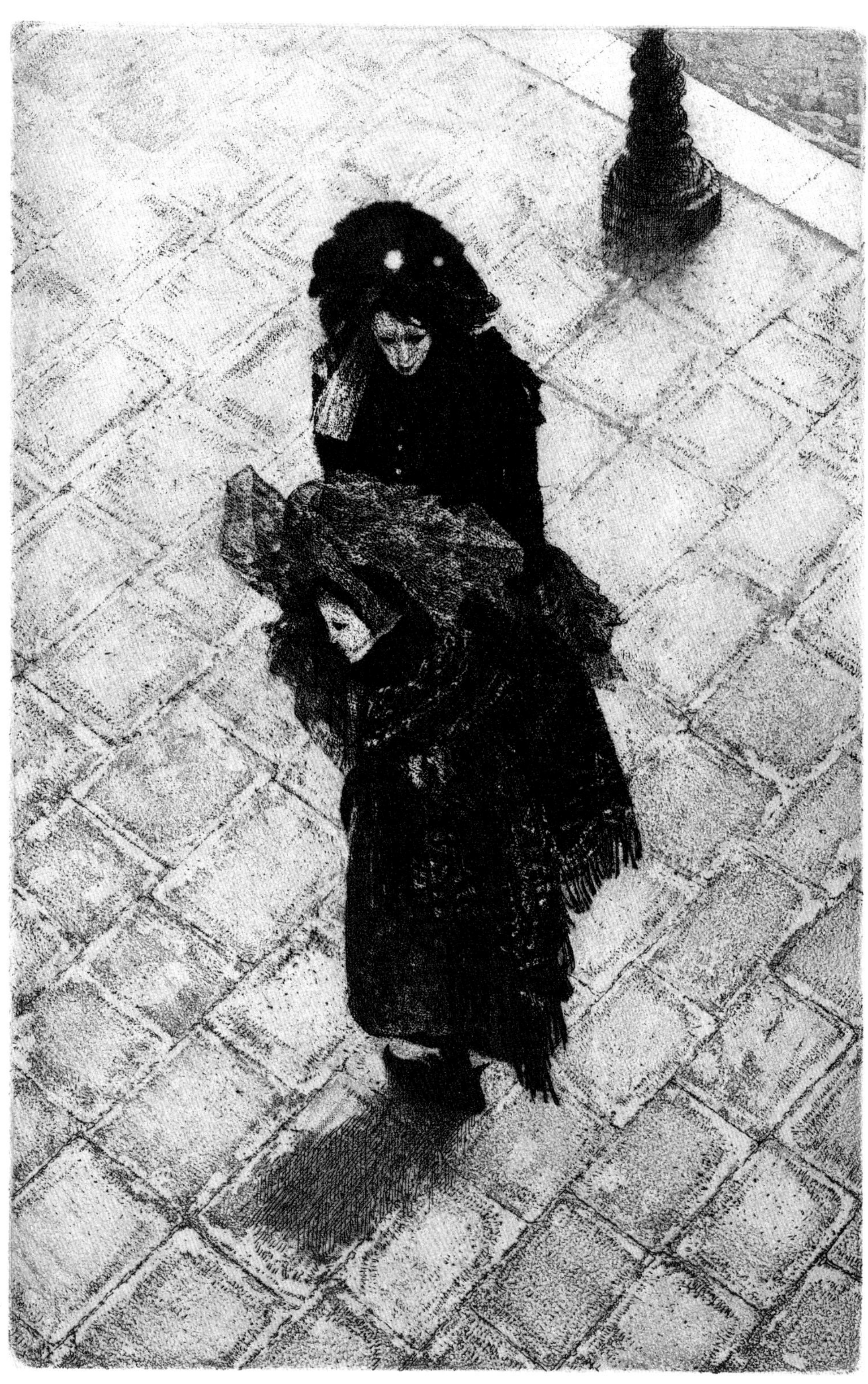

48. Venice Carnival, Witches. 1988. E/A $8 \times 5\frac{1}{4}$ (132)

All plates are copper unless otherwise stated. Measurements in inches, height before width.

ABBREVIATIONS
RA Royal Academy
RE Royal Society Painter-Etchers and Engravers
RSA Royal Scottish Academy
LE Line engraving
E. Etching
A. Aquatint
SG Soft ground etching
D. Drypoint

The first number in the entries below is the number of prints taken from each of the working states of the plate. The second number is that of the working state, eg 1/4 means that there is one proof of the fourth state. The details of the states, and the evolution of a plate, *Traghetto* (25), can be found on page 16.

1932

1. **Landscape with Ivied Tree**
E. $5\frac{3}{4} \times 5\frac{1}{2}$
No working proofs. Not exhibited

1933

2. **Joan Dressing her Hair**
E. $7\frac{1}{2} \times 6$
States 2/1
Exh: RE 1934. RA 1934. Atkinson Art Gallery, Southport 1934. Bankside Gallery 'Five Man Show' 1987 (109)
Reproduced *Arts Review*

3. **The Little Garden**
E. $6\frac{1}{4} \times 6$
States 1/1. 1/3. 1/4. 1/5
Exh: RE 1934

4. **The Doorway (The Arrival)**
E. $10 \times 6\frac{1}{2}$
Royal College of Art Diploma Plate (Engraving School)
Plate and working states retained by The Royal College of Art
Exh: RE 1934. RA 1934. Bankside Gallery 'Five Man Show' 1987 (113)
Reproduced *Studio*
Purchased Blackburn Art Gallery 1937, Contemporary Art Society 1939 (A M Hind)

5. **Shetley Brook No.1**
E. $5 \times 4\frac{1}{2}$
States 1/1. 1/2. 1/3. 1/4. 1/5
Exh: RE 1934. Harris Institute, Preston 1934. Bankside Gallery 'Five Man Show' 1987 (110)

6. **Scotshaw Brook**
E. 5×5
States 2/1. 1/2. 1/3. 1/4. 1/5
Exh: RE 1934

7. **Morning**
E. $7\frac{1}{2} \times 6\frac{1}{2}$
States 3/1. 2/2. 1/3. 2/4. 1/5. 1/6. 1/7. 1/8. 2/9
Plate for Special Subject, Rome Scholarship Competition 1934
Exh: RE 1934. Bankside Gallery 'Five Man Show' 1987 (117)

1934

8. **Plants**
E. $6 \times 4\frac{1}{2}$
States 3/1. 1/2. 1/3. 1/4. 1/5
Exh: RE 1935. RA 1935
Reproduced *Studio*

9. **Shetley Brook No.2**
E. $5\frac{1}{4} \times 4\frac{1}{2}$
States 2/1. 1/2. 1/3. 1/4. 1/5
Exh: RE 1935

10. **Winona (Joan)**
E. $6 \times 4\frac{1}{2}$
States 3/1. 1/2
Exh: RE 1935. RA 1935. Blackburn Art Gallery 1937. RA Red Cross Exhibition 1940. Phoenix Gallery, Lavenham 1963. Bankside Gallery 'Five Man Show' 1987 (112)
Reproduced *Fine Prints* 1934

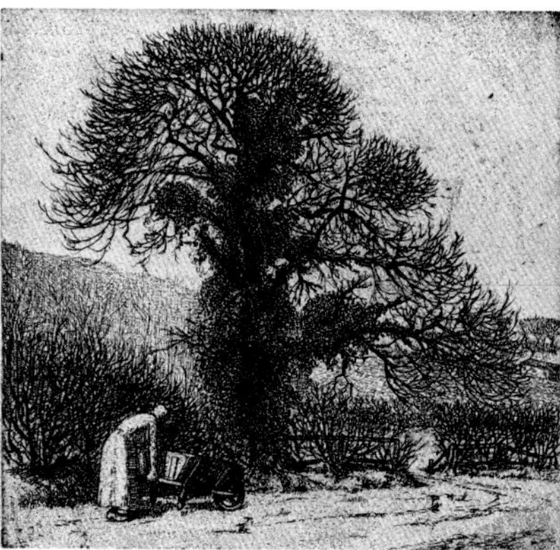

1

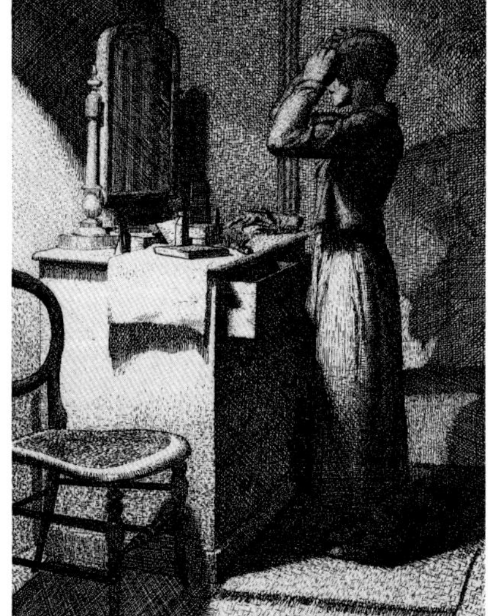

2

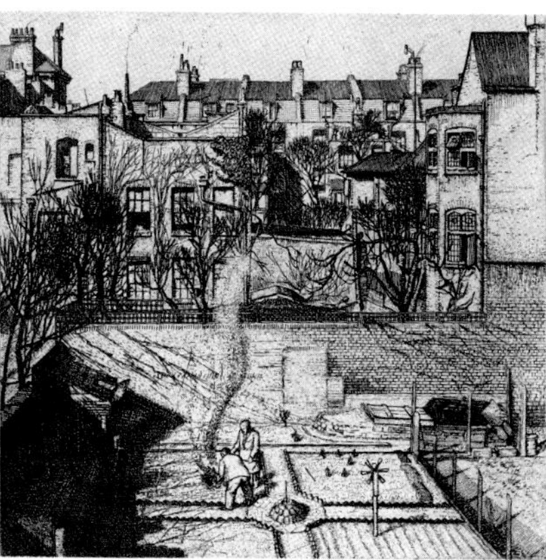

3

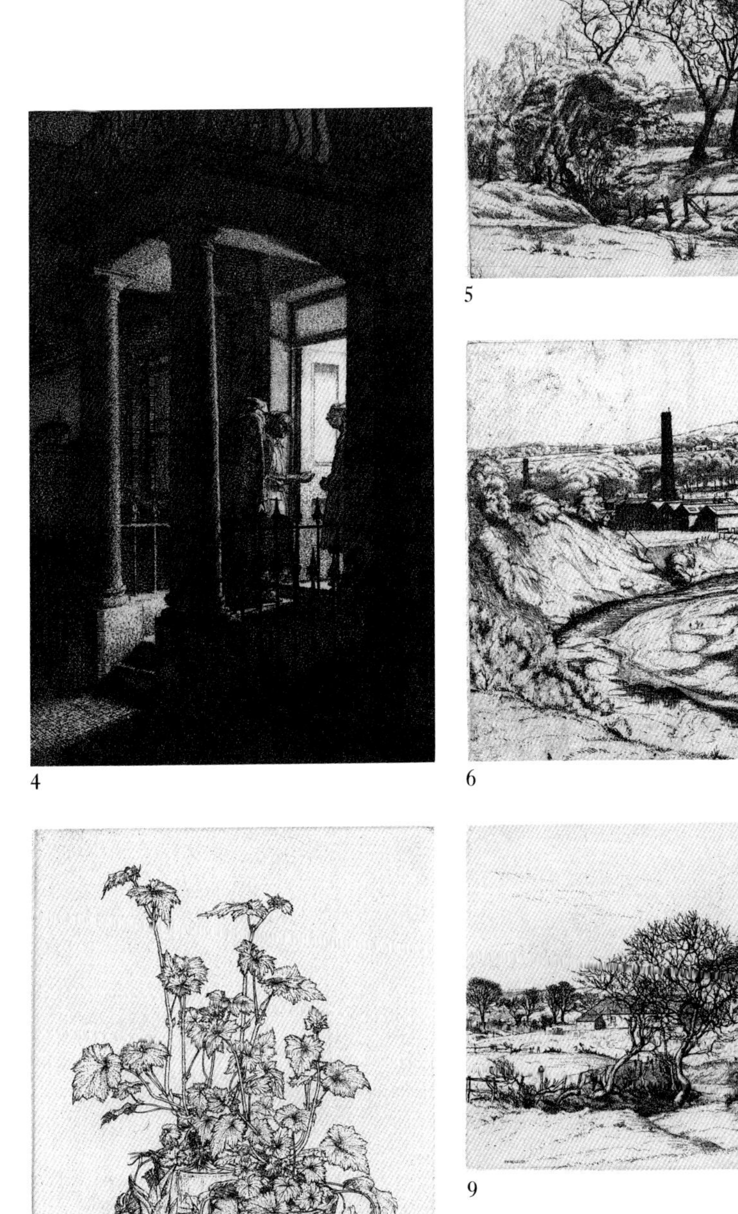
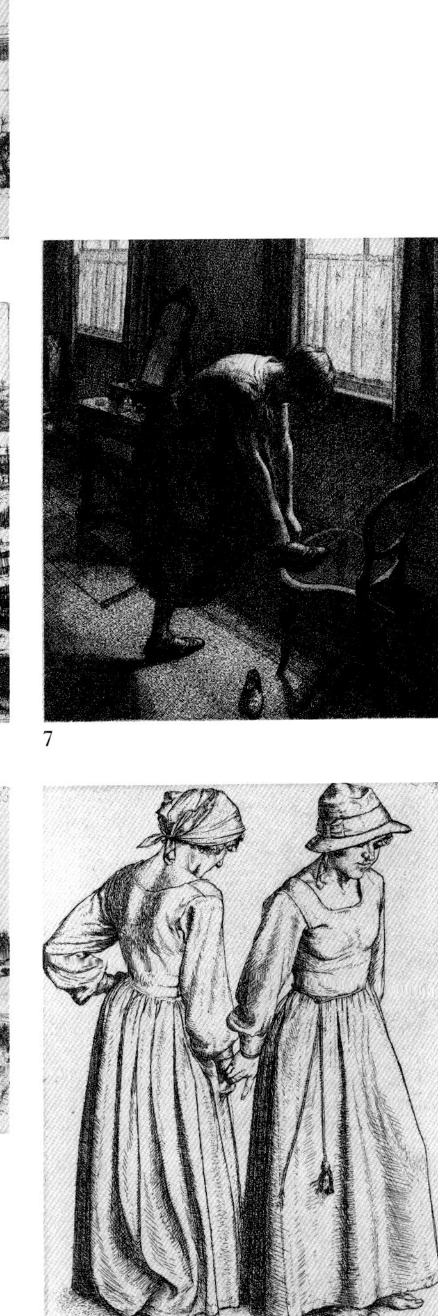

11. Ruth
E. $5 \times 5\frac{1}{2}$
States 1/1. 1/2. 1/3
Exh: None

12. The Letter
E. $5\frac{1}{2} \times 5$
States 2/1. 1/2. 1/3. 1/4
Exh: RE 1935

13. Rome from the Pincio
E. $4\frac{1}{4} \times 4\frac{1}{4}$
States 5/1. 1/2. 1/3. 1/4. 2/5. 1/6
Exh. RE 1935. Walker Gallery, Liverpool
1935

14. Landscape, Aqua Acetosa
E. 4×5
States 2/1. 2/2. 1/3. 1/4. 2/5
Exh: None

1935

15. Praying Peasant
E. $4 \times 5\frac{1}{4}$
States 2/1. 1/2. 3/3
Exh: None

16. Peasant Women
E. $5\frac{1}{2} \times 6\frac{1}{2}$
States 3/1. 1/2. 1/3. 1/4. 3/5
Exh: RE 1936
Reproduced *Fine Prints* 1935

17. Garden Tools
E. 5×4
States 3/1. 5/2
Exh: RE 1936. Phoenix Gallery, Lavenham
1963 (30). New Ashgate Gallery, Farnham
1983. Bankside Gallery 'Five Man Show'
1987 (122)

18. Valley of the Tescio, Assisi
E. $3\frac{3}{4} \times 6\frac{1}{2}$
States 2/1. 1/2. 1/3. 1/4
Exh: RE 1936

19. Olives, Assisi
E. $6\frac{1}{2} \times 6\frac{1}{4}$
States 2/1. 1/2. 1/3. 1/5. 2/6
Exh: RE 1937

20. The Spanish Mule
LE $6\frac{3}{4} \times 8$
States 2/1. 2/2. 1/3. 1/4
Exh: RE 1937. RA 1937. Art Institute of
Chicago 1937. RSA 1938. British Council
Scandinavian Tour 1939/40. Phoenix Gal-
lery, Lavenham 1963 (20). New Ashgate
Gallery, Farnham 1978. RE Spring Exhibi-
tion Special Show 1983 (154). Bankside
Gallery 'Five Man Show' 1987 (114)
Reproduced Colnaghi Prospectus, May
1938

21. Peasant Conversation
LE $5\frac{3}{4} \times 6\frac{1}{2}$
States 2/1. 1/2. 2/3. 1/4. 2/5
Exh: RE 1937
Reproduced *Fine Prints* 1936. Colnaghi
Prospectus, May 1938

22. El Potro, Cordoba, MCMXXXVI
LE $6\frac{3}{4} \times 5\frac{1}{4}$
States 1/1. 1/3. 1/4. 1/5. 1/7. 1/8. 1/10
Exh: RE 1937, 1940. RSA 1938. Interna-
tional Print Makers, Los Angeles 1938

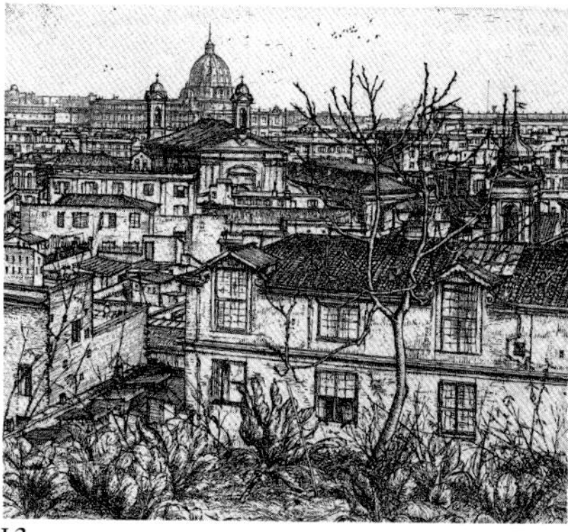

13

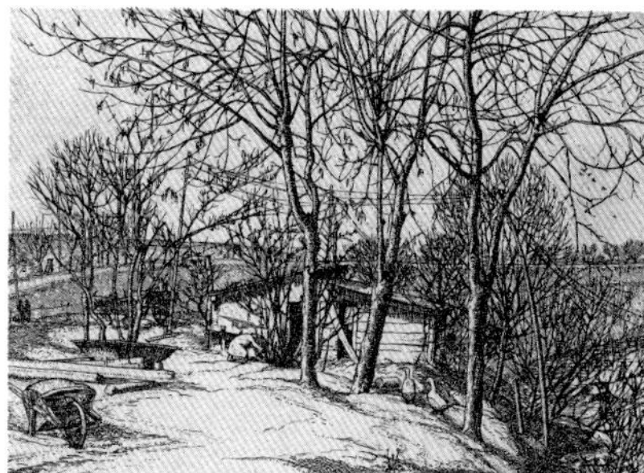

14

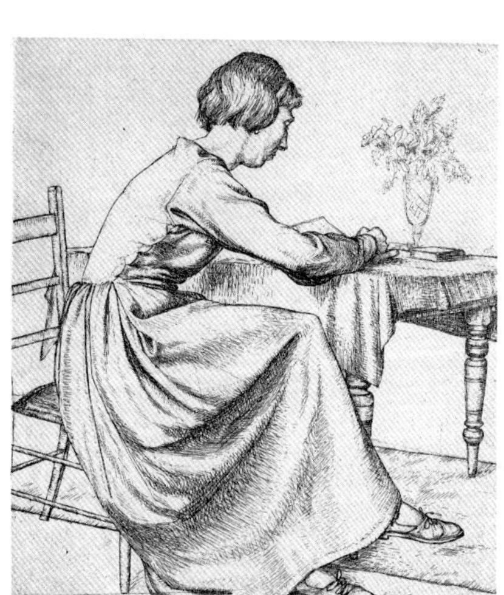

11

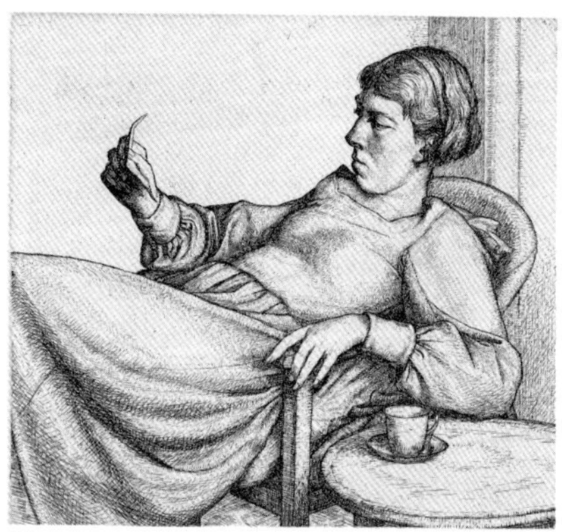

12

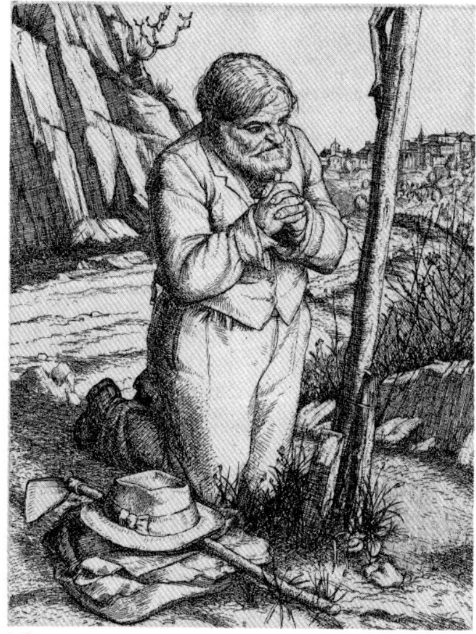

15

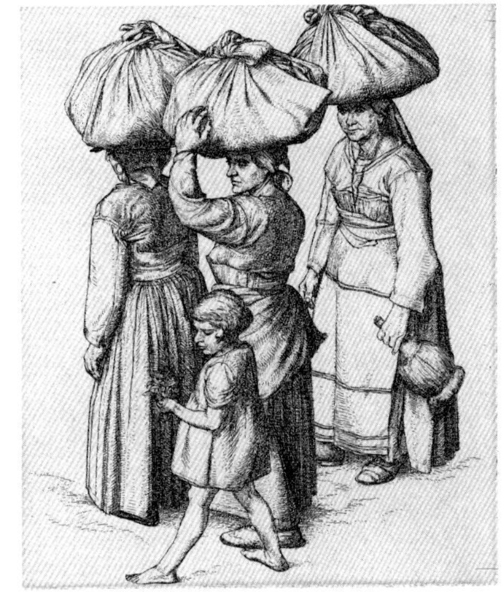

16

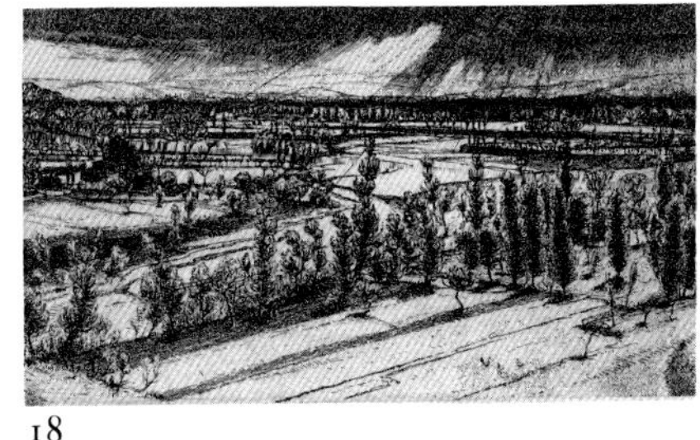

18

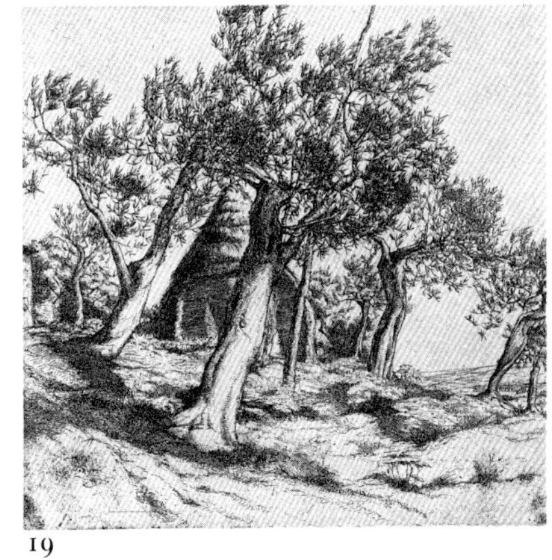

19

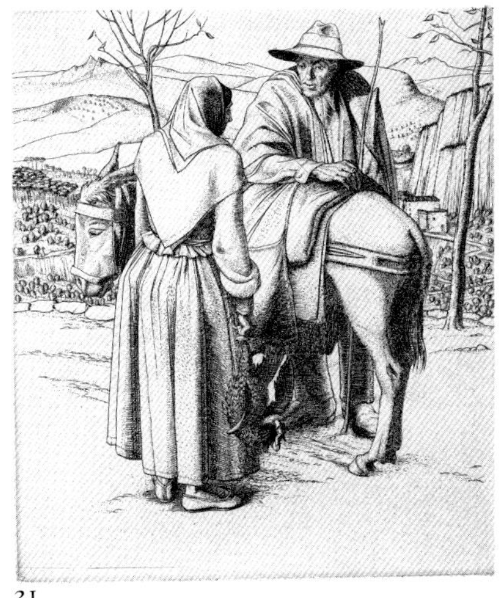

21

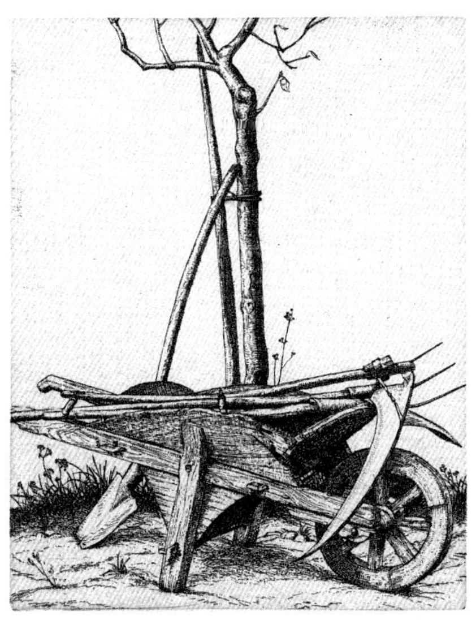

17

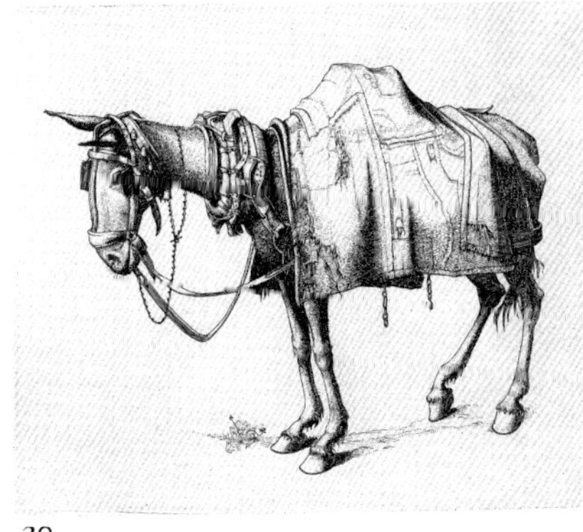

20

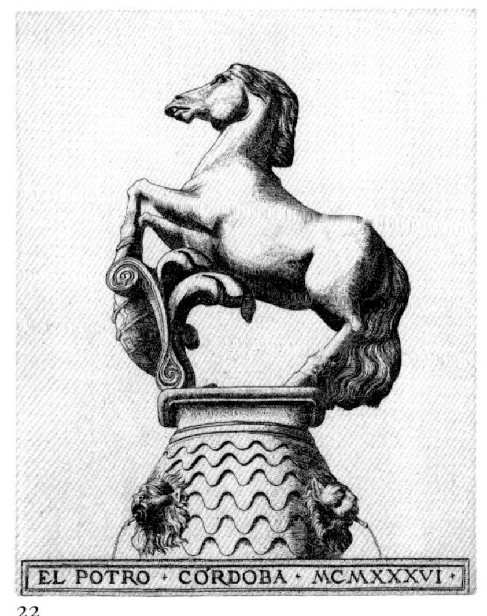

22

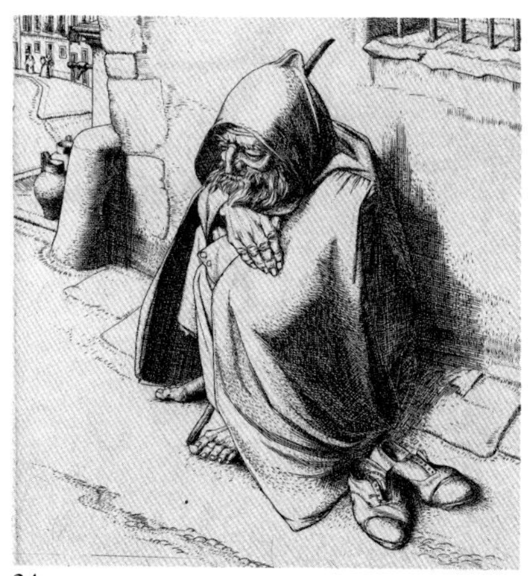

24

1937

23. El Kantara, Toledo
E. $9\frac{3}{4} \times 13$
Plate re-worked in drypoint 1974 (see 83)
States 2/1. 1/2. 1/4. 1/5. 1/6. 1/8
Exh: RE 1937, 1940. RA 1937. Hudders-
field Art Gallery 1937. Phoenix Gallery,
Lavenham 1963 (portfolio). New Ashgate
Gallery, Farnham 1980
Reproduced *Fine Prints* 1937. Colnaghi
Prospectus, May 1938

24. The Spanish Beggar
LE 6×5
States 2/1. 1/2. 3/3. 1/4. 1/5. 1/6
Four final proofs before letters P.C.
Exh: RE 1938. Phoenix Gallery, Lavenham
1963 (portfolio). Plate for Print Collectors
Club 1938. Bankside Gallery 'Five Man
Show' 1987 (118)

25. Traghetto
LE $7\frac{1}{4} \times 8\frac{1}{2}$
Plate re-worked in etching/drypoint 1981
(see 105)
States 2/1. 2/2. 1/3. 2/4. 2/5
Exh: RE 1938. Phoenix Gallery, Lavenham
1963 (portfolio)
Purchased Contemporary Art Society 1939
(A M Hind)
Reproduced *Print Collectors Quarterly*
February 1938 p.115. Colnaghi Prospectus,
May 1938

26. Palma Cathedral
E. 10×14
Plate re-worked in drypoint 1970 (see 75)
States 2/1. 2/2. 2/3. 1/4. 1/5. 2/6. 2/7
Exh: RE 1938. RA 1938. Phoenix Gallery,
Lavenham 1963 (portfolio)
Reproduced *Fine Prints* 1938. Colnaghi
Prospectus, May 1938

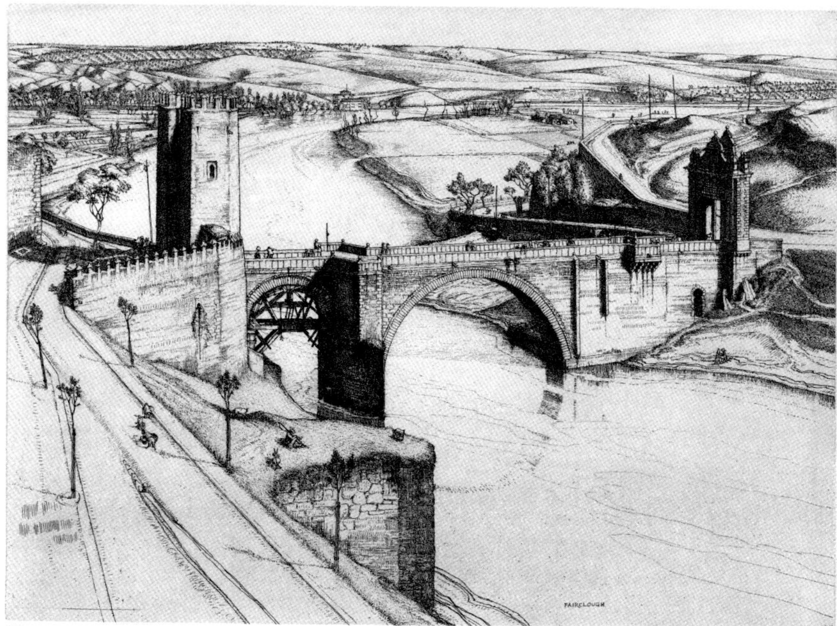

23

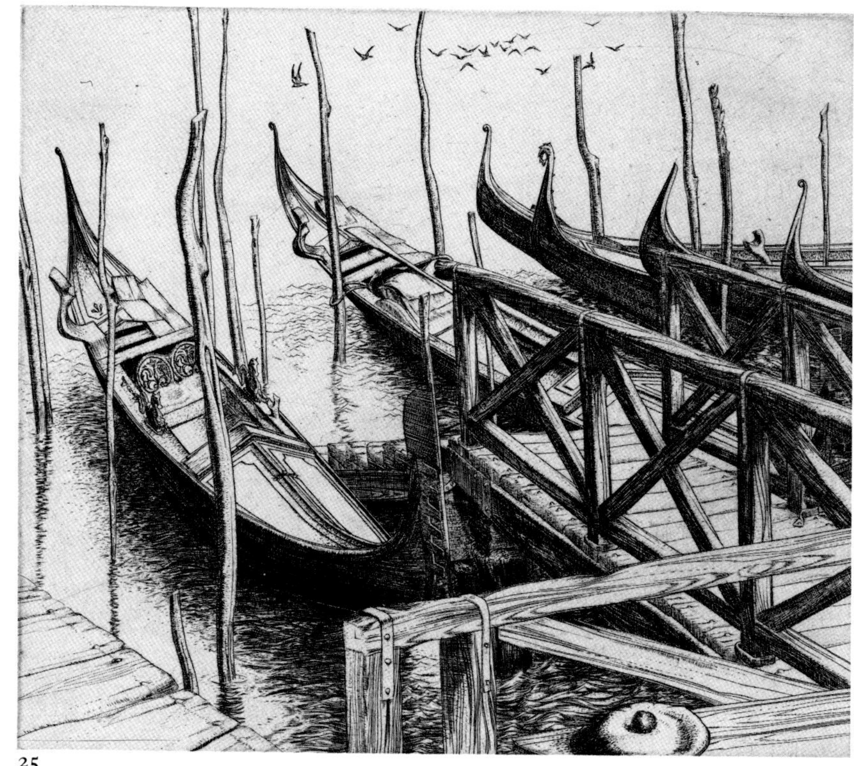

25

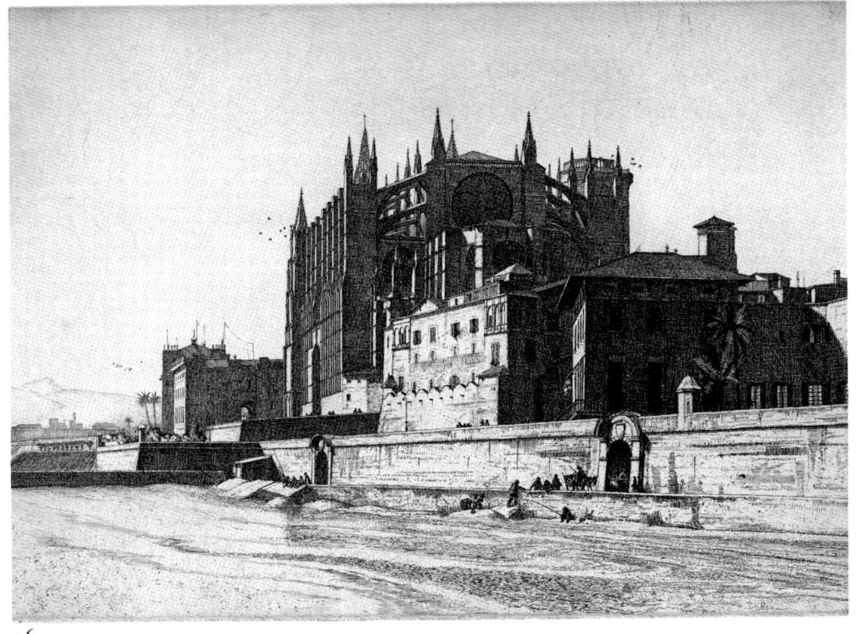

26

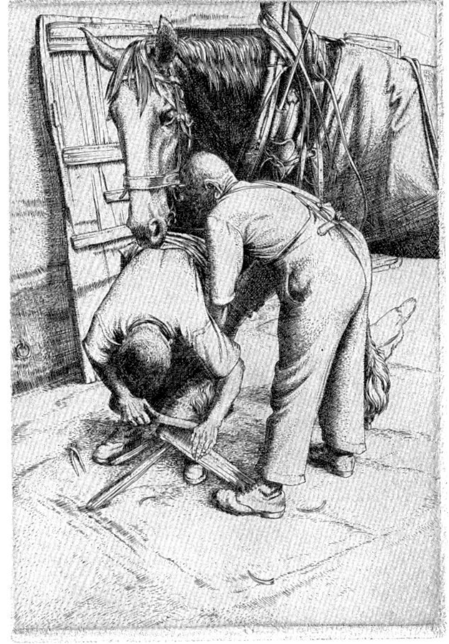

27

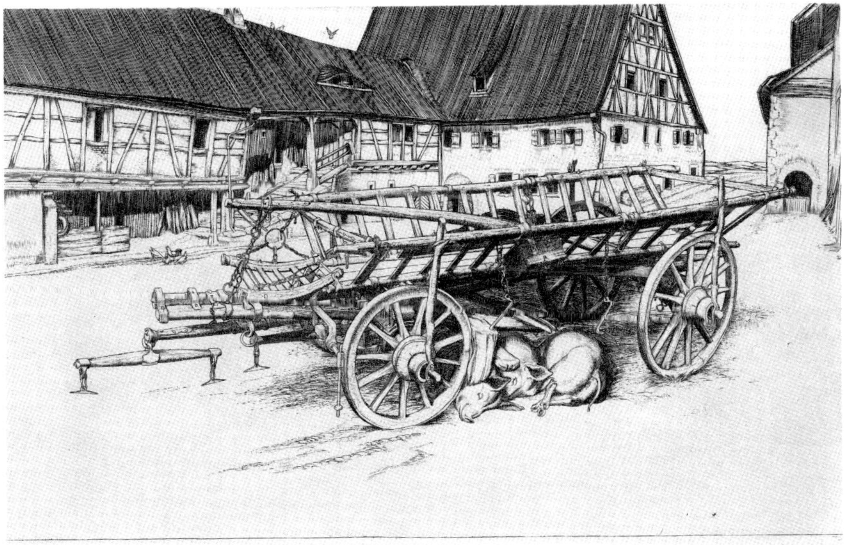

28

· JOHN · FVLLER · GODBOLT · ESQ · MCMXXXVIII ·

29

1938

27. Farriers
LE $6\frac{1}{4} \times 4\frac{1}{2}$
States 2/1. 2/2. 1/3. 2/4. 5/5
Exh: RE 1938. Phoenix Gallery, Lavenham 1963 (7). New Ashgate Gallery, Farnham 1980 (19). Bankside Gallery 'Five Man Show' 1987 (125)
Reproduced Colnaghi Prospectus, May 1938

28. The Large Cart, Rothenburg
LE $8 \times 12\frac{1}{2}$
States 3/1. 2/2. 3/4
Exh: RE 1939. RA 1939. British Council Scandinavian Tour 1939/40. Phoenix Gallery, Lavenham 1963 (10). New Ashgate Gallery, Farnham 1978, September 1980 (20). Bankside Gallery 'Five Man Show' 1987 (111)
Purchased Gothenburg Museum 1940

29. John Fuller Godbolt
LE 10×8
States 2/1. 2/2. 1/3. 2/4
Exh: Rejected for exhibition RE 1938
Plate destroyed

30. Three Heraldic Book Plates for Charles Henry Vereker
(1) LE $5\frac{1}{4} \times 3\frac{1}{4}$
(2) LE $6\frac{1}{4} \times 4$
(3) LE $7\frac{1}{4} \times 4\frac{1}{2}$
States: no record
Engraved to be hand coloured

31. Das Gänsemännchen, Nürnberg, MCMXXXVIII
LE $8\frac{1}{2} \times 5\frac{1}{2}$
States 3/1
Exh: RE 1939. Bradford 1946. Phoenix Gallery, Lavenham 1963 (portfolio). New Ashgate Gallery, Farnham 1980 (21). Bankside Gallery Christmas 1981

1940

32. Reggie Gould
E. $8\frac{1}{2} \times 6$
States: one state only
The subject was a LCC evacuee at Rustington Camp, near Littlehampton

33. Magdalen College, Oxford
E. $16 \times 18\frac{1}{4}$
Plate re-worked in drypoint 1975 (see 90)
States 3/1. 3/2
Exh: RE. RA. Bradford 1949. RA 1957. RA tour 1957/58. Phoenix Gallery, Lavenham 1963 (portfolio)

1943

34. Hambleden Orchard
LE $7\frac{1}{2} \times 11$
States 4/1. 4/2. 4/3
Exh: RE. Bradford 1949. Phoenix Gallery, Lavenham 1963 (portfolio). New Ashgate Gallery, Farnham 1980 (18). Bankside Gallery 'Five Man Show' 1987 (119)
Purchased Contemporary Art Society (A M Hind)

1949

35. Book Plate for the Hon. Mr Arnold Palmer
LE $2\frac{3}{4} \times 2\frac{3}{4}$
States 1/1. 1/2
Exh: RE? Bradford 1950. Bankside Gallery 'Five Man Show' 1987 (120b)

1950

36. Burnley Building Society, Head Office
E. $11\frac{3}{4} \times 12\frac{3}{4}$
States: no record

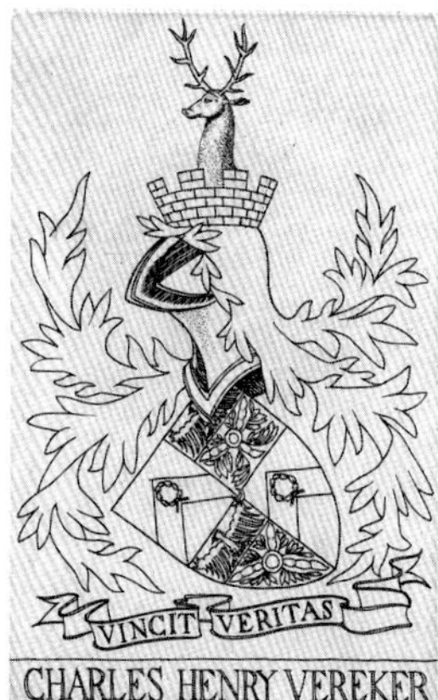

30 (1)

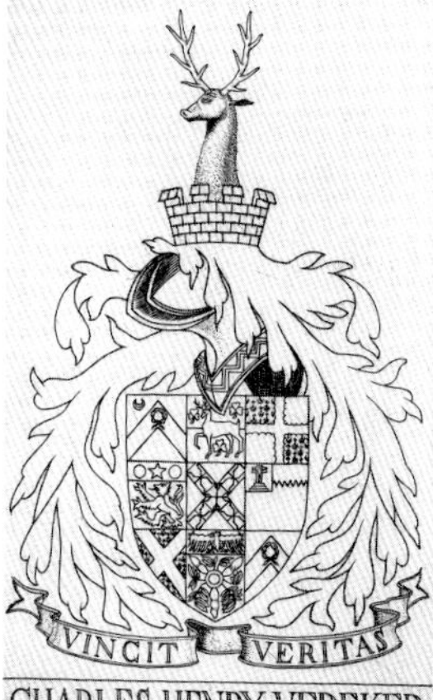

30 (2)

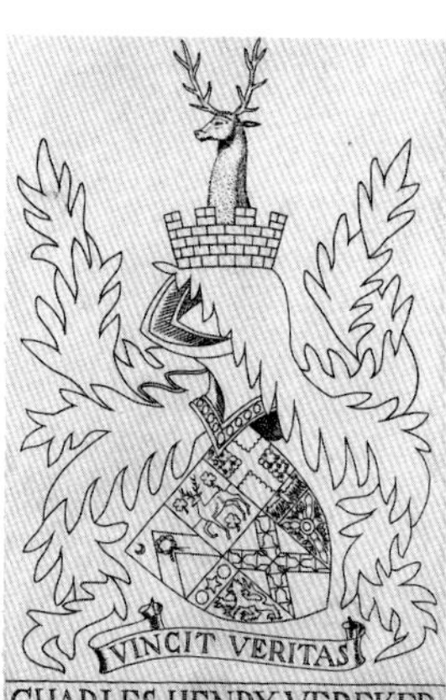

30 (3)

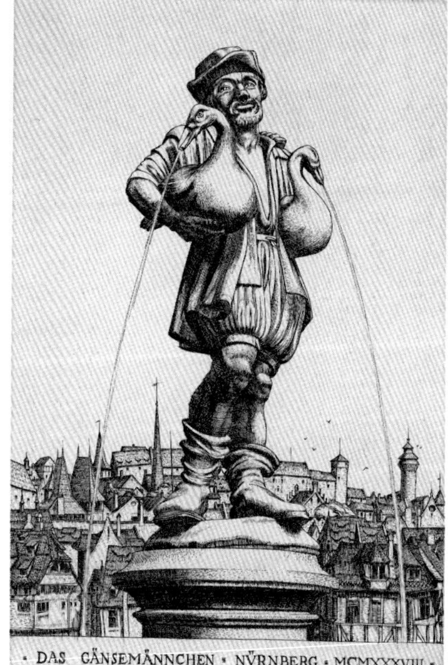
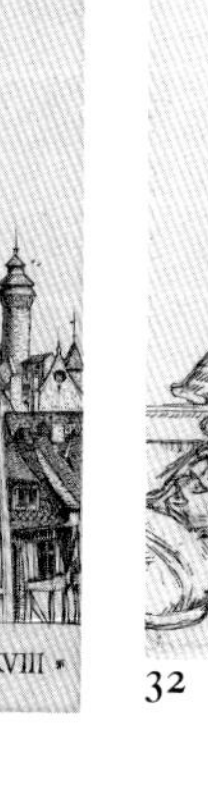

31

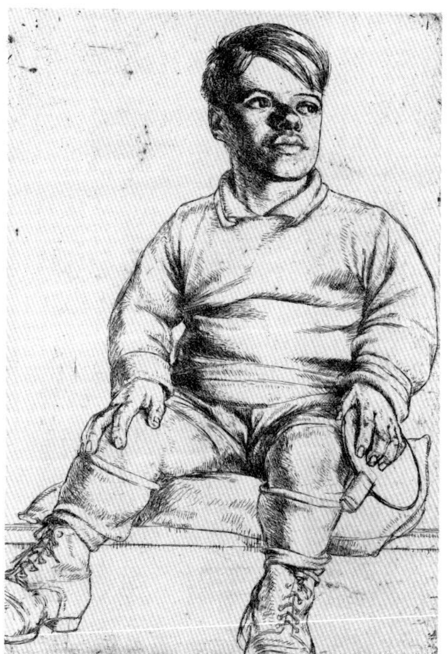
32

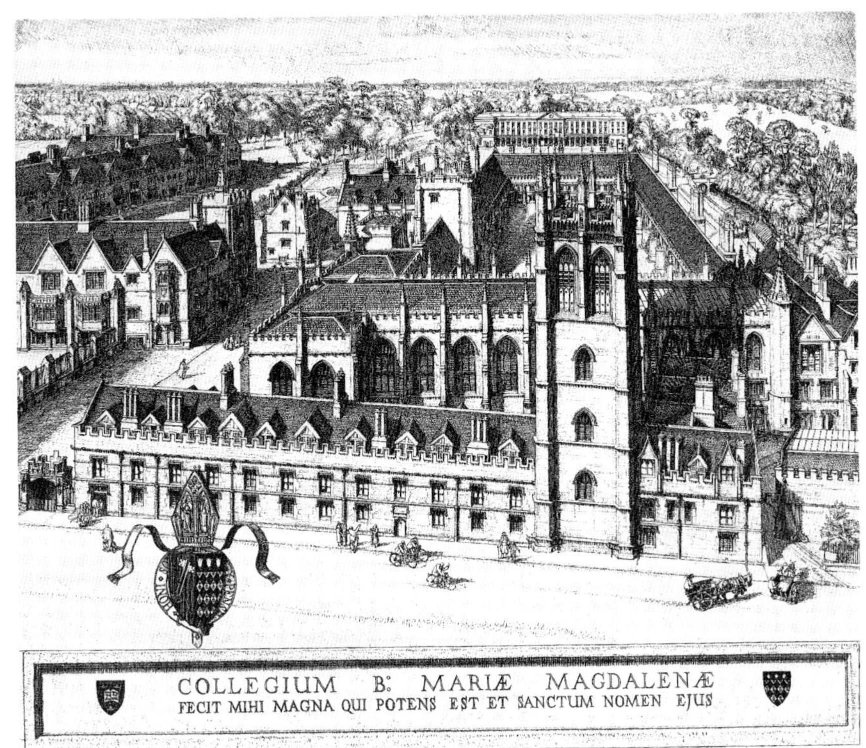

33

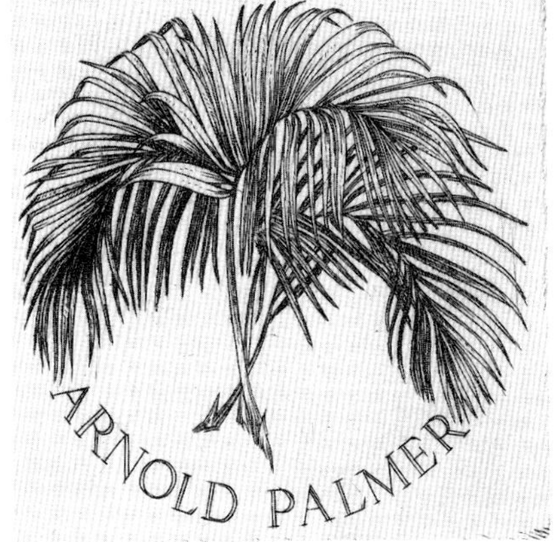

35

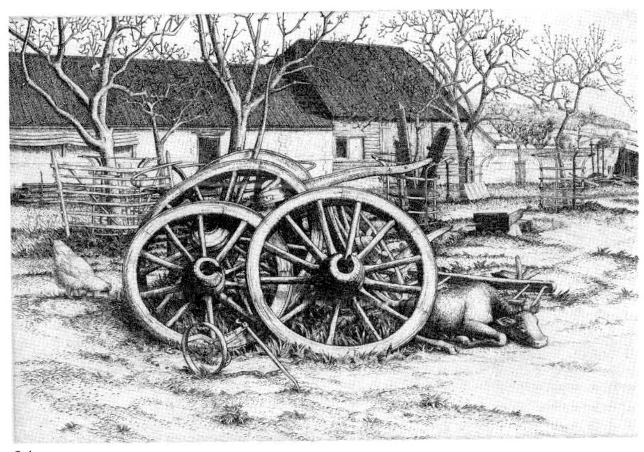

34

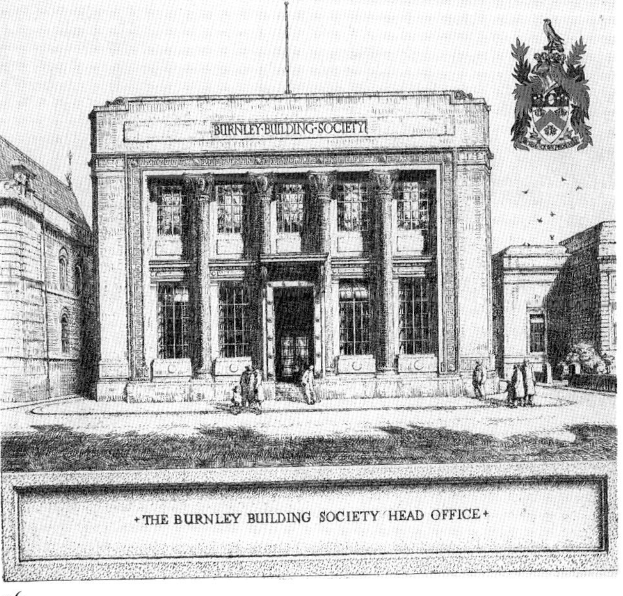

36

37. Book Plate for Wye College
E. $4\frac{1}{2} \times 3\frac{1}{2}$
States : no record
Exh : Bradford 1950. Bankside Gallery
'Five Man Show' 1987 (120a)

1953

38. The Old Lady
E. 7×3
States 1/1. 5/2
Exh : RE 1953. Phoenix Gallery, Lavenham
1963 (portfolio). New Ashgate Gallery,
Farnham 1978 (1)

1954

39. The Camel
E. $8\frac{1}{2} \times 8$
States 3/1
Exh : RE 1954. Phoenix Gallery, Lavenham
1963 (portfolio)

40. Puppets
E. $10 \times 7\frac{1}{2}$
States 3/1
Exh : RE 1954. Rome Scholars Exhibition,
Festival Hall 1959 (46). Phoenix Gallery,
Lavenham 1963 (portfolio)

1955

41. Donkeys
E. $7 \times 8\frac{3}{4}$
States 3/1
Exh : RE 1955

**42. Miss Hattie Jacques, Players'
Theatre**
E. $8\frac{3}{4} \times 5$
States 3/1
Exh : RE 1955. RA 1955. RA Tour 1955/56.
Phoenix Gallery, Lavenham 1963 (4). New
Ashgate Gallery, Farnham 1978 (4). Illus-
trated on catalogue cover

1956

43. Camels (Mother and Child)
E. 9×8
States 2/1
Exh : RE 1956. Phoenix Gallery, Lavenham
1963 (portfolio)

44. Bellcage, East Bergholt
E. 8×10
States 2/1
Exh : RE 1956. RA 1956. Phoenix Gallery,
Lavenham 1963 (9). New Ashgate Gallery,
Farnham 1978 (9)

45. Olivelli's
E. $9 \times 5\frac{1}{2}$
States 2/1
Exh : RE 1956. RA 1956. RA Tour 1956/57.
Phoenix Gallery, Lavenham 1963 (5). New
Ashgate Gallery, Farnham 1978 (4). Bank-
side Gallery Christmas 1981

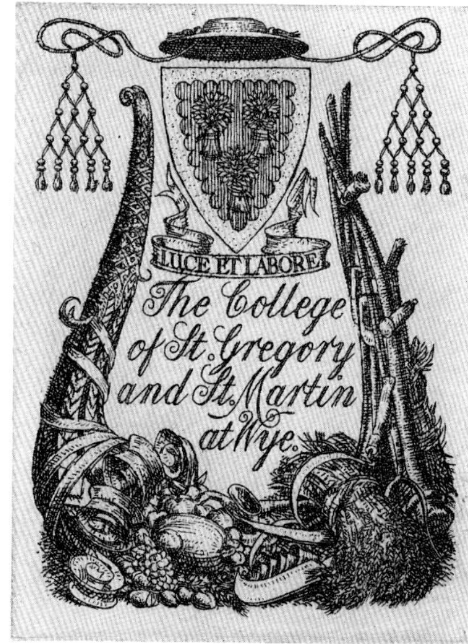

37

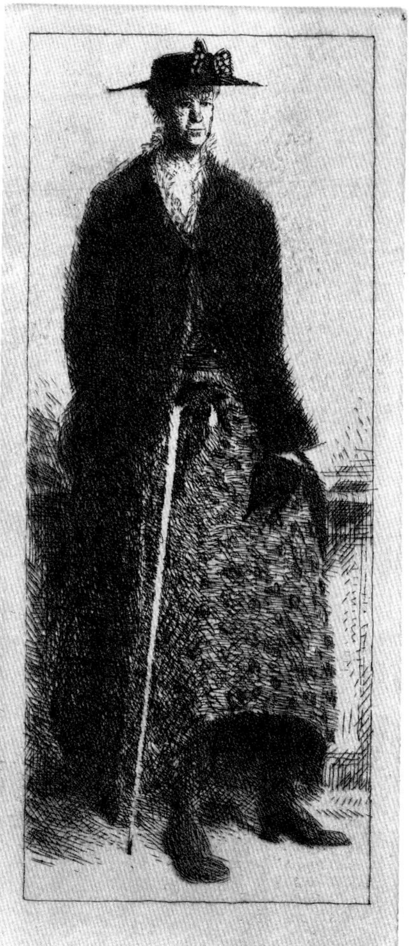

38

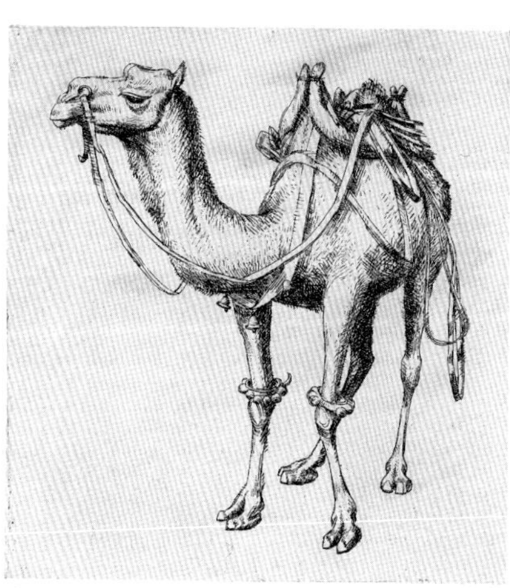

39

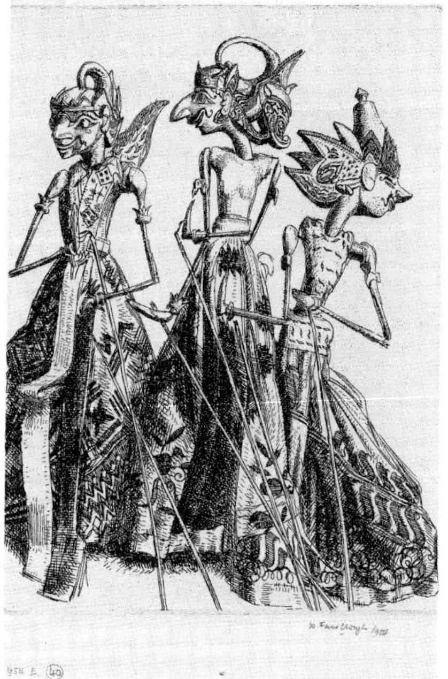

40

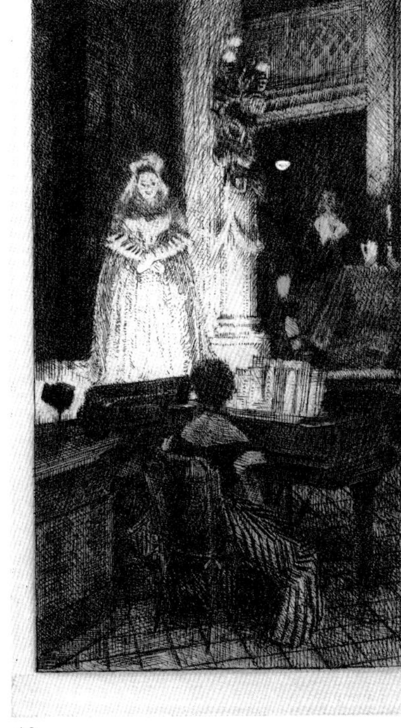

41

42

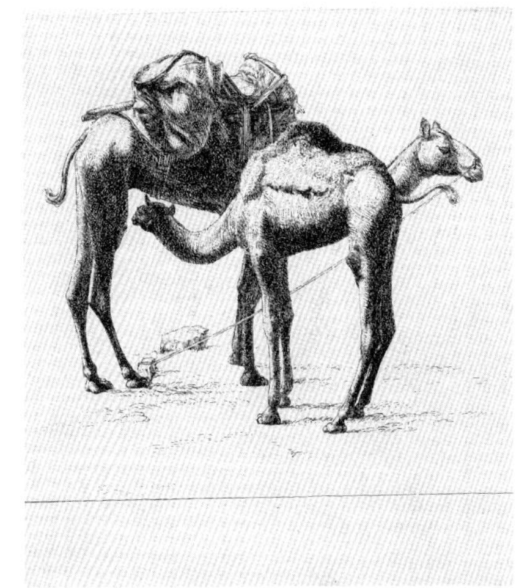

43

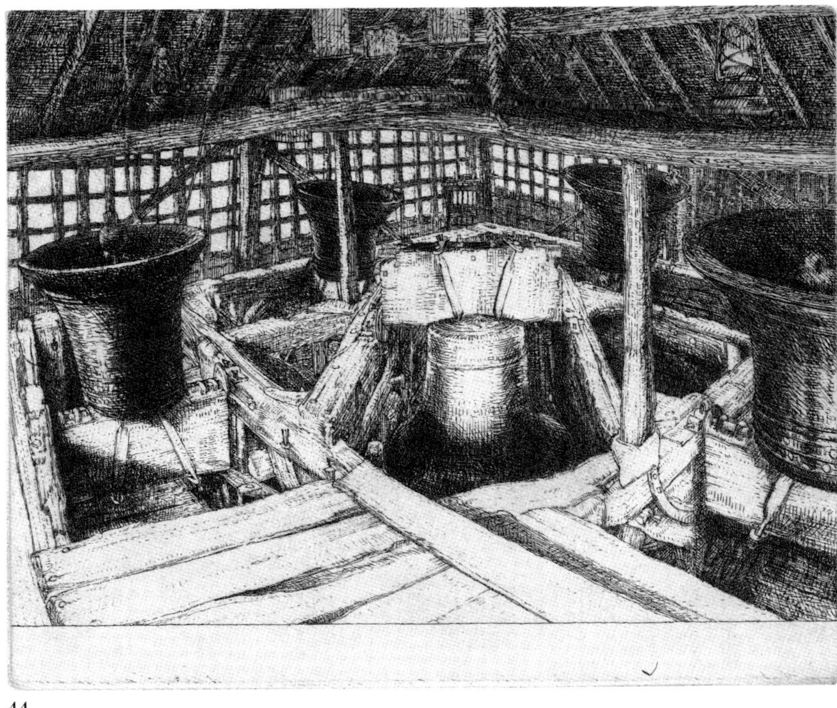

44

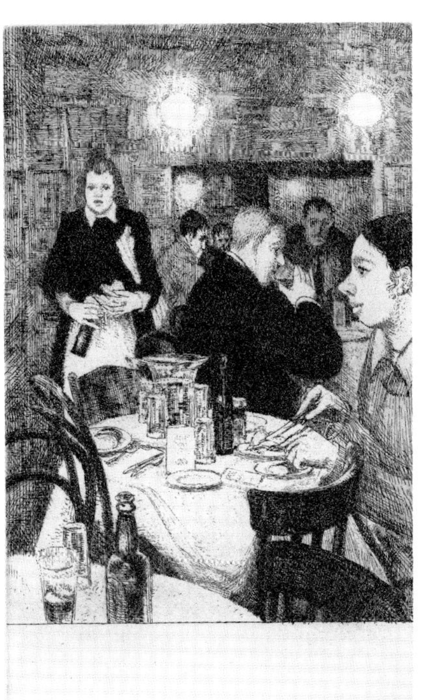

45

46. Angel and Bell
E. 10 × 8
States 2/1
Exh : RE 1956. Invitation, Southport,
Atkinson Art Gallery 1956. Phoenix Gal-
lery, Lavenham 1963 (portfolio)

1957

47. Covent Garden, Grand Tier
E. 7 × 8
States 1/1. Second state – final state
Exh : RE 1957. RA 1957. Phoenix Gallery,
Lavenham 1963 (6). New Ashgate Gallery,
Farnham 1978 (5). Bankside Gallery
Christmas 1981. Bankside Gallery 'Five
Man Show' 1987 (131)
Plate for Print Collectors Club 1957

48. The Stoic
E. 10 × 8
States 1/1. 1/2
Exh : RE 1957. RA 1957. Phoenix Gallery,
Lavenham 1963 (portfolio)

49. Two Ladies on a Beach
E. 6 × 8
States 1/1. Second state – final state
Exh : RE 1957. Atkinson Art Gallery
Southport 1957. Phoenix Gallery, Laven-
ham 1963 (15). New Ashgate Gallery, Farn-
ham 1983. Bankside Gallery Christmas
1983

50. Gaiety Theatre
E. 9 × 12
States 2/1. 1/2
Exh : RE 1957 (18). RA 1958 (1156). Rome
Scholars Exhibition, Festival Hall 1959.
Phoenix Gallery, Lavenham 1963 (14).
Bankside Gallery 'Five Man Show' 1987
(116)
Plate commissioned by the English Electric
Company Ltd, who retain the plate

51. Bedford Box, Covent Garden
E. 7 × 4¼
States. Complete in 1st state, no further
work required
Exh : RE 1957. RA 1958. Phoenix Gallery,
Lavenham 1963 (28). New Ashgate Gallery,
Farnham 1978 (6). RE Spring Exhibition
(172), Special Exhibition 1983

**52. Jacques String Orchestra, Hampton
Court**
E. 6½ × 10
States 1/1. 2nd state – final state
Exh : RE 1958. Atkinson Art Gallery
Southport 1958. Rome Scholars Exhibition,
Festival Hall 1959 (47). Phoenix Gallery,
Lavenham 1963 (12). New Ashgate Gallery,
Farnham 1978 (7)

53. Cherubs and Trophies
E. 6½ × 8
States 2/1. 2nd state complete. Final state
Exh : RE 1958. Atkinson Art Gallery
Southport 1958. Phoenix Gallery, Laven-
ham 1963 (portfolio)

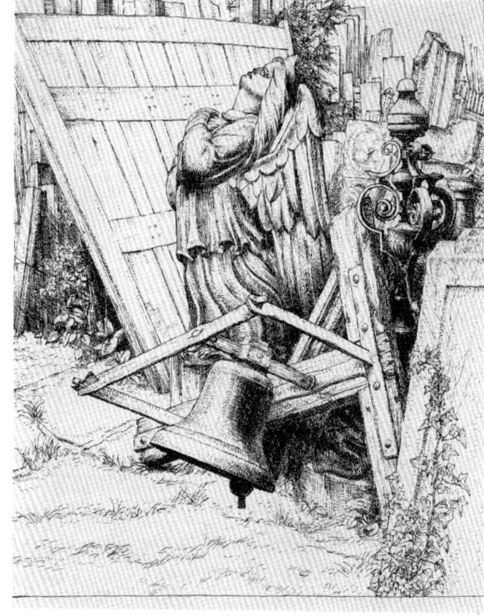

46

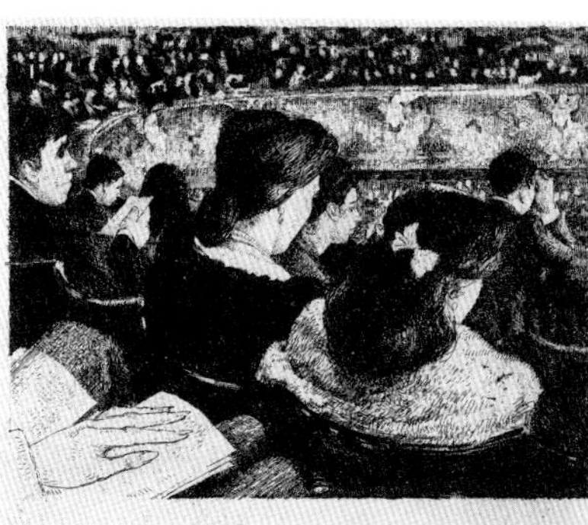

47

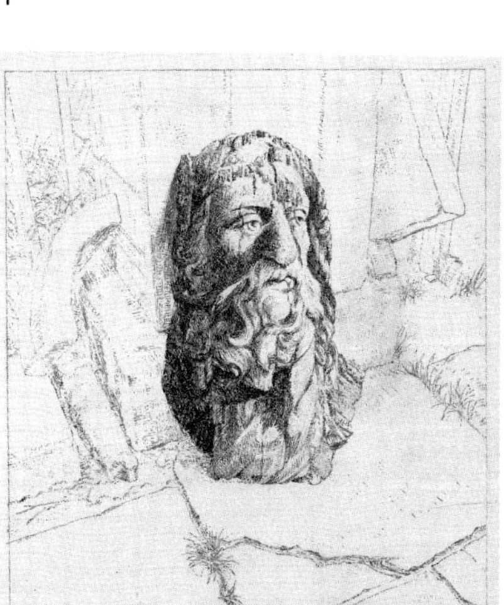

48

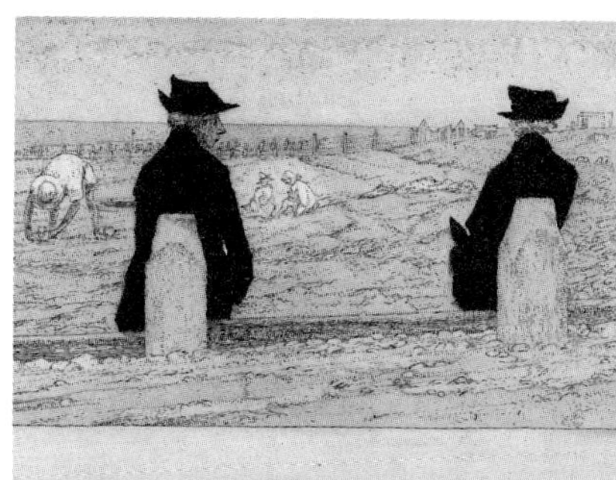

49

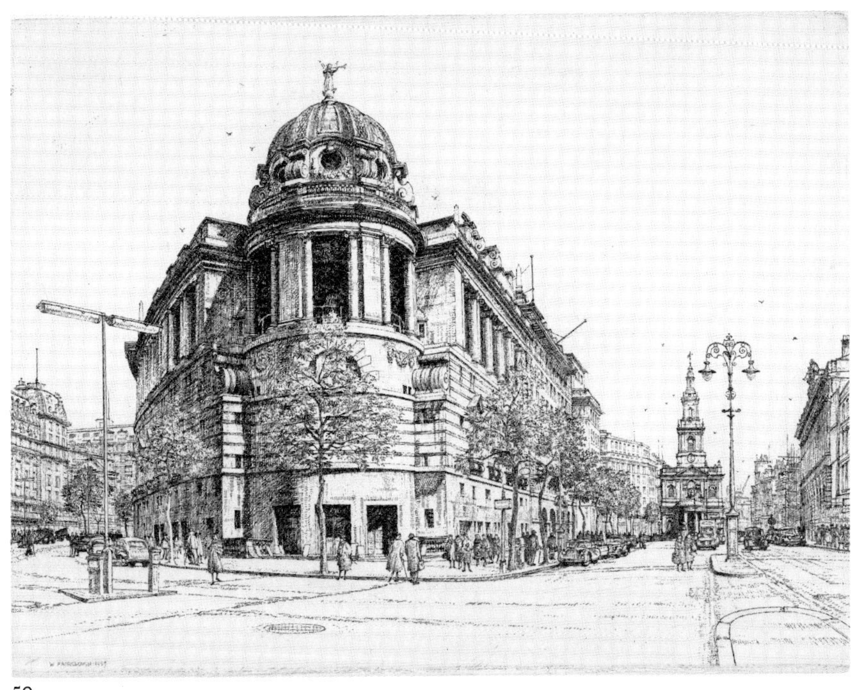

50

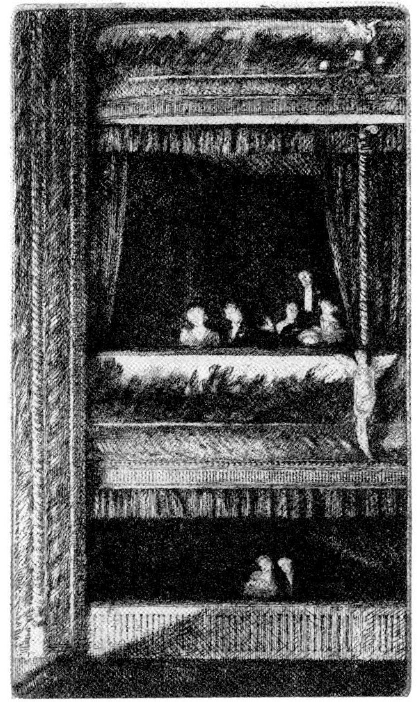

51

52

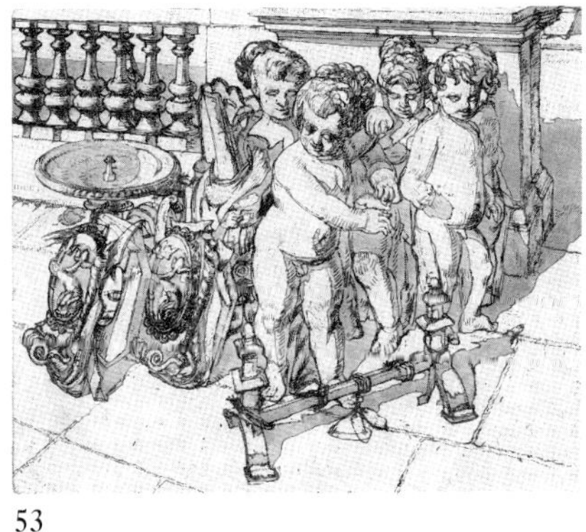

53

1959

54. Radcliffe Camera, Oxford
E. $11\frac{1}{4} \times 12\frac{1}{4}$
States 2/1
Exh: RE 1959 (16). RA 1959 (1248). Atkinson Art Gallery 1960. Phoenix Gallery, Lavenham 1963 (11). New Ashgate Gallery, Farnham 1980 (17). RE Spring Exhibition, Special Exhibition 1983 (153)

55. Bullock Team, Burgos
E. $7\frac{1}{2} \times 11$
States 2/1. 2/2
Exh: RE 1959 (6). Phoenix Gallery, Lavenham 1963 (2). New Ashgate Gallery, Farnham 1983. Bankside Gallery Christmas 1983

56. Covent Garden, Wings
E. $12 \times 6\frac{1}{4}$
States 2/1
Exh: RE 1959 (80). RA 1959 (1212). Phoenix Gallery, Lavenham 1963 (18). Atkinson Art Gallery, Southport 1961. New Ashgate Gallery, Farnham 1978 (18). Bankside Gallery Christmas 1982. RE Spring Exhibition. Special Exhibition 1983 (171). Bankside Gallery 'Five Man Show' 1987 (139)

1960

57. La Capricciosa, The Lady and The Fool
SG two plates (colour) $10\frac{1}{2} \times 5\frac{1}{2}$
States: no record
Exh: RE 1960 (55). RA 1960. New Ashgate Gallery, Farnham 1978 (9). Phoenix Gallery, Lavenham 1963 (40). Atkinson Art Gallery, Southport 1960. Rome Scholars Exhibition, Festival Hall 1960. Bankside Gallery 'Five Man Show' 1987 (137)

58. Magdalen College Tower and Bridge
E. $10\frac{1}{4} \times 11$
States 3/1. 1/2
Exh: RE 1960 (182). RA 1963 (1069). Rome Scholars Exhibition, Festival Hall 1960. South London Art Gallery 1960. Phoenix Gallery, Lavenham 1963 (portfolio). Bankside Gallery 'Five Man Show' 1987 (115)

1961

59. Giselle, Peasant Dance
SG $10 \times 10\frac{1}{4}$ colour, four plates
States: no record
Exh: RE 1961 (28). RA 1961 (1081). Phoenix Gallery, Lavenham 1963 (29). Atkinson Art Gallery 1964. Bankside Gallery 'Five Man Show' 1987 (133)

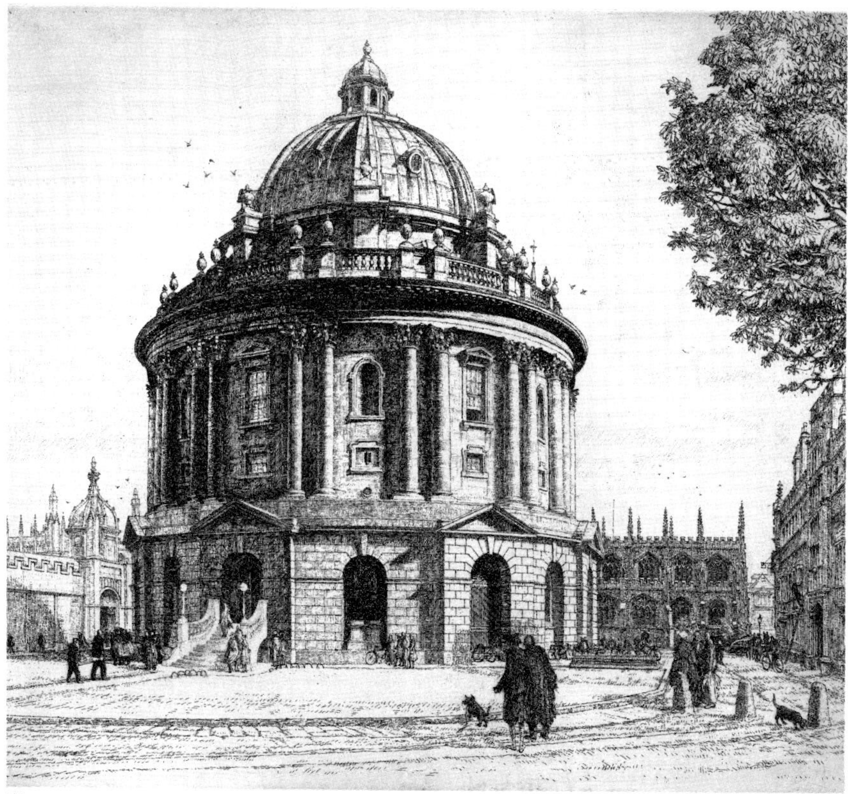

54

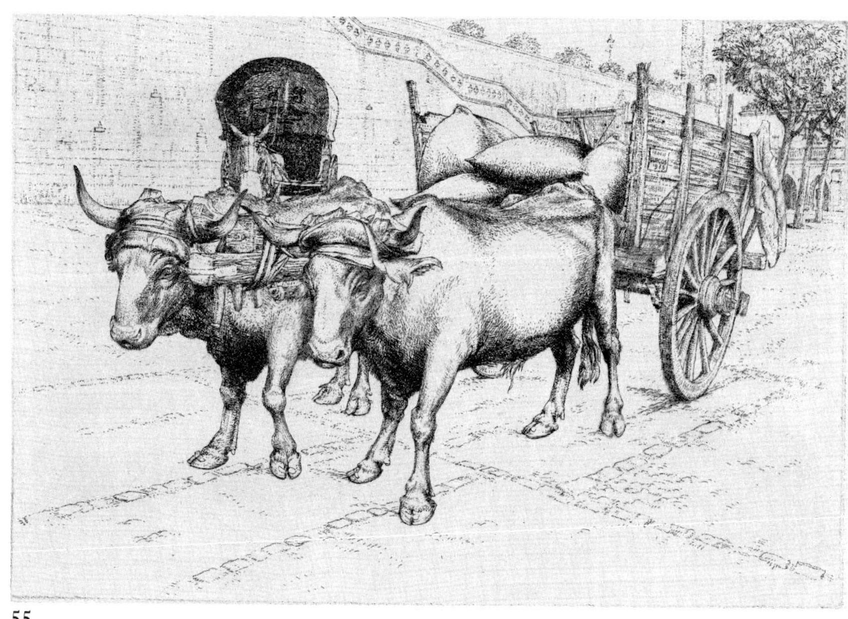

55

60. Christ Church, Oxford
E. 11×11 (plate cut 1967 $10\frac{1}{4} \times 11$)
States 4/1. 4/2
Exh: RE 1961 (170). RA 1961 (1146). Phoenix Gallery, Lavenham 1963 (13). South London Gallery 1961. New Ashgate Gallery, Farnham 1989 (16)

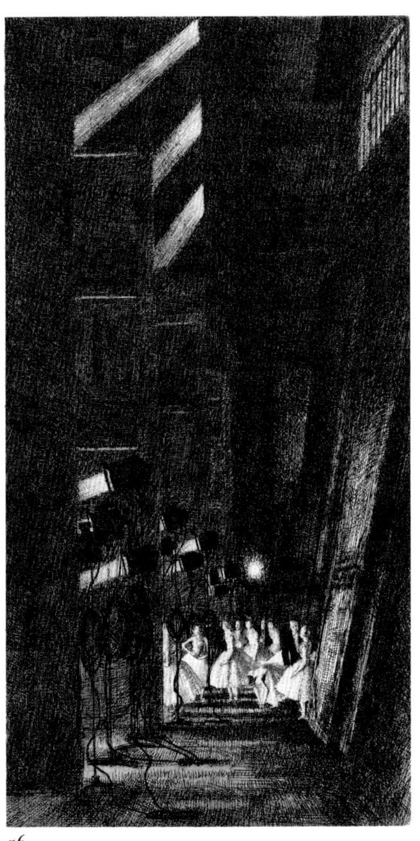

56

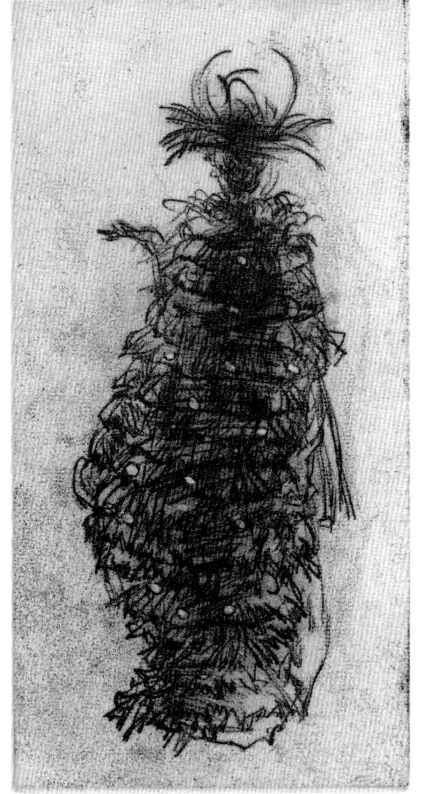

57

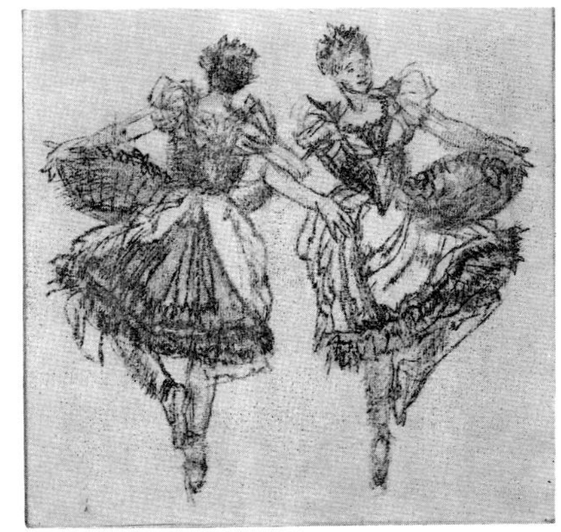

59

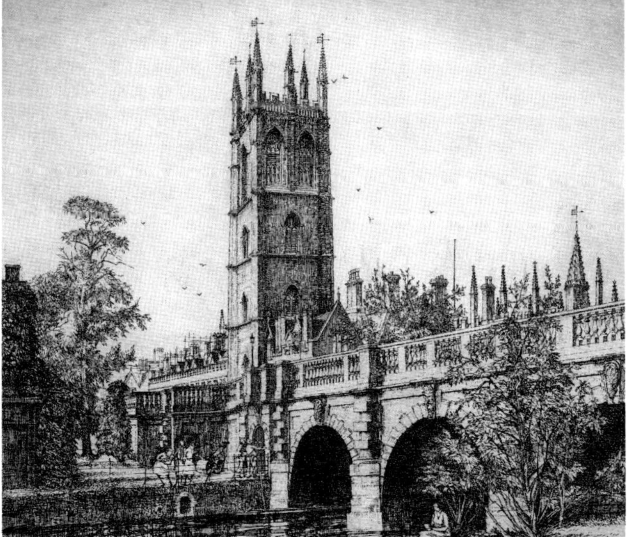

58

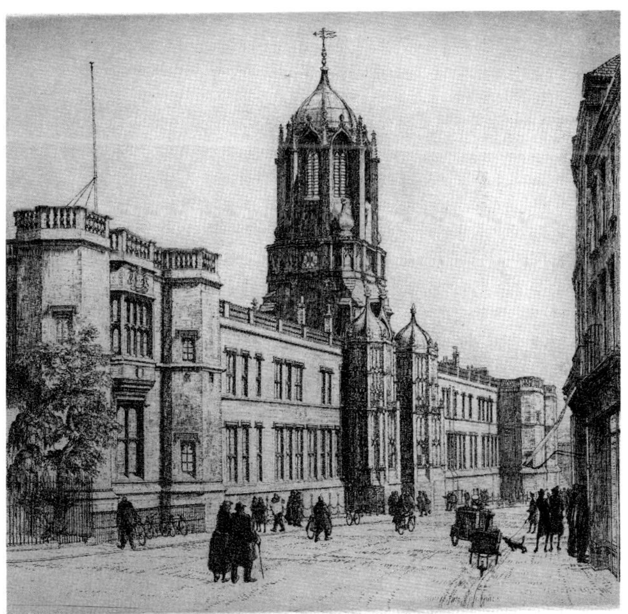

60

1962

61. Mario's Venezia
SG 14 × 18 colour, four plates (zinc). Plates damaged beyond repair (chemical action in envelopes)
States: no record
Exh: RE 1962 (64). Phoenix Gallery, Lavenham 1963 (17)
Purchased Stoke Education Authority

62. The Blue Pool
SG 10½ × 19¾ colour, four plates (zinc). Plates damaged beyond repair (chemical action in envelopes)
States: no record
Exh: RE 1962 (121)

1963

63. Municipal Band, Venice
SG 12¾ × 17 colour, three plates (zinc). Plates damaged beyond repair (chemical action in envelopes)
States: no record
Exh: RE 1963 (337). Phoenix Gallery, Lavenham 1963 (1). Atkinson Art Gallery, Southport 1964.

64. Covent Garden, Perches
SG 18 × 9 colour, one plate (zinc). Plates damaged beyond repair (chemical action in envelopes)
States: no record
Exh: RE 1963 (336). Phoenix Gallery, Lavenham 1963 (8)

1964

65. Boat to Chioggia
E/A 12 × 9 zinc
States 1/1
Plate for Print Collectors Club 1964
Exh: RE 1964. RA 1964 (970). South London Gallery, 'Modern Prints' 1972. Fine Art Society, 'Echoes of Venice', Aldeburgh 1973 (40). Edinburgh 1973. Bankside Gallery 'Five Man Show' 1987 (129).
Reproduced South London Gallery, illustration for poster/invitation card, 'Modern Prints' 1972

66. Wilderness
E. 16 × 10 zinc
States: no record
Exh: RE 1964. RA 1964 (962). Art Exhibitions Bureau, RA Selection 1964. Atkinson Art Gallery, Southport 1965. Phoenix Gallery, Lavenham 1967

1965

67. Lavenham Church
E. 9 × 12¾
States 2/1. 1/2
Exh: RE 1966 (60). RA 1966 (1033). Art Exhibitions Bureau, RA Tour 1966/67. Pendulum Gallery, Selborne 1973. New Ashgate Gallery, Farnham 1983
Purchased Stoke Education Authority

68. Two Gentlemen of Verona
E/A 8 × 10
States 1/1. 2/2
Exh: RE 1966 (49). RA 1967 (1138). Pendulum Gallery, Selborne 1973. New Ashgate Gallery, Farnham 1983. Bankside Gallery Christmas 1983

1966

69. Mario, Venetian Fishmonger
E/A 11 × 8½ (zinc)
Plate damaged by chemical action. Damage repaired except for spots in darks
States 2/1. 1/2. Restored plate six proofs
Exh: RE 1966. RA 1966 (1020). Phoenix Gallery, Lavenham 1967. New Ashgate Gallery, Farnham 1978 (23). Fine Art Society 'Echoes of Venice' Aldeburgh 1973 (41). Phoenix Gallery, Lavenham 1968 (29). Illustrated RA. Illustrated 1966. Purchased Princess Margaret of Hesse: present for Peter Pears, Red House, Aldeburgh

1967

70. Net Mender, Sorrento
E/A 8 × 10 zinc
States 1/1. 1/2
Exh: RE 1967 (82). Phoenix Gallery, Lavenham 1967

71. Connoisseur, Zurich
E/A 11 × 7¼ zinc
Plate damaged beyond repair (chemical action in envelope)
States 2/1. 1/2
Exh: RE 1967 (53). RA 1967 (1144). Phoenix Gallery 1967/68 (30)

1968

72. Sweet Martini
SG/A 12 × 8 zinc
States 2/1
Exh: RE 1968. Fine Art Society Edinburgh 1973. Pendulum Gallery 1973. New Ashgate Gallery, Farnham 1978 (24)

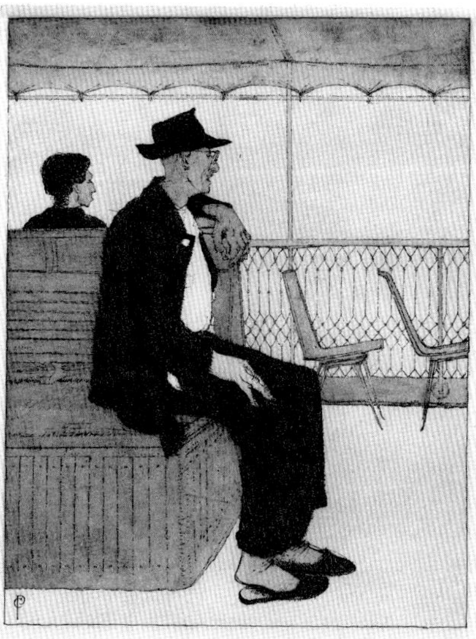

65

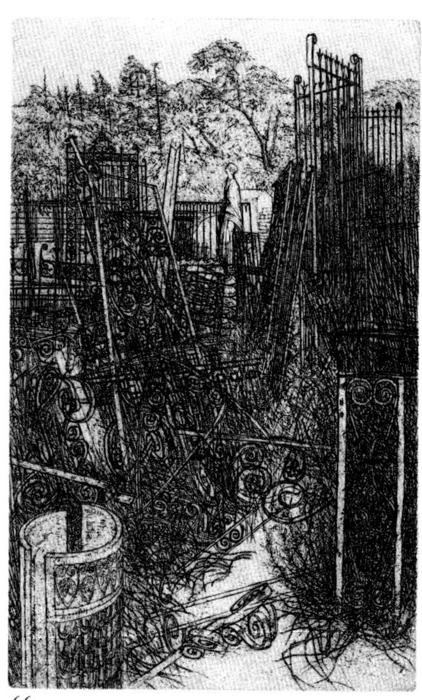

66

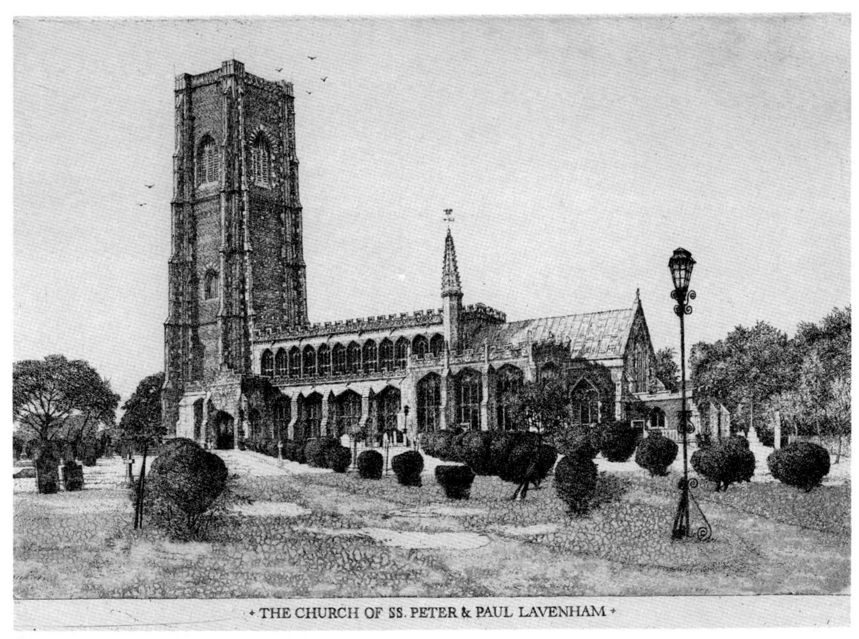

67

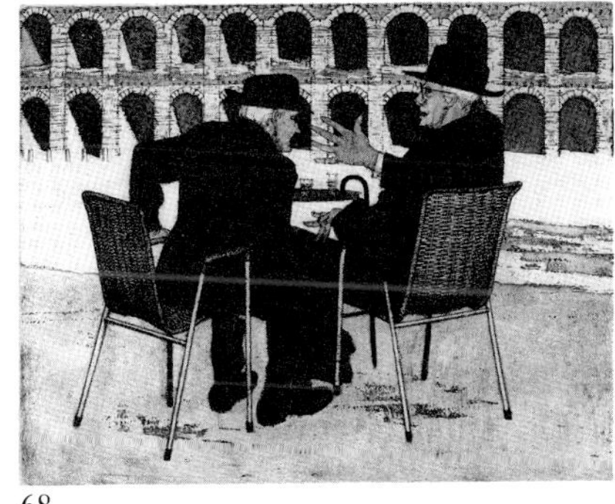

68

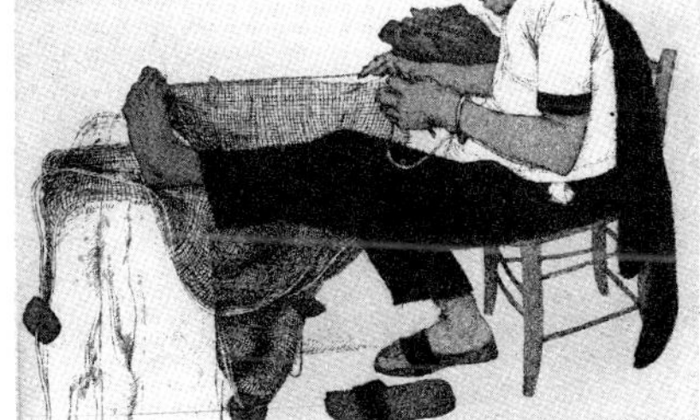

70

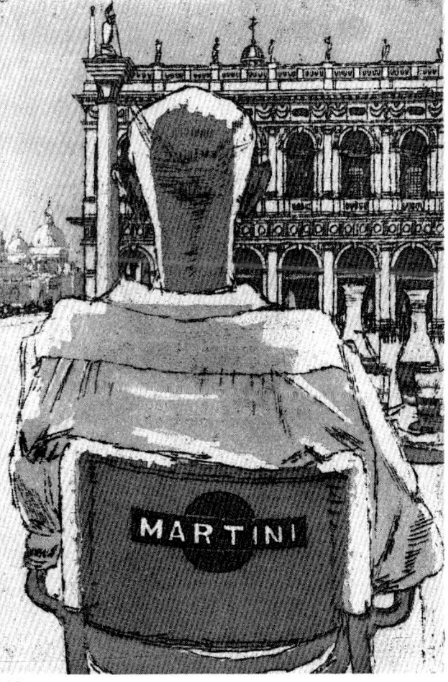

72

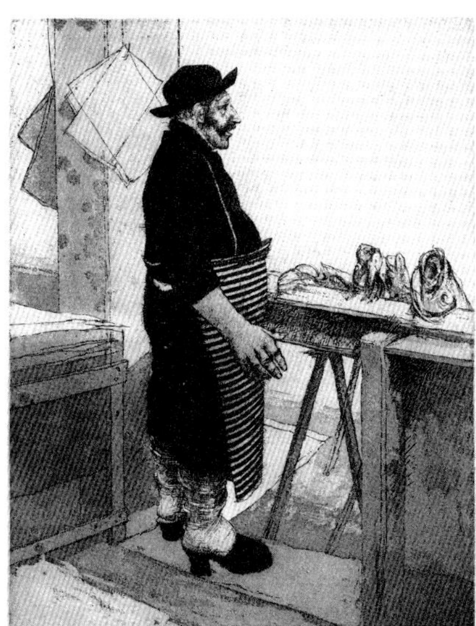

69

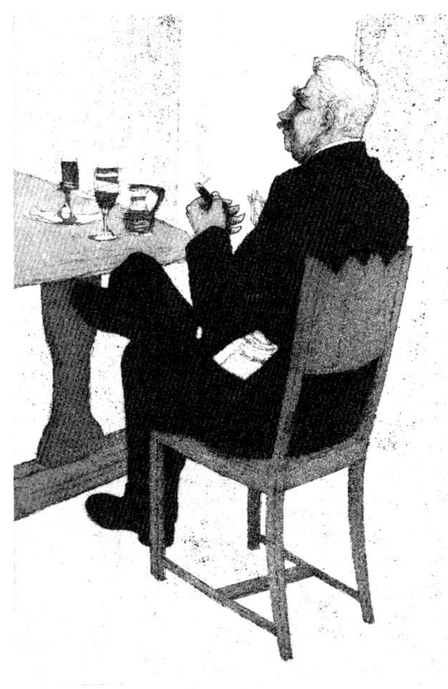

71

1969

73. Conversation, Gubbio
E/A $7\frac{3}{4} \times 9\frac{3}{4}$ zinc
States 2/1. 1/2. 1/3
Exh: RE 1969 (46)

1970

74. Frenchman in Tivoli
E/A $9\frac{1}{4} \times 8$ zinc
States 3/1. 2/2. 2/3
Exh: RE 1970 (42). New Ashgate Gallery,
Farnham 1980 (13). Bankside Gallery
Christmas 1981

75. Palma Cathedral
(see 26)
E. 1937. Re-worked in drypoint 1970
10×14
States: no record
Exh: RE 1970 (52). RA 1970 (736). New
Ashgate Gallery, Farnham 1980 (12)
Phoenix Gallery, Lavenham 1975. RE
Spring 1983, Special Exhibition (151)

1971

76. S Giorgio Maggiore, I Virtuosi di Roma
E. $10 \times 11\frac{1}{4}$
States 2/1. 1/2
Exh: RE 1971 (41). RA 1971 (864). Art
Exhibitions Bureau Tour 1971. Fine Art
Society 'Echoes of Venice', Aldeburgh 1973
(42). Edinburgh 1973

77. Venetian I
E/A $6 \times 4\frac{3}{4}$ zinc
States 2/1
Exh: RE 1971 (114). Fine Art Society
'Echoes of Venice', Aldeburgh 1973 (43).
Edinburgh 1973. Pendulum Gallery,
Selborne 1973. New Ashgate Gallery,
Farnham 1978 (27), 1988. Phoenix Gallery,
Lavenham 1975 (30)

1972

78. Covent Garden, Orchestra Pit
E. $9\frac{3}{4} \times 12\frac{1}{4}$
States 2/1. 1/2. 1/3
Exh: RE 1972 (61). RA 1972 (956). RE
Special Exhibition 1983 (168). Phoenix
Gallery, Lavenham 1975. Paris, Spring
1983. New Ashgate Gallery, Farnham 1978
(11). Bankside Gallery 'Five Man Show'
1987 (135)
Reproduced RE Journal May 1981 No.3,
p5

79. Venetian II
E. 9×7
States 1/1. 1/2. 2/3
Exh: RE 1972 (53). Fine Art Society
'Echoes of Venice', Aldeburgh 1973 (44).
New Ashgate Gallery, Farnham 1978 (22).
Phoenix Gallery, Lavenham 1975. RE
Special Exhibition 1983 (166). Bankside
Gallery 'Five Man Show' 1987 (130)
Illustrated Poster/invitation card, Kingston
Art Gallery, Fine Art Staff Exhibition

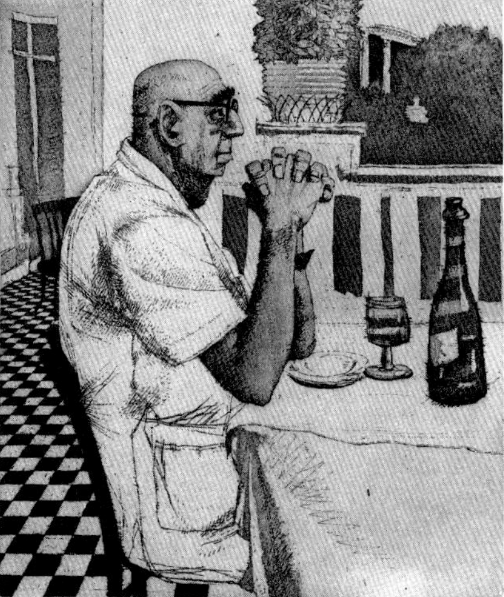

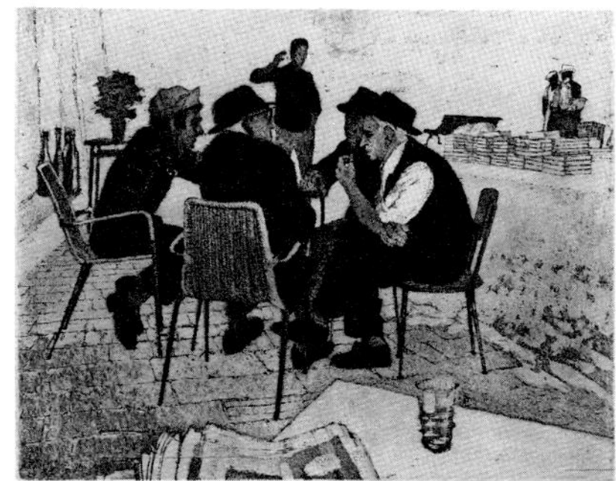

73

74

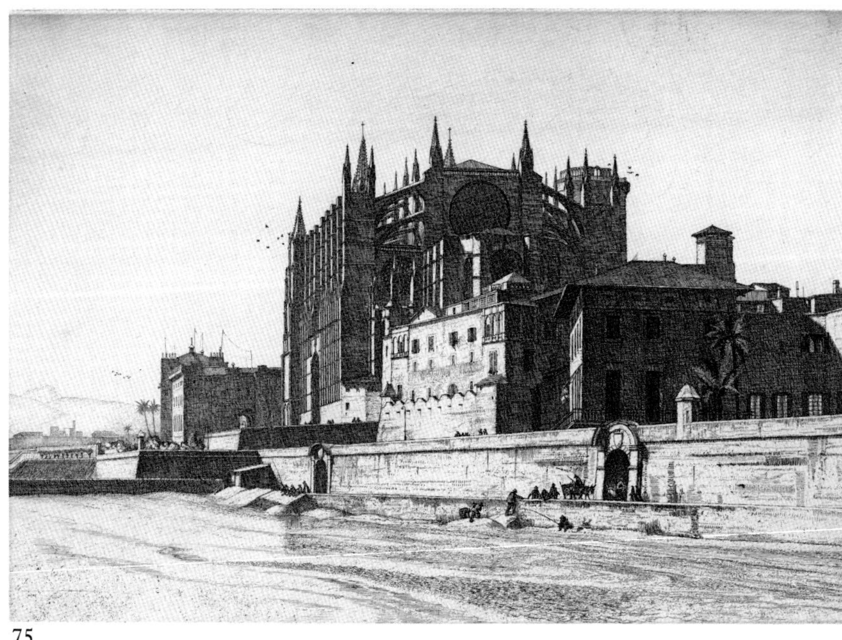

75

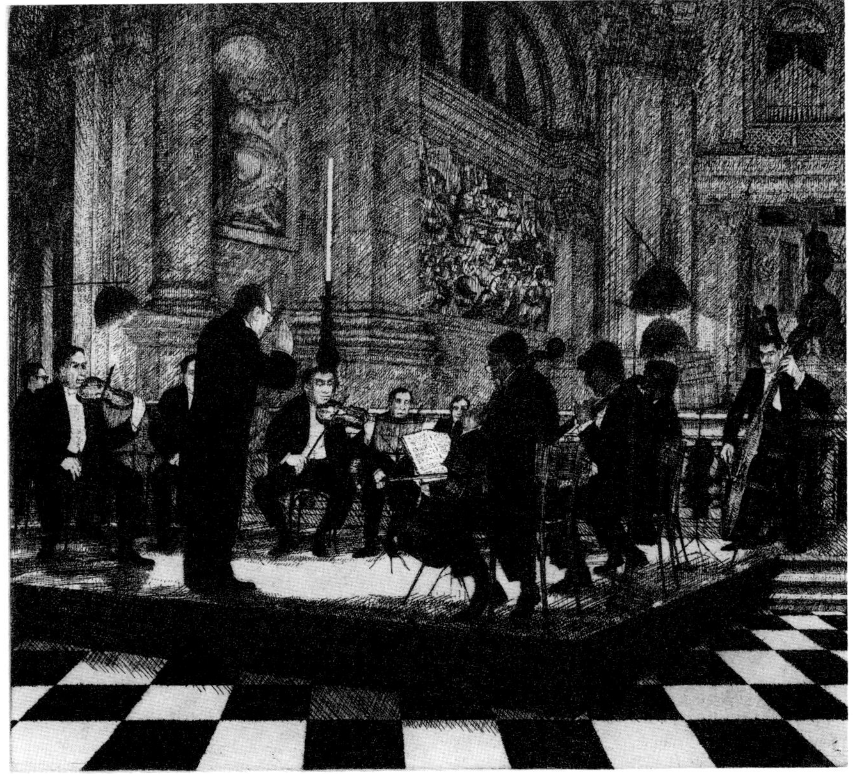

76

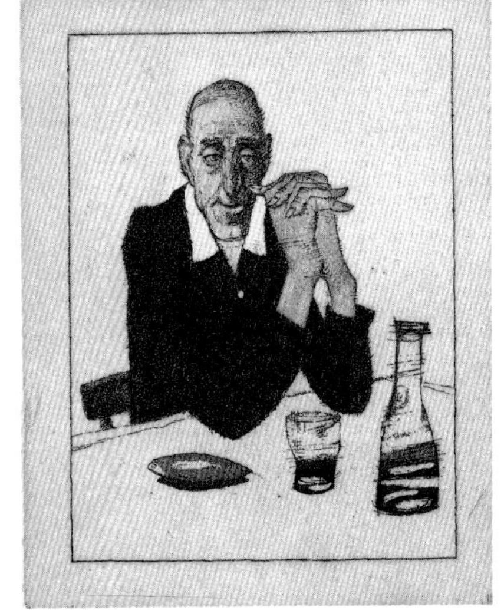

77

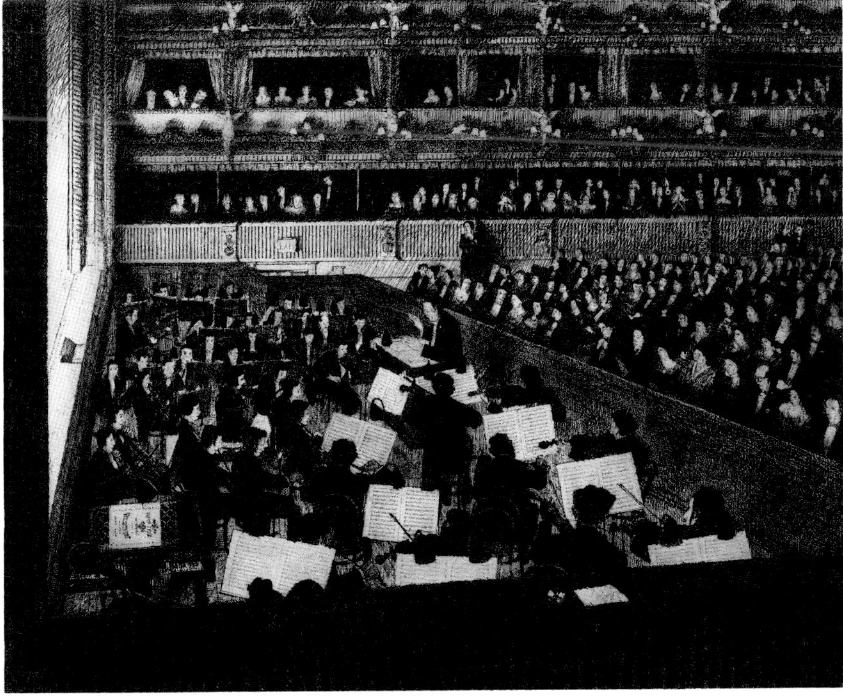

78

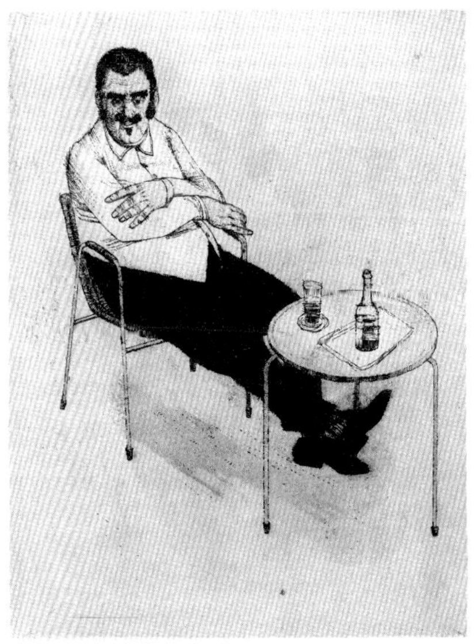

79

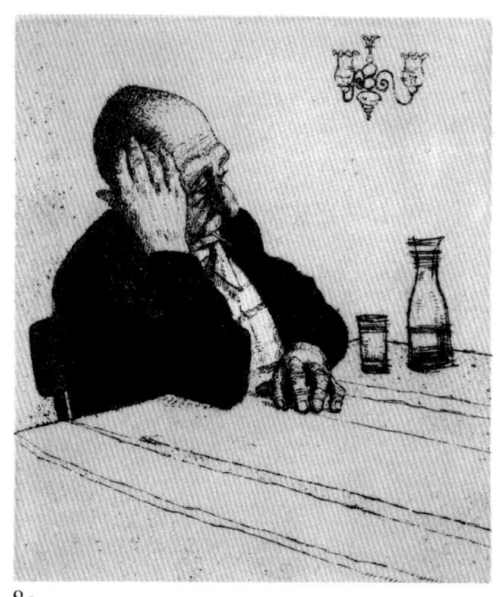

80

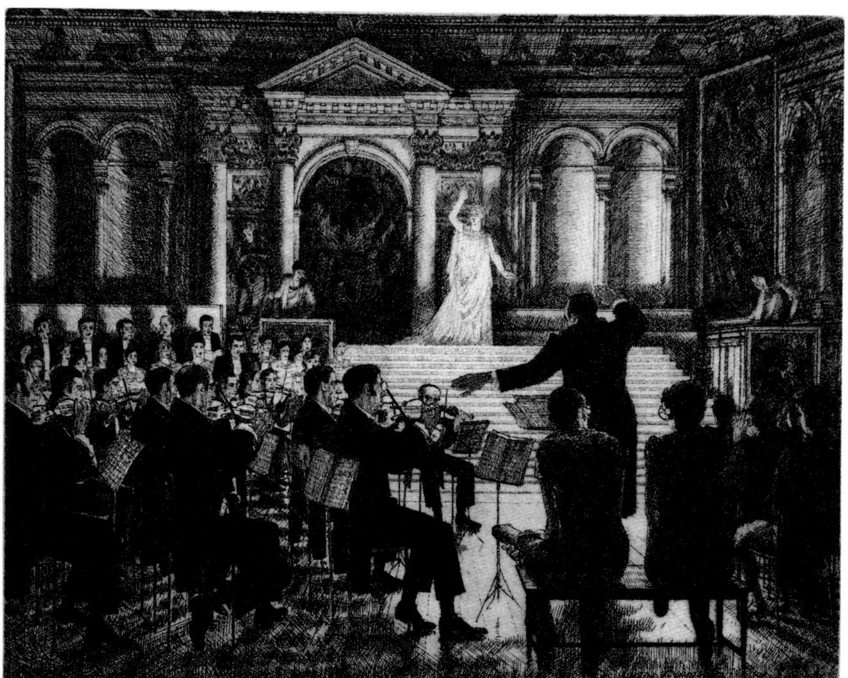

81

1973

80. The Toothpick
E. 7 × 6 zinc
States 1/1. 1/2
Exh: RE 1973 (68). Fine Art Society
'Echoes of Venice', Aldeburgh 1973 (45).
Pendulum Gallery, Selborne 1973. Phoenix
Gallery, Lavenham 1975. New Ashgate
Gallery, Farnham 1938 (25). RE Special
Exhibition Spring 1983 (163)

**81. Juditha Triumphans, Scuola
Grande di San Rocco**
E. $9\frac{3}{4} \times 12\frac{1}{4}$
States 2/1. 1/2. 1/3
Exh: RE 1973 (65). RA 1973 (185). Fine
Art Society 'Echoes of Venice', 1973 (46)
Edinburgh. Art Exhibitions Bureau, RA
Tour 1973. RE Special Exhibition, Spring
1983 (162). New Ashgate Gallery, Farnham
1978 (12). Phoenix Gallery, Lavenham
1975. Bankside Gallery 'Five Man Show'
1987 (136)

82. Venice – Sketch
E. $8\frac{1}{4} \times 11$ zinc
States 2/1
Exh: RE 1973 (63). Fine Art Society
'Echoes of Venice', Edinburgh 1973.
Pendulum Gallery, Selborne 1973. Phoenix
Gallery, Lavenham 1975, 1982

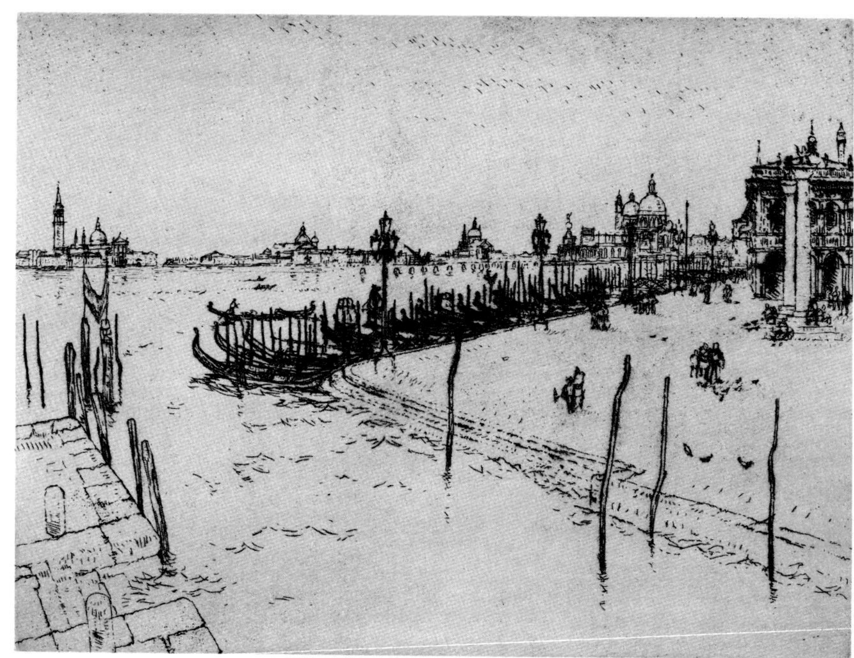

82

1974

83. El Kantara, Toledo
(see 23)
ED $9\frac{3}{4} \times 13$
States: no record
Exh: RE 1974 (53). RA 1974 (987). Phoenix
Gallery, Lavenham 1975, 1982. New Ash-
gate Gallery, Farnham 1986 (11). RE
Special Exhibition Spring 1983 (155)

84. Le Procope, Paris
E. 8 × 11
States 1/1
Exh: RE 1974 (39). Phoenix Gallery,
Lavenham 1975. New Ashgate Gallery,
Farnham 1978 (13)

85. Venice from the Dogana
E. 8 × 11
States: no record
Exh: RE 1974 (45). New Ashgate Gallery,
Farnham 1980 (10). Phoenix Gallery,
Lavenham 1975/82

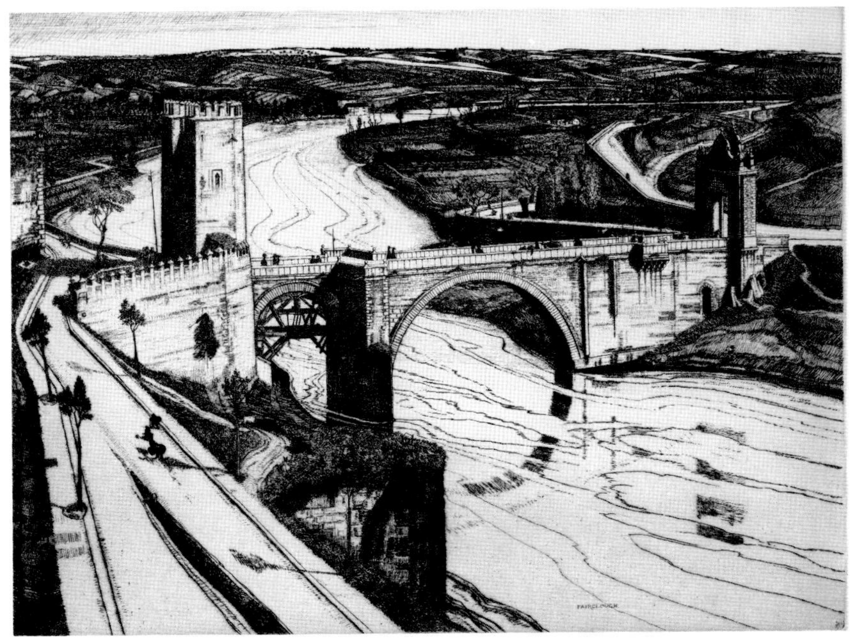

83

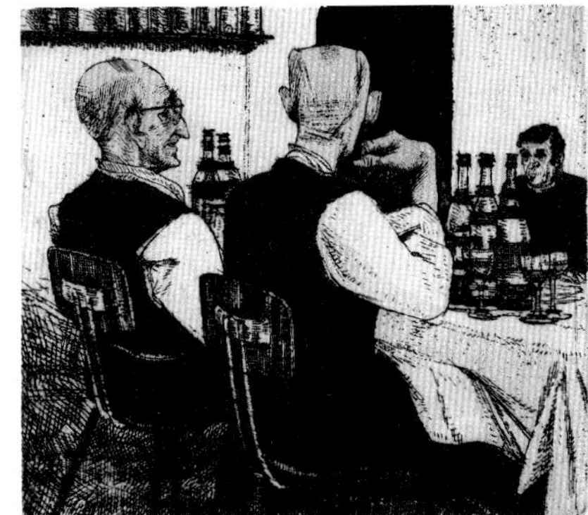

86

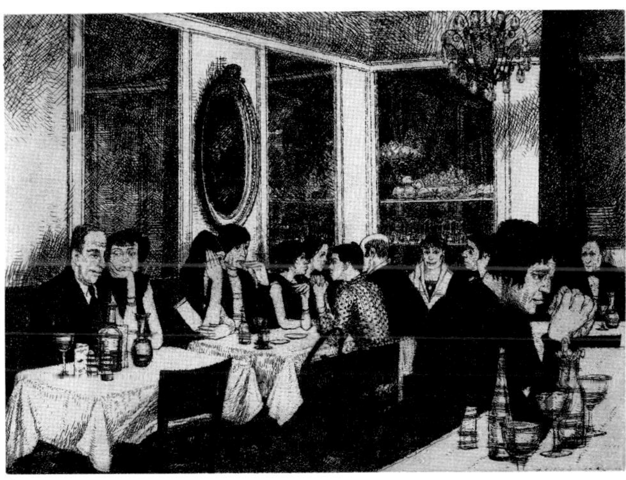

84

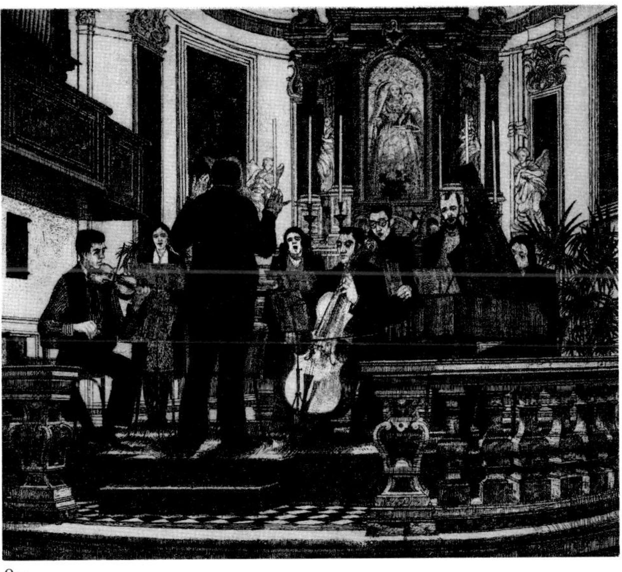

87

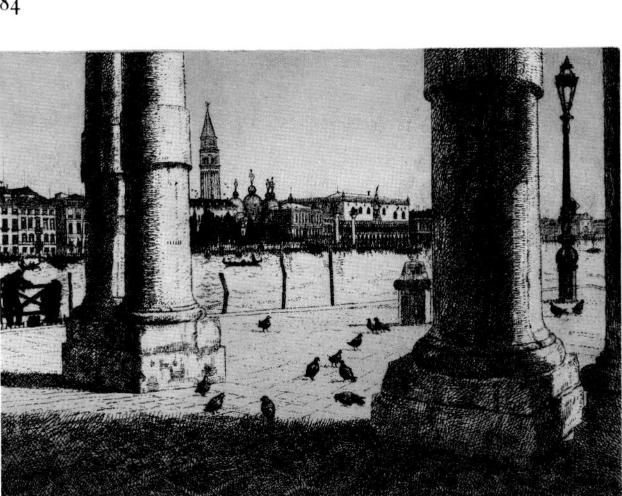

85

86. Orvieto Wedding, Three Bottle Men
E. $6\frac{1}{4} \times 6\frac{3}{4}$ zinc
States 2/1. 1/2
Exh: RE 1974 (3). Phoenix Gallery, Lavenham 1975. New Ashgate Gallery, Farnham 1978 (20)

1975

87. I Musici Cantori, Rehearsal, Bergamo
E. $9\frac{1}{2} \times 11$
States 2/1
Exh: RE 1975 (65). RA 1978 (1103). New Ashgate Gallery, Farnham 1978 (14). Phoenix Gallery, Lavenham 1975. RE Special Exhibition Spring 1983 (161)

99

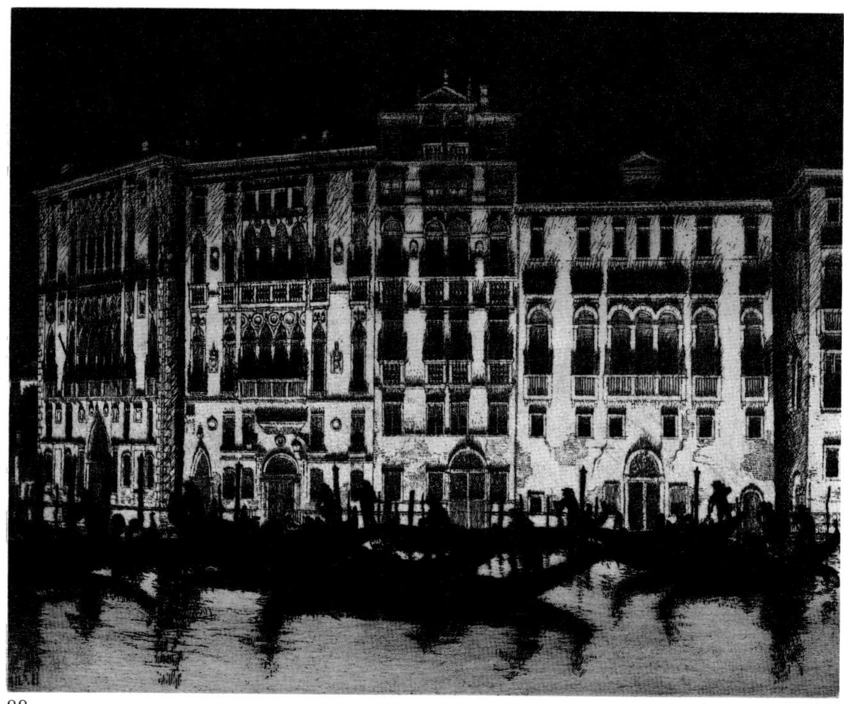

88

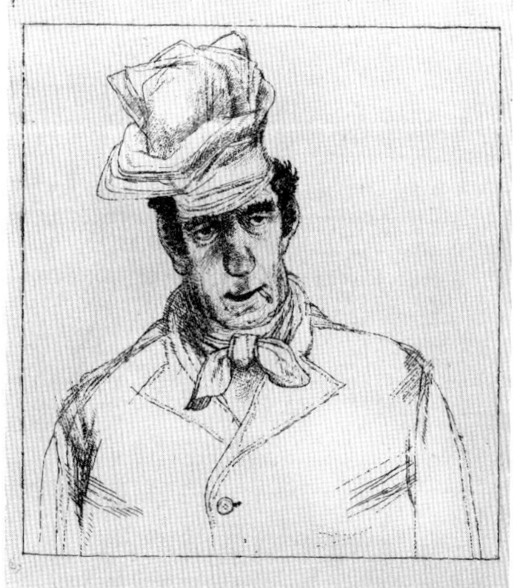

89

88. Venice, Night
E. 8 × 10
States 2/1
Exh: RE 1975 (52). Phoenix Gallery,
Lavenham 1975. New Ashgate Gallery,
Farnham 1978 (15).

89. The Chef, Bergamo
E. 7 × 6
States 2/1
Exh: RE 1975 (72). New Ashgate Gallery,
Farnham 1978 (19), 1982. Phoenix Gallery,
Lavenham 1975. Bankside Gallery Christ-
mas 1981, 1983. RE Special Exhibition
Spring 1983 (165). Bankside Gallery 'Five
Man Show' 1987 (147)

90. Magdalen College, Oxford
(see 33)
ED 13½ × 18¼
States 1/1. 1/2. 1/3. 1/4. 1/5. 1/6. 1/7. Plus
three proofs of alterations – New Buildings.
Exh: RE 1976 (48). Phoenix Gallery,
Lavenham 1975. New Ashgate Gallery,
Farnham 1980 (14)

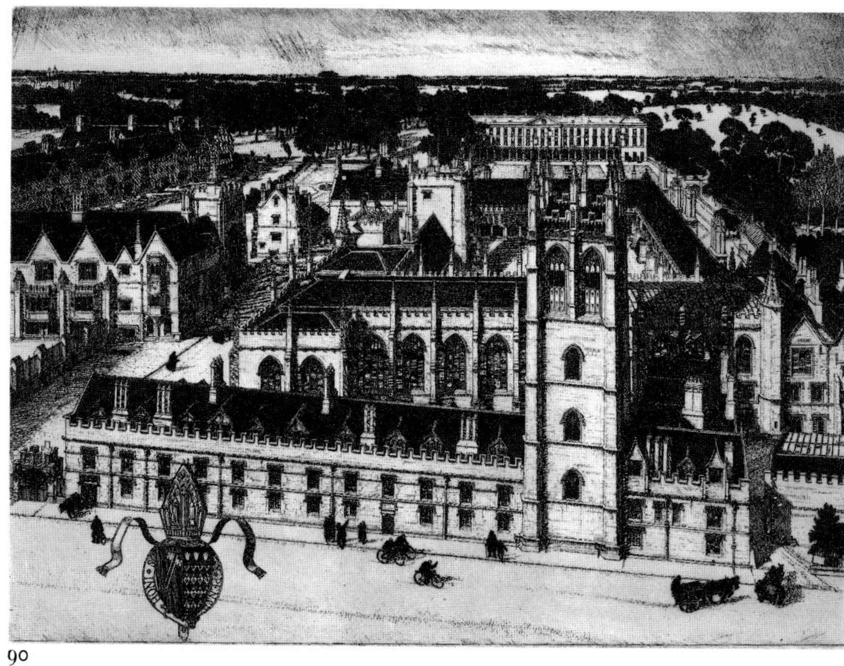

90

1976

91. Venice, Mefistofele Fantasia
E. 9 × 11½
States 3/1. 14/2. The eight sales up to 1982
are 2nd states. The bell of the French Horn
removed 1982
Exh: RE 1976 (137). RA 1977 (1103). New
Ashgate Gallery, Farnham 1978 (16). Bankside Gallery Christmas 1982, 1983. Bankside Gallery 'Five Man Show' 1987 (153)

92. Venice, Palazzo Dario
E. 8 × 10¼
States 3/1
Exh: RE 1976 (59). RA 1978 (1088). New
Ashgate Gallery, Farnham 1978 (17). RE
Special Exhibition Spring 1983 (170).
Bankside Gallery 'Five Man Show' 1987
(140)

93. The Sleeper
E. 8¼ × 5¼
States 3/1
Exh: RE 1976 (63). New Ashgate Gallery,
Farnham 1982

1977

94. Venice, Regatta Band Rehearsal
E. 7¾ × 10
States 2/1. 2/2
Exh: RE 1978 (48). RA 1984 (1657). New
Ashgate Gallery, Farnham 1978 (17). RE
Special Exhibition Spring 1983 (48). Bank-
side Gallery 'Five Man Show' 1987 (134).
Bankside Gallery Christmas 1988.

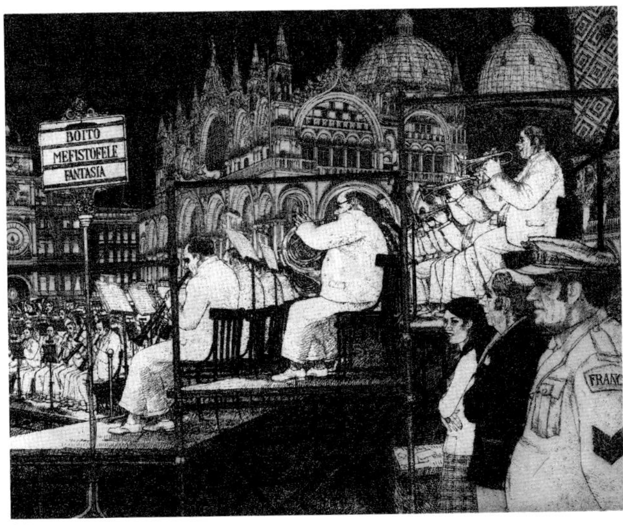

91

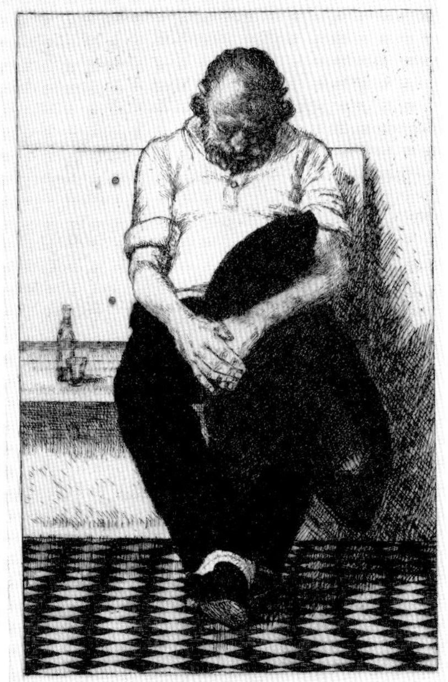

93

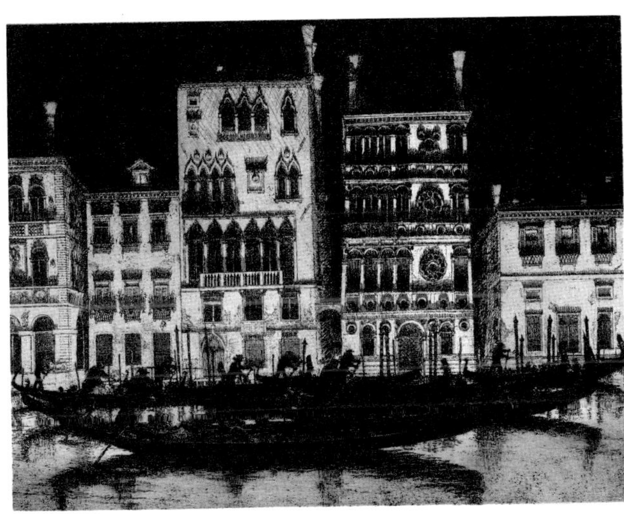

92

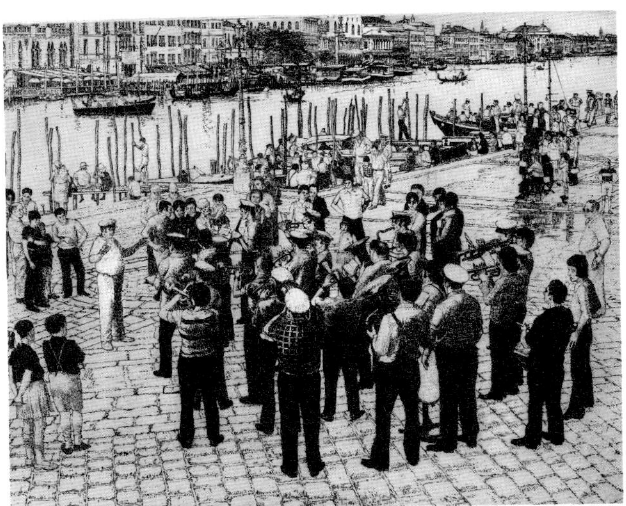

94

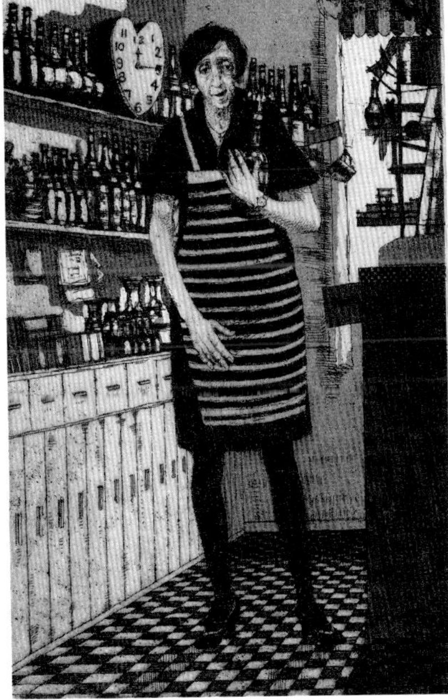

95

95. Venetian Barmaid
E/A $9\frac{1}{2} \times 6$
States 2/1. 2/2
Exh: RE 1978 (57). New Ashgate Gallery,
Farnham 1980 (9)

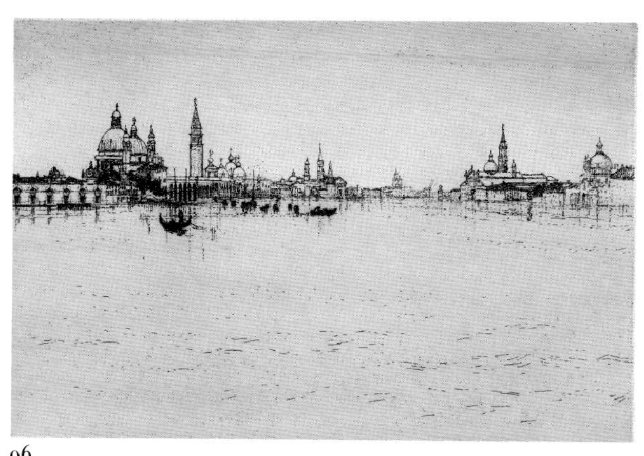

96

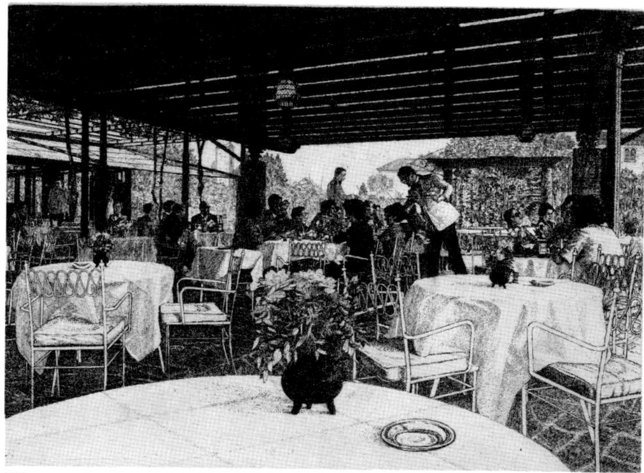

97

1978

96. Venice from the Giudecca
E. 8 × 12
States 2/1. 2/2
Exh: RE 1978 (65). Phoenix Gallery,
Lavenham 1978. New Ashgate Gallery,
Farnham 1980 (8)

1979

97. Venice, Lunch at Torcello
E. 7½ × 10½
States 2/1. 1/2
Exh: RE 1979 (61). RA 1979. RE Paris
1983. New Ashgate Gallery, Farnham 1980
(7), 1988. RE Special Exhibition Spring
1983 (160). Bankside Gallery 'Five Man
Show' 1987 (149)

98. Venice, La Fenice, Solo Violin
E. 7½ × 9¼
States 2/1. 1/2. 1/3
Exh: RE 1979 (55). New Ashgate Gallery,
Farnham 1980 (6). RE Special Exhibition
Spring 1983 (157).

99. Venice, The Rose and the Writ
EA 9 × 6½
States 2/1. 1/2. 1/3. 1/4. 1/5. 1/6
Exh: RE 1979 (78). RA 1983 (97). New
Ashgate Gallery, Farnham 1980 (5). RE
Special Exhibition Spring 1983 (164).
Bankside Gallery Christmas 1982.

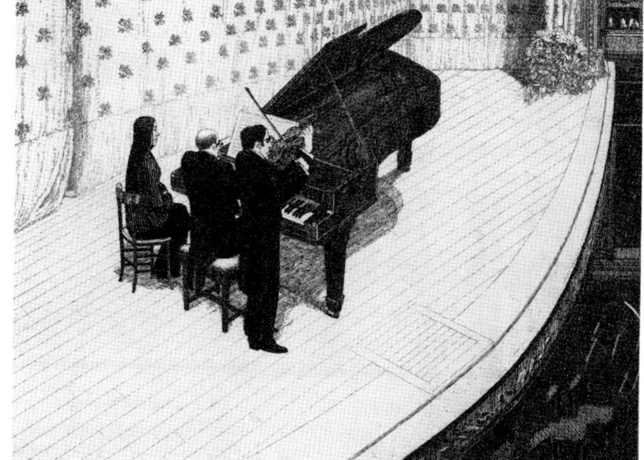

98

1980

100. Family Reunion
EA 8 × 11
States 3/1. 2/2
Exh: RE 1981 (141). New Ashgate Gallery,
Farnham 1980 (4). RE Special Exhibition
Spring 1983 (174).

**101. Venice, Vivaldi, Chiesa di Santa
Maria della Pietà**
E. 9 × 11½
States 2/1. 1/2
Exh: RE 1980 (145). New Ashgate Gallery,
Farnham 1980 (3). Bankside Gallery
Christmas 1981

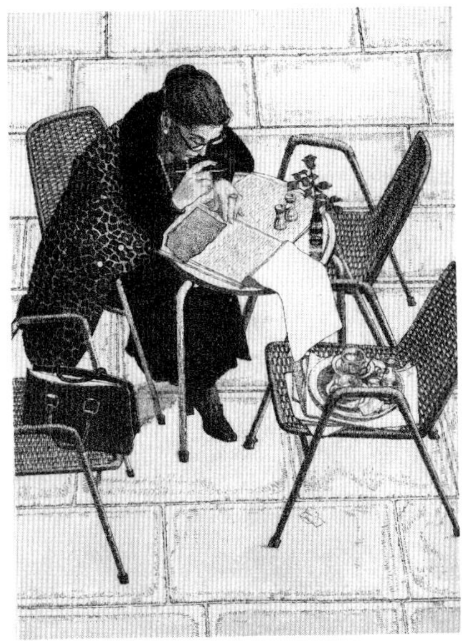

99

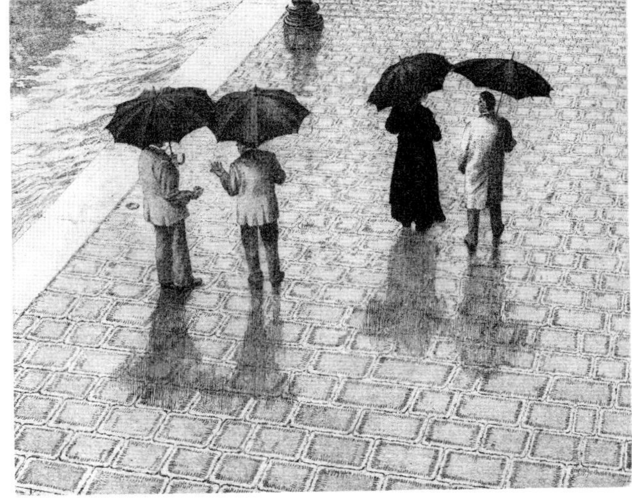

103

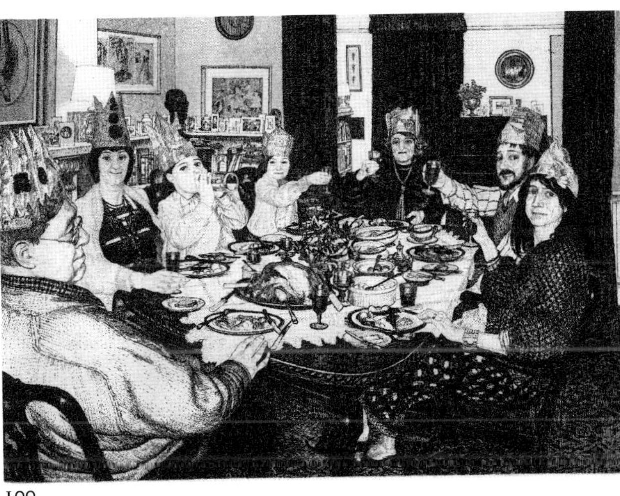

100

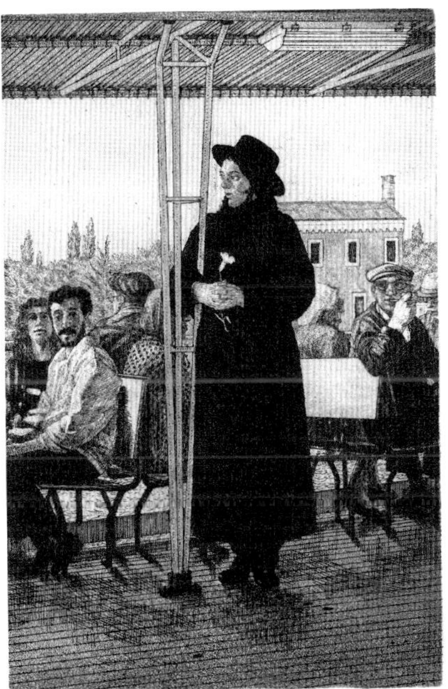

102

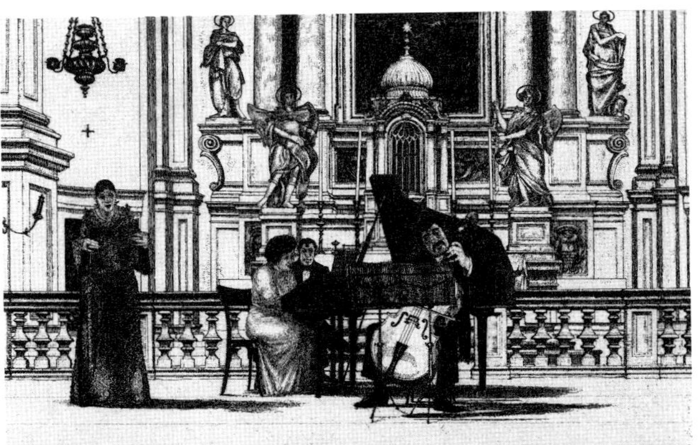

101

102. Boat from Torcello. The White Carnation
EA 9 × 6
States 2/1. 1/2. 2/3
Exh: RE 1981 (112). New Ashgate Gallery, Farnham 1980 (2).

103. Venice, Two by Two
EA 7 × 9
States 2/1. 1/2. 1/3
Exh: RE 1981 (116). RA 1982 (899). New Ashgate Gallery, Farnham 1980 (1).

104. Venice from the Lido
E. $4\frac{1}{4} \times 12\frac{1}{4}$
States 3/1. Final state
Exh: RE 1981 (45). RA 1985. RE Special
Exhibition Spring 1983 (156). New Ashgate
Gallery, Farnham 1983.

105. Traghetto del Giglio
(see 25)
LE / E. / D. $7\frac{1}{4} \times 8\frac{1}{2}$
States 2/1. 1/2
Exh: RE 1981 (209). RA 1982 (883). RE
Special Exhibition Spring 1983 (158). New
Ashgate Gallery, Farnham 1983. Bankside
Gallery 'Five Man Show' 1987 (151)

1981

106. Mario
EA $9 \times 5\frac{1}{2}$
States 2/1. 1/2. 1/3. 1/4. 1/5. 1/6. 1/7
Exh: RE 1981 (266). New Ashgate Gallery,
Farnham 1982

1982

107. Lucerne, Selected Duets
E. $8\frac{1}{4} \times 5\frac{3}{4}$
States 3/1. 2/2. 1/3
Exh: RE 1982 (55). RA 1982 (884). New
Ashgate Gallery, Farnham 1983

108. Watendlath, Cumbria
SG $6 \times 9\frac{1}{2}$
States 3/1. 1/2. 3/3. 1/4
Exh: RE 1982 (85). New Ashgate Gallery,
Farnham 1983

109. Venice, Torcello Afternoon
E. 8×11
States 2/1. 1/2. 1/3
Exh: RE 1982 (115). New Ashgate Gallery,
Farnham 1983

110. Ullswater, Aira Force
E. $9\frac{1}{4} \times 6$
States 1/1. 1/2
Exh: RE 1982 (6). RE Special Exhibition
Spring 1983 (173). Paris Spring 1983. New
Ashgate Gallery, Farnham 1983. Bankside
Gallery Christmas 1983, 1985

1983

111. Venice, Storm
EA $6\frac{1}{2} \times 9$
States 2/1. 1/2. 1/3
Exh: RE 1983 (169). RA 1983 (832). RE
Special Exhibition Spring 1983 (169).
Bankside Gallery 'Five Man Show' 1987
(155). New Ashgate Gallery, Farnham
1983, 1986

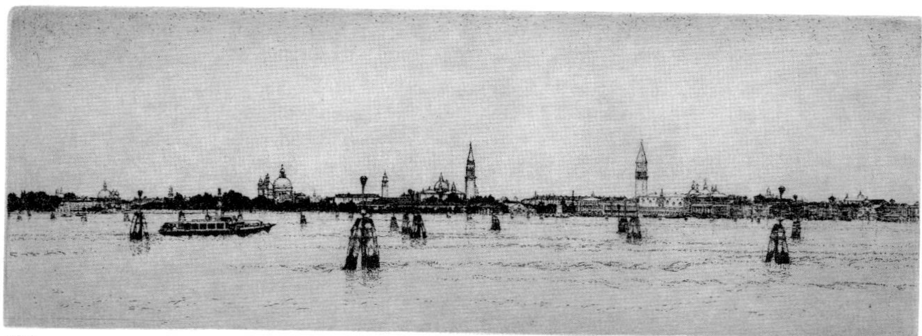

104

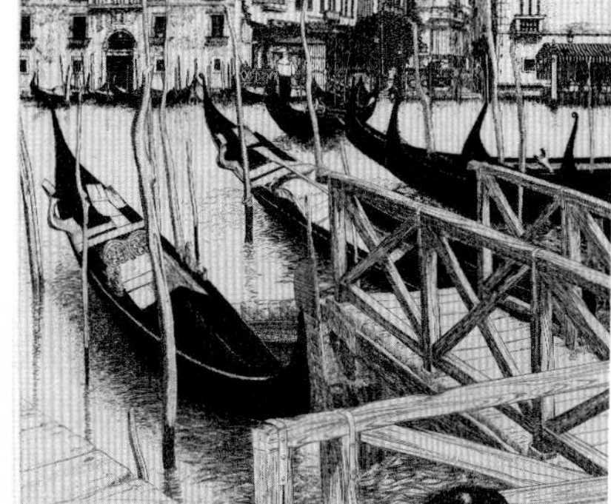

105

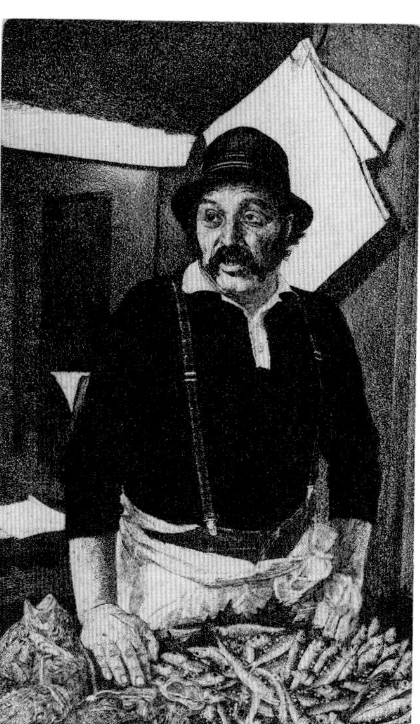

106

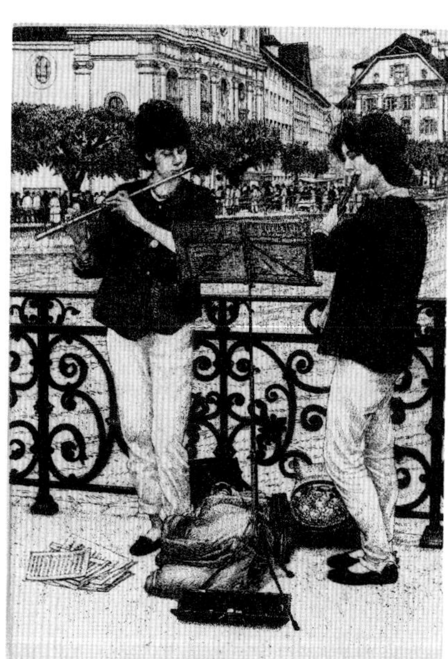

107

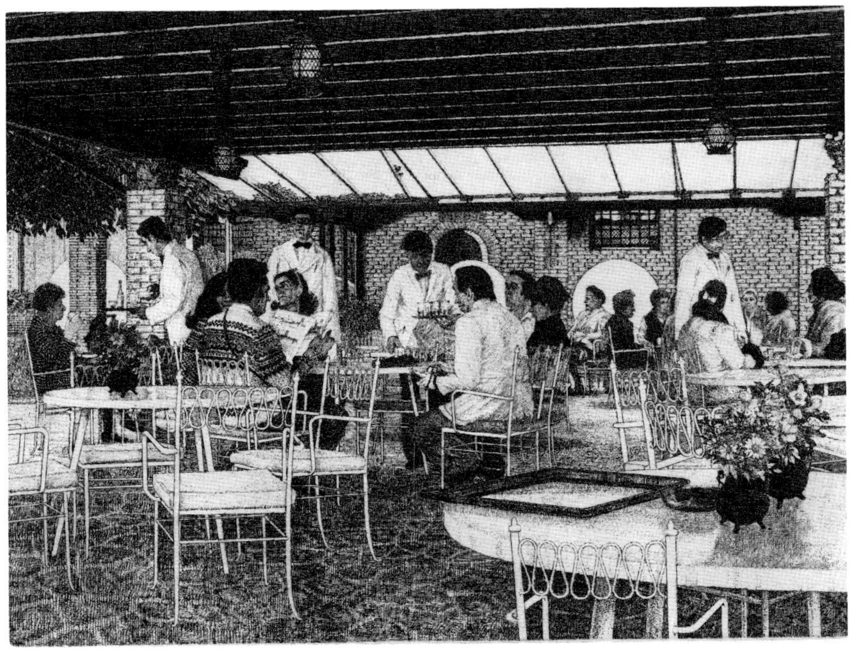

109

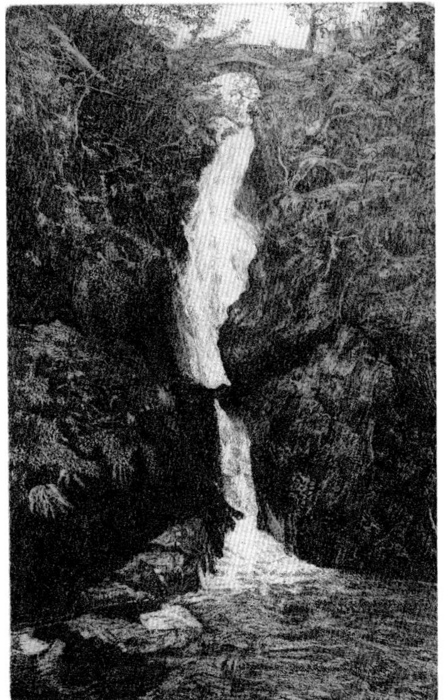

110

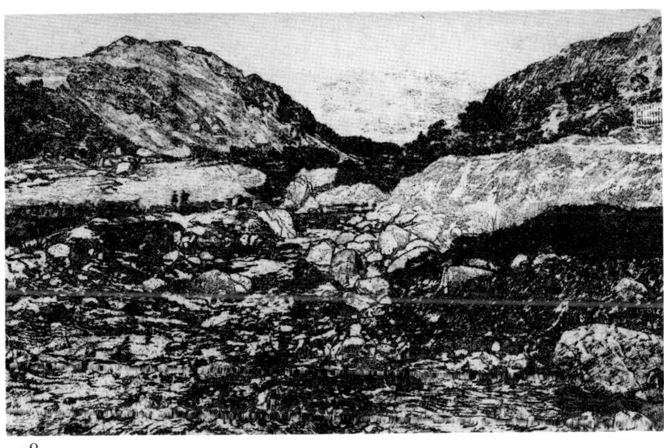

108

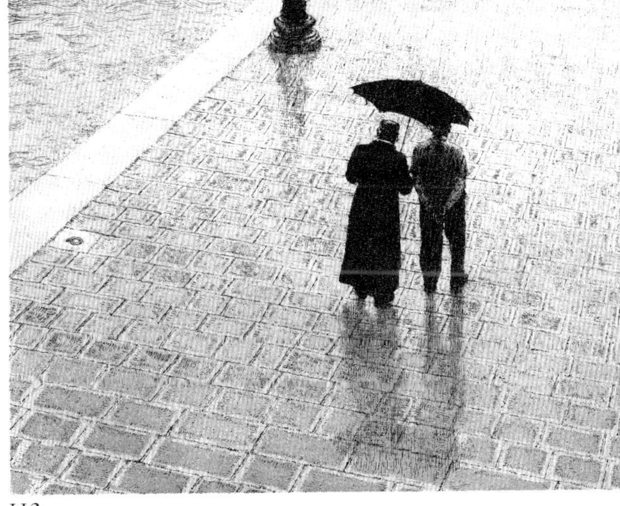

112

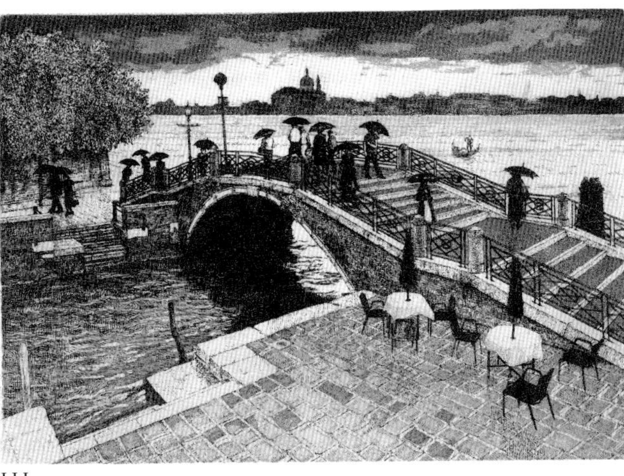

111

112. Venice, Two to One
EA $6\frac{1}{2} \times 8$
States 2/1. 1/2. 1/3
Exh: RE 1983 (159). RA 1984 (1656). New
Ashgate Gallery, Farnham 1983. Bankside
Gallery Christmas 1985. Bankside Gallery
'Five Man Show' 1987 (152). Bankside Gal-
lery Special Exhibition Spring 1983 (159)

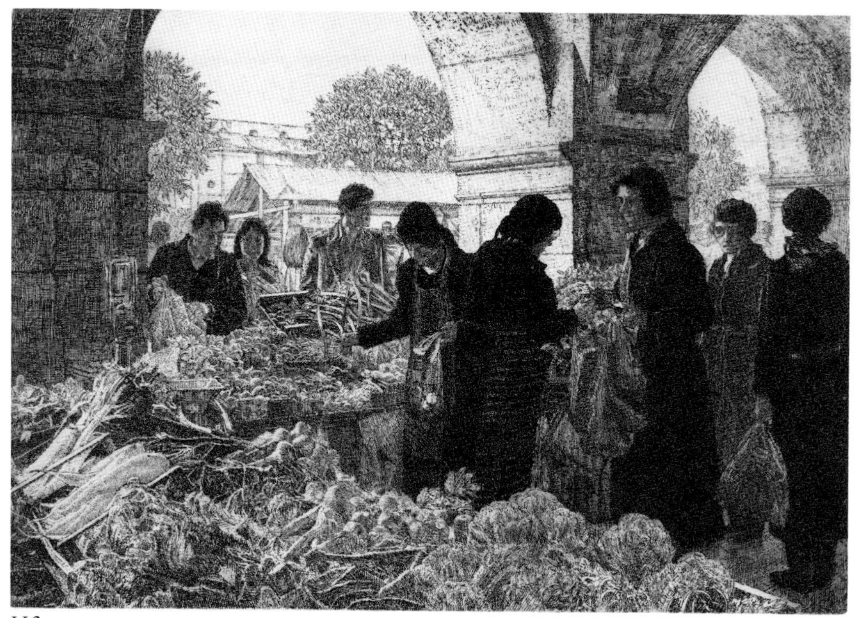

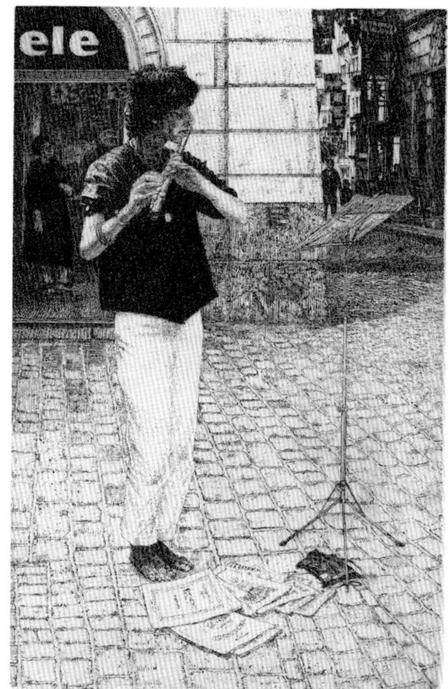

113

114

113. Lucerne Market
E. 7×10
States $2/1$. $1/2$. $2/3$
Exh: RE 1983 (129). RA 1984 (1655).
Bankside Gallery Christmas 1985

114. Lucerne, Solo Flute and Flags
E. $8\frac{1}{4} \times 5\frac{1}{4}$
States $2/1$. $2/2$. $1/3$
Exh: RE 1983 (128)

1984

115. Venice, On Parade
E. $5\frac{3}{4} \times 10\frac{1}{2}$
States $2/1$. $2/2$
Exh: RE 1984 (194). RA 1985 (1583).
Bankside Gallery 'Five Man Show' 1987
(158). Bankside Gallery Christmas 1988

116. Venice, The Chef
E. $7\frac{3}{4} \times 5\frac{3}{4}$
States $2/1$. $2/2$
Exh: RE 1984 (210). Bankside Gallery
'Five Man Show' 1987 (147). Bankside Gal-
lery Special Exhibition 1983 (165). Christ-
mas 1988. New Ashgate Gallery, Farnham
1988

**117. Lucerne Market, Bread and
Cheese**
EA $7\frac{1}{2} \times 10$
States $2/1$. $1/2$. $1/3$
Exh: RE 1984 (54). RA 1985 (1584). Bank-
side Gallery 'Five Man Show' 1987 (148).
New Ashgate Gallery, Farnham 1986.
Bankside Gallery Christmas 1985

118. Venice, La Signora
E. $8\frac{1}{4} \times 6$
States $2/1$. $1/2$. $1/3$. $1/4$
Exh: RE 1984 (55)

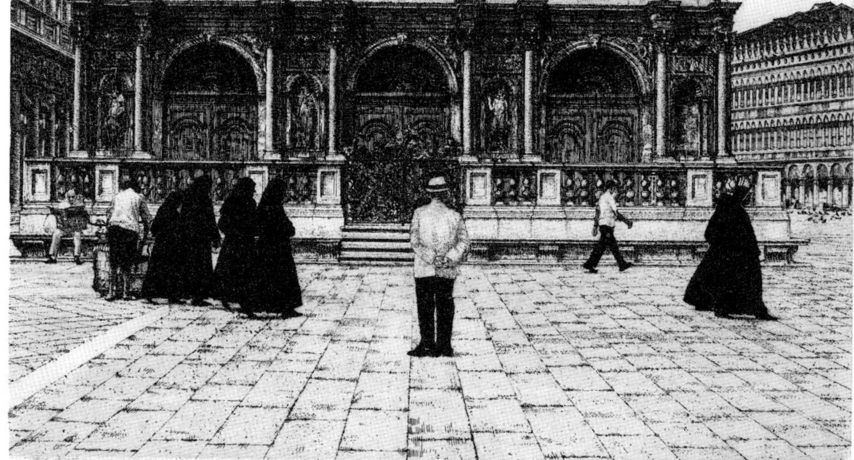

115

1985

119. Venice, Light Music
ED 7×9
States $2/1$. $1/2$. $1/3$
Exh: RE 1985. Cumberland Hotel XX^c Art
1988. Bankside Gallery Christmas 1988.
New Ashgate Gallery, Farnham 1986

120. Lucerne Market, Cacti
E. $7\frac{3}{4} \times 8$
States $2/1$. $1/2$. $1/3$. $2/4$
Exh: RE 1985. Bankside Gallery Christmas
1985

121. Burano Wedding, Il Gatto Nero
EA $7\frac{1}{4} \times 10$
States $1/1$. $1/2$. $1/3$
Exh: RE 1985 (210). Bankside Gallery
'Five Man Show' 1987 (157). New Ashgate
Gallery, Farnham 1986, 1988. Bankside
Gallery Christmas 1985

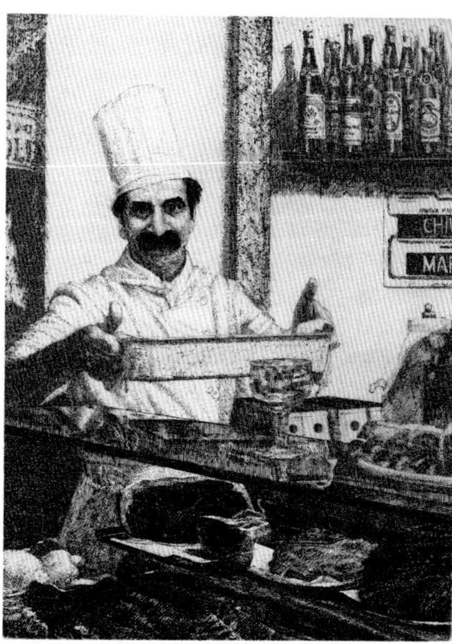

116

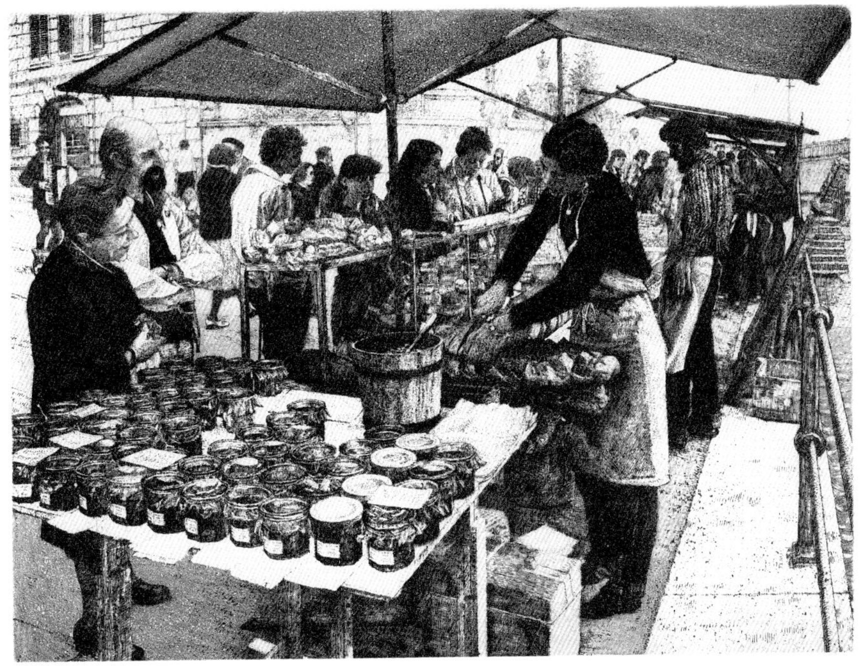

117

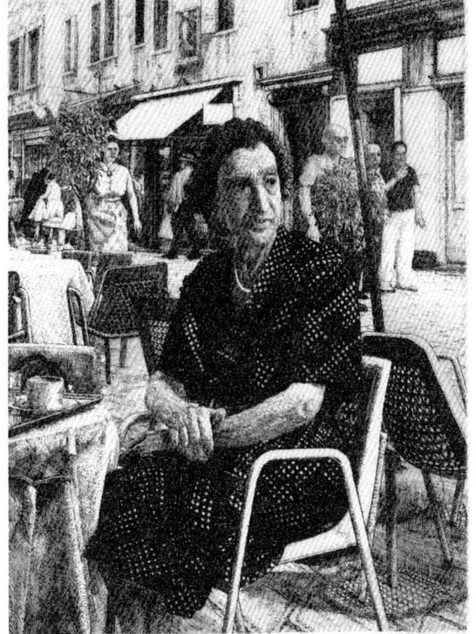

118

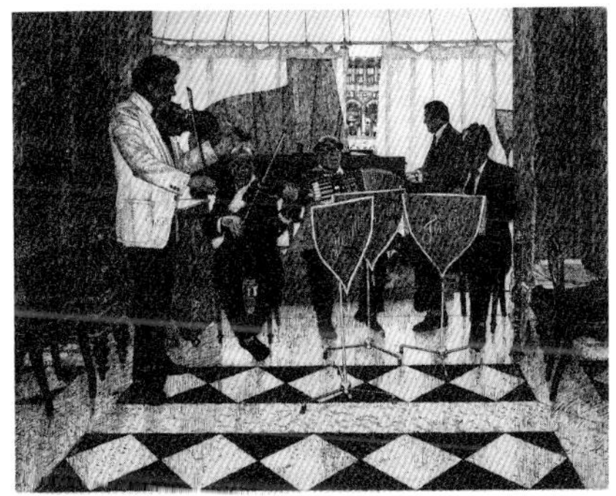

119

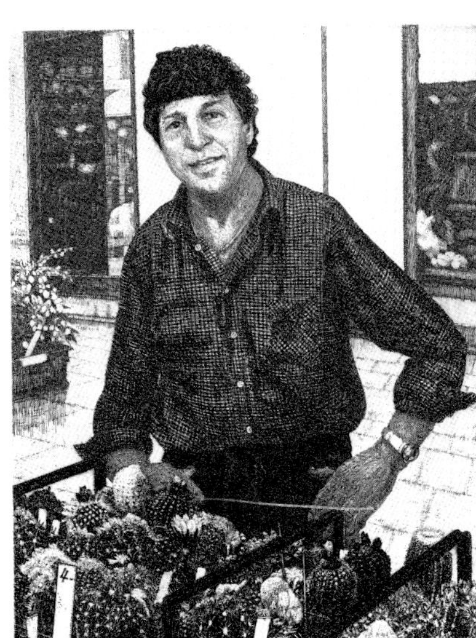

120

121

122. Venice Carnival, Make Up I
E. $8\frac{1}{2} \times 5\frac{1}{4}$
States 1/1. 1/2. 1/3
Exh: RE 1985 (71). RA 1986 (1405). New
Ashgate Gallery, Farnham 1988. Bankside
Gallery Christmas 1988

123. Venice Carnival, Paris in Venice
E. $5\frac{1}{2} \times 8\frac{3}{4}$
States 2/1. 1/2. 2/3
Exh: RE 1986 (94). New Ashgate Gallery,
Farnham 1988

1986

124. Venice Carnival, Masks
EA $7 \times 4\frac{1}{2}$
States 2/1. 1/2. 2/3
Exh: RE 1986 (84). CCA Galleries plc
Award £500 for the artist of the outstand-
ing print in the Exhibition. Bankside Gal-
lery Christmas 1988

125. Lucerne Fishmarket, Onlookers
E. $5\frac{1}{2} \times 9$
States 2/1. 2nd state, final proof
Exh: RE 1986 (158). RA 1988 (1178).
Bankside Gallery 'Five Man Show' 1987
(150). Bankside Gallery Christmas 1988

126. Venice Carnival, Nozze
EA $7\frac{1}{4} \times 4\frac{3}{4}$
States 2/1. 2nd state, final proof
Exh: RE 1986 (50). RA 1989 (165). Bank-
side Gallery 'Five Man Show' 1987 (165).
Bankside Gallery Christmas 1988

127. Lucerne Pike
EA $4\frac{3}{4} \times 10$
States 2/1. 2nd state, final proof
Exh: RE 1986 (174). Bankside Gallery
Christmas 1988

1987

128. Lucerne Market, Flower Girl
EA $5\frac{1}{2} \times 8$
States 2/1. 1/2. 1/3. 1/4. 5th state, final state
Exh: RE 1987 (199). Bankside Gallery
'Five Man Show' 1987 (156)

129. Venice Carnival, Clown
EA 5×7
States 2/1. 1/2. 1/3. 1/4. 1/5. 6th state final
state
Exh: RE 1987 (201). RA 1990 (244). Bank-
side Gallery 'Five Man Show' 1987 (161).
Bankside Gallery Christmas 1988

130. Venice Carnival, Man in Black
EA $7\frac{1}{4} \times 5$
States 2/1. 1/2. 1/3. 1/4
Exh: RE 1987 (30). Bankside Gallery 'Five
Man Show' 1987 (164). New Ashgate Gal-
lery, Farnham 1988

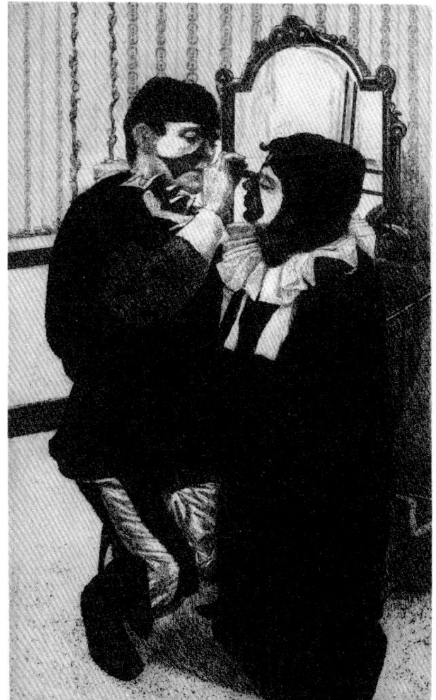

122

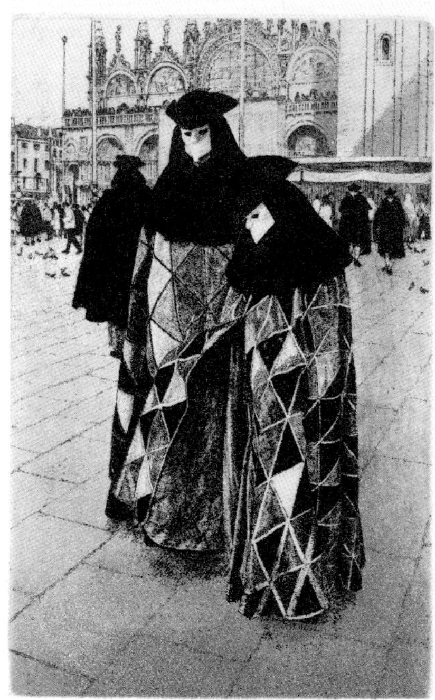

124

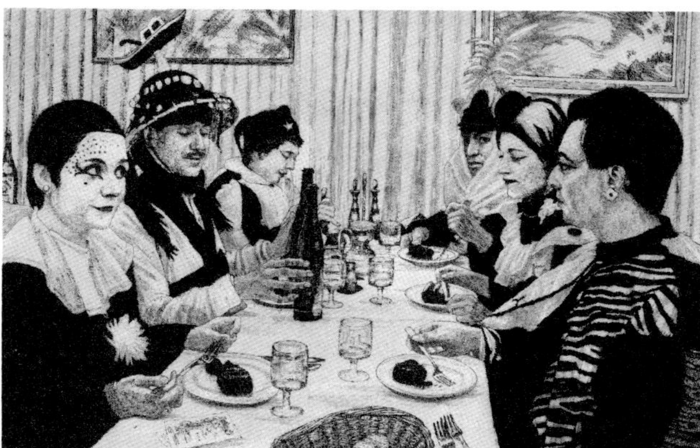

123

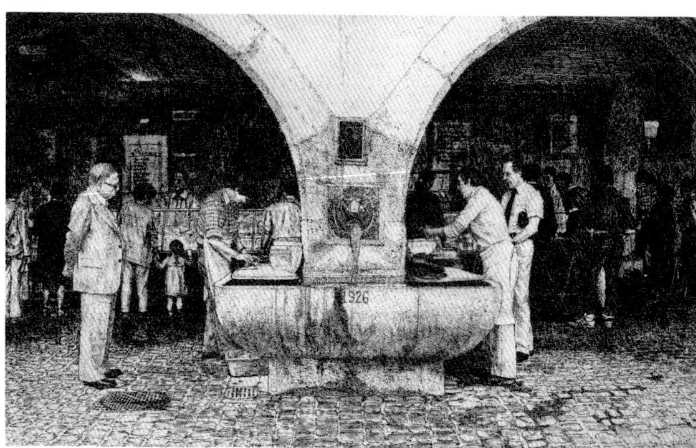

125

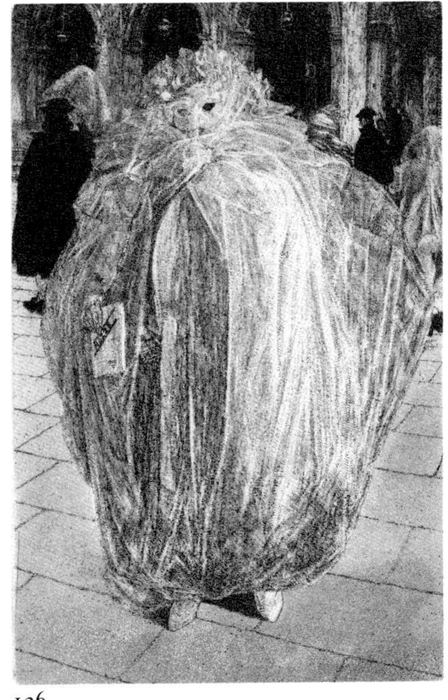

126

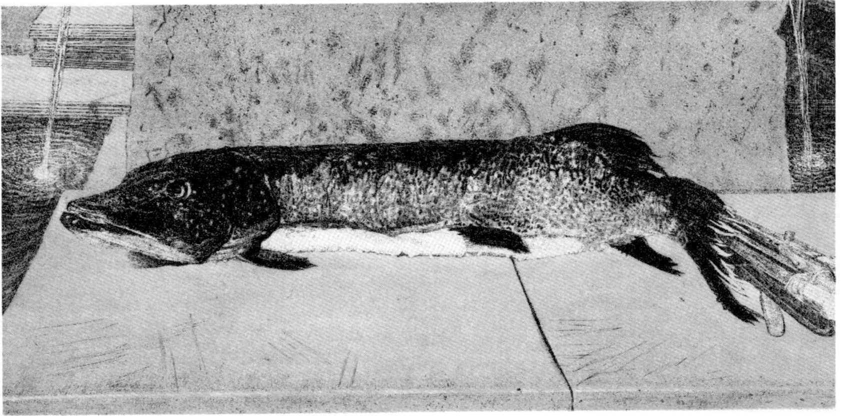

127

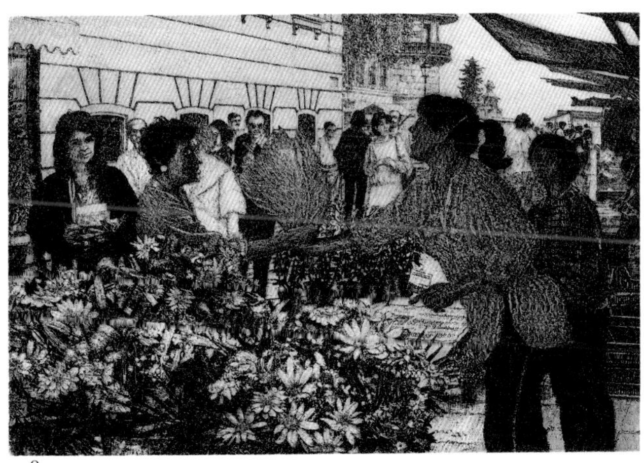

128

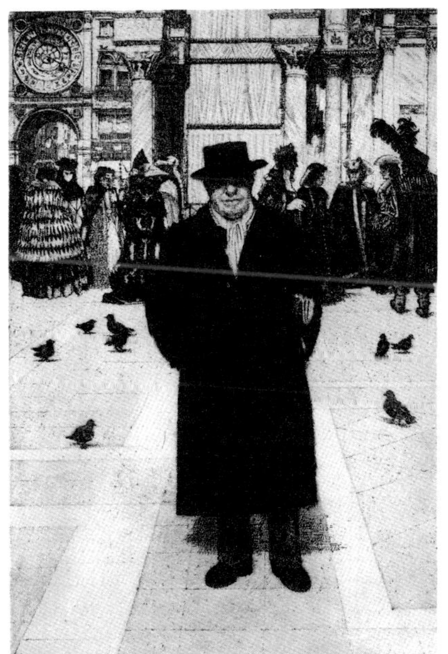

130

129

131. **Lucerne, Market Gossip**
E. $7 \times 5\frac{1}{4}$
States 2/1. 1/2. 1/3. 1/4
Exh: RE 1987 (26)

1988

132. **Venice Carnival, Witches**
EA $8 \times 5\frac{1}{4}$
States 2/1. 1/2. 1/3. 1/4. 1/5. 1/6
Exh: RE 1988 (86). RA 1989 (159). Bank-
side Gallery Christmas 1988

133. **Venice Carnival, Make Up II**
E. $8 \times 5\frac{1}{2}$
States 2/1. 1/2. 1/3. 1/4. 1/5
Exh: RE 1988 (90). Bankside Gallery
Christmas 1988

134. **Venice Carnival, Dancers**
EA $8 \times 5\frac{1}{4}$
States 2/1. 1/2. 1/3. 1/4. 1/5
Exh: RE 1988
Reproduced *Arts Review*, 23 September
1988 p.642

1989

135. **Palazzo Grimani and Rio di San
Luca**
E. $7 \times 9\frac{1}{2}$
States 2/1. 1/2. 1/3
Exh: RE 1989 (127)

136. **Piazza San Marco, Light Music**
E. $6 \times 8\frac{1}{2}$
States 2/1. 1/2. 1/3
Exh: RE 1989 (129)

137. **Venice Carnival, Secrets**
EA $7\frac{3}{4} \times 5\frac{1}{4}$
States 2/1. 1/2. 2/3. 1/4. 1/5. 1/6
Exh: RE 1989 (128)

1990

138. **Venice Carnival, Fur, Feathers and
Garter**
EA $7\frac{7}{8} \times 5$
States 2/1. 1/2. 2/3
Exh: RE 1990 (163)

139. **Venice, The Tetrarchs (I Mori)**
EA $8\frac{5}{8} \times 4\frac{7}{8}$
States 2/1. 1/2. 2/3. 2/4
Exh: RE 1990 (161)

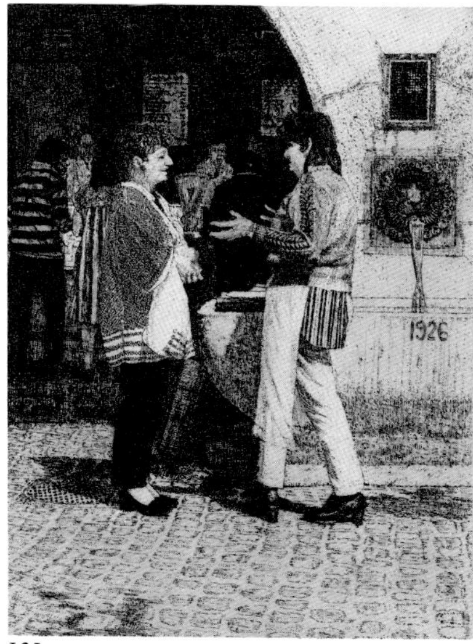

131

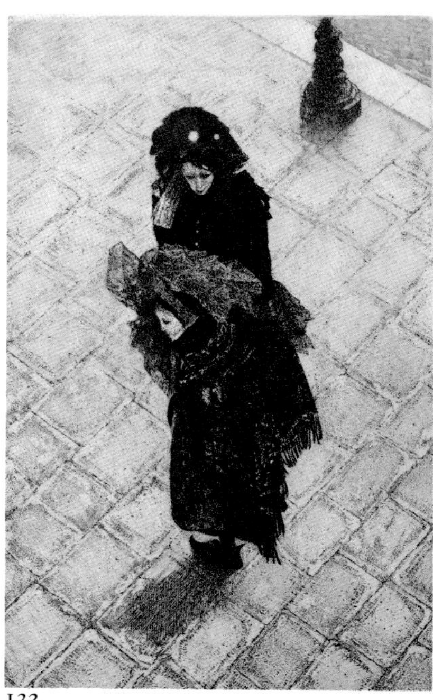

132

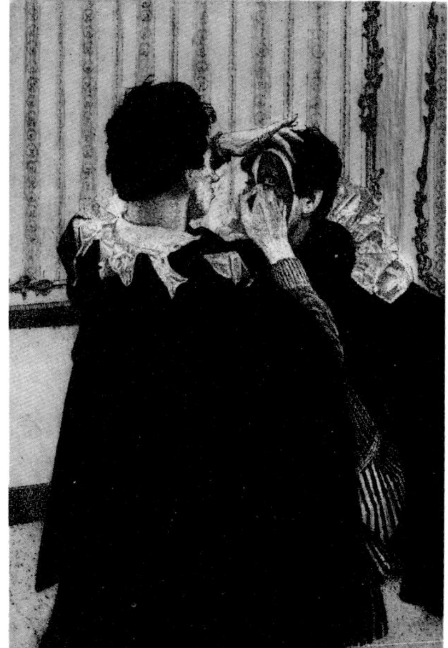

133

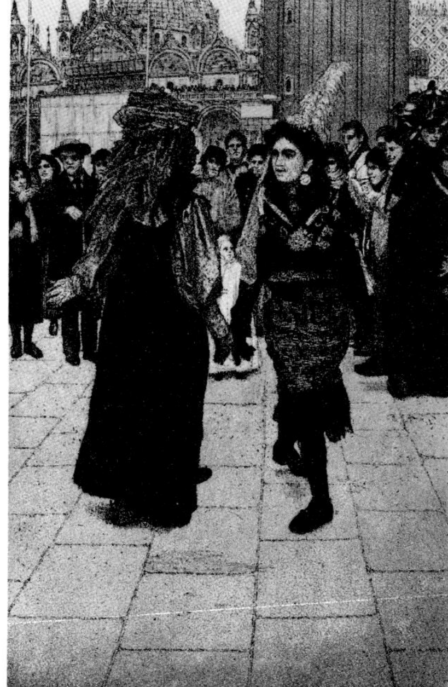

134

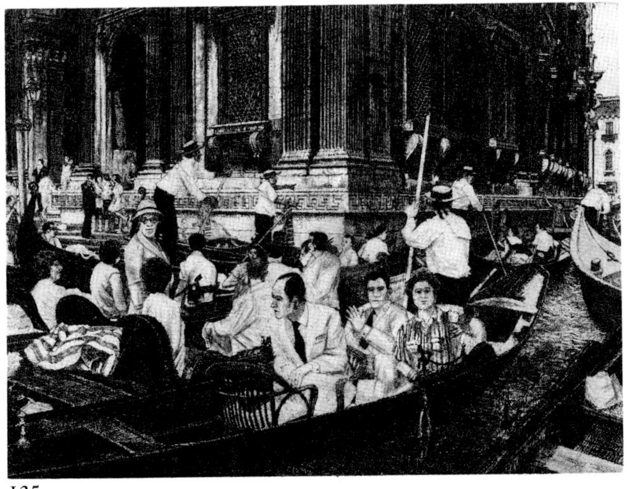

135

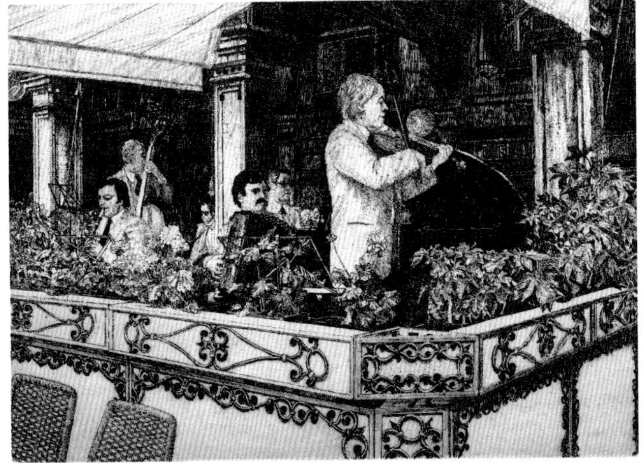

136

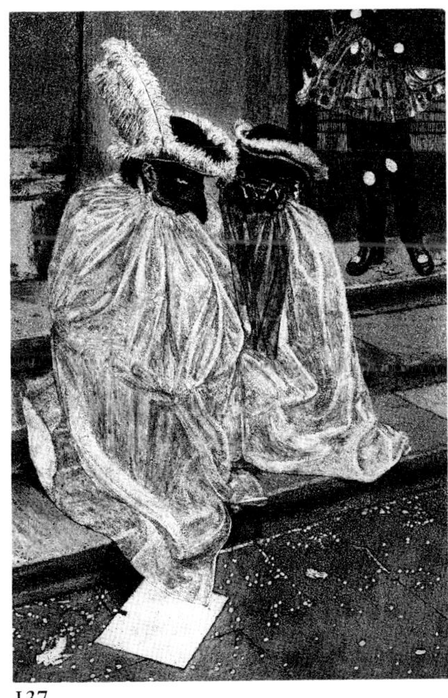

137

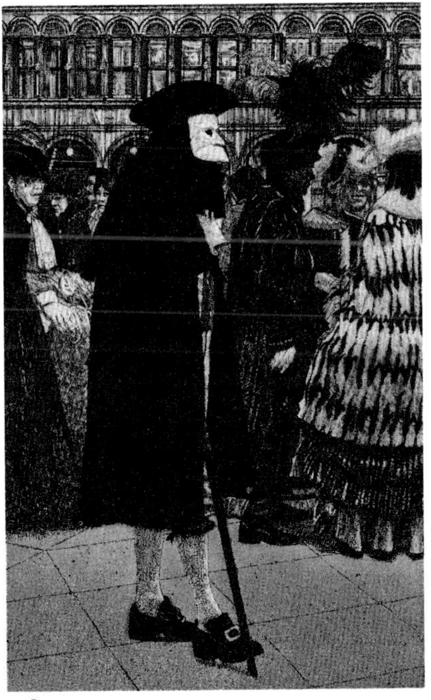

138

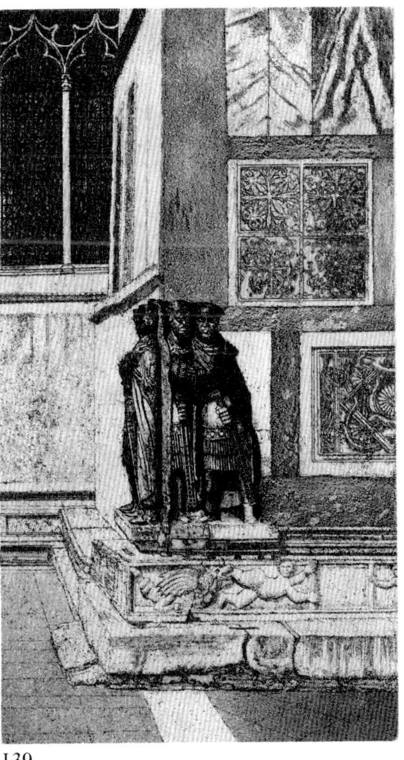

139

List of unpublished plates

Life drawings direct on to the plate, portraits, landscapes

1931

1. Van Dyck Head
(copy)
E. $6\frac{1}{2} \times 5\frac{1}{2}$

1932

2. The Wings, Blackburn Theatre Royal
E. $6\frac{1}{2} \times 5\frac{1}{2}$

3. The Bedroom
D. $7\frac{1}{4} \times 10$

4. Head of a Man
D. $5\frac{3}{4} \times 4\frac{1}{2}$

5. The Orators
EA $6 \times 8\frac{1}{2}$

6. Edward Biggs
E B was appointed to the staff of All Saints' Elementary School (Church School) on being demobilised in 1918. He taught English, Geography, Drawing and Music. He was the first person to encourage W F to draw. He introduced W F to the writings of G B Shaw, H G Wells and W H Hudson, also to the music of Beethoven, Mozart, Schubert and Dvorak. He was a member of the Cecil Sharp Society of Folk Song and Dancing. He trained a team of the children of All Saints School which competed successfully for three years at the Blackpool Musical Festival in Country, Morris and Sword Dancing. The friendship lasted from the age of eleven until E B's death in 1943.

7. George Whalley
(close friend of Edward Biggs)
E. $5\frac{3}{4} \times 4\frac{1}{2}$

1933

8. Studies from Life, Back View, Fanny Bell
E. $4\frac{3}{4} \times 3\frac{1}{4}$

9. Young Boy
E. $4\frac{1}{2} \times 3\frac{1}{4}$

10. Keyhole Katey
E. $4\frac{1}{2} \times 3$

11. Carmen Watson
E. 5×4

12. Three Studies Seated, Legs etc
E. $4\frac{3}{4} \times 6\frac{1}{4}$

13. Blackburn Golf Course
E. $3\frac{1}{2} \times 6\frac{1}{2}$

14. Studies from Life, Model Standing by Throne
E. $5\frac{3}{4} \times 2\frac{3}{4}$

15. Three-quarter-length Negress, Head turned away
E. $5 \times 2\frac{3}{4}$

16. Back View of Seated Woman, other details
E. 5×3

17. Haymakers
E. $6\frac{1}{2} \times 9\frac{1}{4}$

18. Small Self Portrait
E. $2\frac{3}{4} \times 2$

19. Back Garden, Cathcart Road
E. 7×7

1934

20. Crockery on Table, Hollywood Road
E. $5\frac{1}{4} \times 5\frac{1}{4}$

21. Sleeping Girl
E. $5\frac{1}{2} \times 5\frac{1}{4}$

22. Woman cutting Bread
E. $7\frac{1}{2} \times 5$

23. Large Self Portrait
E. $5\frac{3}{4} \times 4\frac{1}{2}$

24. Weeds
E. 6×5

25. Peasant Women
(1st plate)
E. $6\frac{1}{2} \times 4\frac{1}{4}$

1935

26. Sheet of Details (figure)
E. 5×6

27. Half-length of Female, Lit from rear
E. $4\frac{1}{2} \times 3$

28. Two Peasants and a Dog
E. 6×5

29. Three-quarter-side view of Large Female (de la Questa)
E. $5 \times 3\frac{1}{2}$

1936

30. Seated Woman holding Ankle
E. $4\frac{3}{4} \times 4$

31. Female Torso
E. $3\frac{3}{4} \times 3$

32. Ronda Washerwomen
E. $4 \times 6\frac{1}{2}$

33. Seville, Women Ironing
E. $5 \times 7\frac{1}{4}$

34. Ronda, In the Valley
E. 4×8

1982

35. Ullswater, Aira Force
SG. $9\frac{1}{4} \times 6$